HOLLOW HEROES

HOLLOW HEROES

AN UNVARNISHED LOOK AT
THE WARTIME CAREERS OF
CHURCHILL,
MONTGOMERY
AND
MOUNTBATTEN

MICHAEL ARNOLD

CASEMATE

Philadelphia & Oxford

Published in the United States of America and Great Britain in 2015 by
CASEMATE PUBLISHERS
908 Darby Road, Havertown, PA 19083
and
10 Hythe Bridge Street, Oxford, OX1 2EW

ISBN 978-1-61200-273-6
Digital Edition: ISBN 978-1-61200-274-3

Cataloging-in-publication data is available from the Library of Congress and
the British Library.

10 9 8 7 6 5 4 3 2 1

Printed and bound in the United States of America.

For a complete list of Casemate titles please contact:

CASEMATE PUBLISHERS (US)
Telephone (610) 853-9131, Fax (610) 853-9146
E-mail: casemate@casematepublishing.com

CASEMATE PUBLISHERS (UK)
Telephone (01865) 241249, Fax (01865) 794449
E-mail: casemate-uk@casematepublishing.co.uk

CONTENTS

INTRODUCTION—
AN UNHOLY TRINITY

Legends are persistent, and delusions tenacious.
—BASIL LIDDELL HART, *The German Generals Talk*

To describe Sir Winston Churchill, Field Marshal Bernard Montgomery and Lord Louis Mountbatten as 'hollow heroes' may at first sight seem absurd because they had all emerged from World War II with glittering reputations—they were a veritable triumvirate in the pantheon of British World War II leaders. The truth may come as a shock because none of them were heroes of truly solid integrity. In each case there was an unsavoury, hollow core hidden beneath their surface image, an essence that was ignored in what was in the national interests in time of war and for some time thereafter, largely due to acceptance of convention. Concealed amongst these hidden agendas were murky and distasteful dealings, acts of contrivance, and in a number of cases outright lies. All three were men of huge egos with massive personal ambitions and who had little or no time for anyone else.

Whilst carrying out research for one of my earlier books, *The Sacrifice of Singapore: Churchill's Biggest Blunder,*[1] I was surprised to uncover that in the case of each of these three men there was a totally different side, which showed that much of their reputations was built on contrived results, deceptions and dishonesty. As the title of my previous book suggests, this was particularly true of Churchill, but on digging deeper and employing the Socratic principle of 'following the evidence wherever it leads', it emerged that there was evidence demonstrating similar contradictions of the popular images of Montgomery and, especially, Mountbatten. Churchill and Montgomery each wrote their own self-serving versions of events, the former going so far as to state that history would be kind to him because he would be writing the history.

The expression that 'truth is the first casualty of war' was originally attributed to the 5th-century BC Greek dramatist Aeschylus and was repeated at about the same time by the Chinese general Sun Tzu; the Prussian military authority Carl von Clausewitz also alluded to it. However, all three of them were referring to the use of truth as a deception strategy or military tactic against an enemy, whereas the more recent comment from American senator Hiram Johnson was an allusion to elected government officials deliberately misleading their own peoples in order to disguise unpalatable facts and avoid a popular backlash. The three individuals to be examined here were not so much guilty on that score—although there were instances when that accusation could legitimately be mounted—but in frequently acting dishonestly in order to advance or promote their own careers. These actions were either to the detriment of their peers, or involved the deliberate and unnecessary sacrifices of many lives. Thus, this was not in the traditional sense truth being a 'casualty of war' but the deliberate use of lies (the opposite of truth) to safeguard and/or advance their own positions or reputations.

All three could be said to have had 'a good war'—an expression frequently used to describe how senior commanders had advanced their careers—but how many of the ordinary wartime soldier or sailors who survived would ever have used this phrase about their own experiences? How many army privates or able seamen would have felt anything other than total relief when it was all over? It is an issue that regularly emerges here; although it is an angle that is often lost in the afterglow of victory, it is one that should be kept in mind when the truth behind the heroic images of these three is examined.

Mountbatten did not write his own account, but according to one of his biographers, Philip Ziegler, he took care to ensure that Ziegler's account fell into line with what Mountbatten wanted. Ziegler wrote of him:

> His vanity, though child-like, was monstrous, his ambition unbridled. The truth, in his hands, was swiftly converted from what it was, to what it should have been. He sought to re-write history with cavalier indifference to the facts to magnify his own achievements.[2]

Despite this apparent condemnation, Ziegler's admiration was such that he confessed to having a note pinned above his desk reading, 'Remember that, after all, he was a great man.' It is difficult to understand how any biographer can even profess impartiality if, having made such a damning assessment, he still admits to being constrained by such a self-imposed caveat.

Both Churchill and Mountbatten had a propensity for self-aggrandisement on such a scale that, if not actually dishonest, certainly manufactured and distorted facts; and, of course, a war was the ideal stage for each of them. Churchill and Mountbatten both came from backgrounds of distinct social privilege. Churchill was born at Blenheim Palace, Oxfordshire, the eldest son of Lord Randolph Churchill and a direct descendent of the Duke of Marlborough. Mountbatten was born at Frogmore House in the grounds of Windsor Castle, the youngest child of Prince Louis of Battenberg who was a great-grandson of Queen Victoria, and Mountbatten himself was a second cousin of King George VI.

Montgomery was a different case altogether, one where the illusion of an enormous ego seems in fact to have been a cover for insecurity and an inferiority complex; the apparently aggressive personality being a compensating mechanism. He was a general of reasonable competence who, through cleverly concealed opportunism, managed to beguile the world into believing he was a genius by manipulation of facts and consistent self-promotion. This will be examined later in greater detail and many of the classic symptoms of an inferiority complex—the fear of making mistakes, a tendency to be rude and aggressive, excessive seeking of attention, the criticism of others, for example—are documented and so completely characteristic of Montgomery that the hypothesis seems quite rational. Indeed this interpretation has already been put forward before, Antony Beevor in his book *D-Day: The Battle for Normandy*[3] saying that Montgomery 'suffered from a breathtaking conceit that almost certainly stemmed from some sort of inferiority complex'. It is time that the reality behind the public image of the British military genius of World War II, largely contrived by Montgomery himself and fanned by an adoring British media, was put into a context of dispassionate reality. Free of emotion and the constraints of convention we shall see someone who was a capable military commander but not much more. Montgomery is under scrutiny here to evaluate his actual performance against his own claim to greatness.

Churchill and Montgomery had loveless childhoods, and although such parental attitudes may not have been much worse than the norm for a certain strata of society in 19th- and early 20th-century England, it seems likely that the experience left its mark, each of them in their different ways evolving into self-centred individuals of ruthless ambition. Mountbatten's childhood by comparison seems to have been fairly happy, although even at a young age he showed self-confidence way beyond his years, a trait that along with his increasing vanity would cause him to be detested by those with whom he worked in government.

While researching my book about the fall of Singapore, my first inkling that there was rather more to the popular image of Churchill than met the eye arose from a comment made by military historian Correlli Barnett in a Singapore edition of *The Straits Times* in 1997. In the correspondence section of that paper discussing the reasons for the fall of Singapore to the Japanese in 1942, Barnett wrote that Churchill, more than anyone else, had been responsible and that 'His fingers were all over it'. Up until that point I had accepted the conventional accounts that attributed the Singapore debacle solely to ham-fistedness and bungling by the military at a local level against a badly equipped and inferior force. I discovered that the truth was quite different and began to uncover a veritable mine of hidden issues and facts that had been deflected by the individuals concerned or ignored by authors in the interests of orthodoxy.

By sheer accident I also uncovered concrete (literally) evidence that in fact the Japanese army was far larger than had previously been thought. This is revealed by a monument in the Japanese cemetery in Singapore that is there today for all to see. From 1977 to 1995 Barnett had been Keeper of the Archives at Churchill College, Cambridge and was therefore in a unique position to offer an opinion. Intrigued by his assessment of Churchill, I began my own investigations and found a wide range of opinions and accounts of the man. These varied from the expected hagiographies to the more recent dissections: in 1993 by Professor John Charmley,[4] in 1994 by Clive Ponting[5] and in 1995 by Professor Richard Overy.[6] Then in 2006 came ex-army officer Gordon Corrigan's *Blood, Sweat and Arrogance: The Myths of Churchill's War,*[7] followed by his 2010 book *The Second World War: A Military History.*[8] All uncovered facts, issues and personality traits that were revealing in the extreme, and all of them laid bare unpleasant truths about the man as a whole, but particularly so from the standpoint of his behaviour in World War II that had hitherto been virtually unknown or even imagined.

Also emerging from the research for my earlier book was a picture of Mountbatten that was completely at odds compared to the conventional wartime heroic image. Some years earlier I had acquired a copy of Stephen Harper's 1985 book *Miracle of Deliverance: The Case for the Bombing of Hiroshima and Nagasaki.*[9] I bought the book at the time simply because I had lived in Malaysia for many years, was familiar with most of the Far East and was intrigued by the title. I discovered that a large part of that book was devoted to Operation *Zipper,* which Mountbatten led and which entailed the invasion of Malaya. Despite the fact that the Japanese had already surrendered and that a simple and orderly reoccupation was all that was required, Mountbatten, as Supreme Commander South-East Asia, was determined to have his moment of glory and insisted on invading the country. I had never heard of this operation, and for good reason: *Zipper* cost a large and unnecessary loss of men and equipment and was such a disaster that even now it is very difficult to find any details of what actually went wrong. There appears to have been a determined, official cover-up. Stephen Harper was able to relate what actually happened only because he was there, otherwise the full details of this sad episode would probably have always remained hidden. Harper was an officer on one of the ships of the invading armada and as far as I am aware his book is the only account that describes that fiasco.

It appears that Mountbatten's decision was based entirely on the fact that he wanted to have the glory of commanding a victorious invading force with British troops recapturing enemy-held beaches as they had done on D-Day. In this he had been encouraged by Churchill, who had said that the shame of Singapore—for which he was primarily responsible—could only be assuaged by the capture of that fortress in battle, no matter the casualties. A more cautious commander would have realised that such an invasion was unnecessary and all that was required following the Japanese surrender was for Malaya to be reoccupied in a systematic and methodical manner. Impetuous and irresponsible as ever, Mountbatten insisted on his forces storming ashore at an unreconnoitred beach on the west coast of Malaya. Large numbers of men were drowned and equipment lost as they rapidly sank into the deep, thick mud of the Strait of Malacca. If he was capable of such a cavalier and irresponsible attitude on this occasion, then it seemed likely there might be other examples; and so it has proved. In his 1994 book *Eminent Churchillians*,[10] Andrew Roberts goes even further in debunking the myth of Mountbatten as a wartime hero, describing him as 'a mendacious, intellectually limited hustler'.

It was Churchill who plucked the inexperienced and youthful Mountbatten from relative obscurity and continually championed him, in spite of a series of self-inflicted and costly disasters for which any other officer would at least have been relieved of his command or more probably court-martialled by the Admiralty. Indirectly, therefore, it was Churchill who was also ultimately responsible for the disaster at Dieppe, another example of Mountbatten's grandstanding. Again it had been Churchill who, having no real concept of exactly what was actually being achieved in North Africa, impatiently sacked two of Britain's most capable commanders, generals Archibald Wavell and Claude Auchinleck. He did this in order to save his own political skin following the recent loss of three by-elections and was indirectly responsible for the very lucky appearance on the war stage of Montgomery—lucky for Montgomery, that is.

It was Correlli Barnett in his book *The Desert Generals* who first pricked the bubble of the Montgomery myth and revealed him as nothing more than an average general—able, yes, but nothing brilliant.[11] His reputation was based entirely on what became known as the Second Battle of El Alamein, which can now be demonstrated to have been a conflict that was not fought for reasons of military strategy but one that was required to save a politician, Churchill, and then was so one-sided that Montgomery, or any other general for that matter, would have had difficulty in losing. Like any other politician, Churchill was more concerned with power, and staying in power, than for any sincere concern for the interests of his country.

Montgomery's prestige and renown was procured very largely by self-contrived propaganda and embellished by a British media desperate to produce encouraging news for an eager public at home. When Correlli Barnett's book was first published in 1960, it provoked a considerable amount of irritation, typified by the blustering indignation of Lord Randolph Churchill in the *News of the World*, who commented condescendingly about 'the sergeant who dares to criticise field-marshals', leading one to ponder whether the concept of a mere sergeant having education and intellect was so impossible for him to stomach. Barnett had been in the Intelligence Corps, whereas Randolph Churchill's reputation was such that when a few years earlier he had had a growth removed, the event prompted Evelyn Waugh to comment succinctly, 'It was a typical triumph of modern science to find the one part of Randolph which was not malignant and remove it'.

Attitudes had changed by the time the second edition of *The Desert Generals* was published in 1983. Corelli Barnett commented that Montgomery by then had been 'reduced to life-size, a Plumer rather than a Wellington, and an eccentric rather than a genius'. Since then there has been an increasing acceptance that the received view during the glowing years immediately after World War II had largely been coloured by what Montgomery had said himself—and mostly about himself—and the need to perpetuate the conventional image of a military hero in a war recently won; the same went for Churchill and Mountbatten. The British press had quite naturally championed them all and were most receptive to their frequent press conferences, especially since, whatever the truth, they always produced good news. During the anxieties of war, the people of Britain had needed champions on which to hang their hopes and Churchill, Montgomery and Mountbatten provided convenient and immediate images for encouragement and admiration. Cooler, more measured and less emotional analysis has recently produced rather different conclusions, a question of longer perspectives in time enabling greater impartiality and refined assessments.

In World War II all three of these men were indifferent to casualties in pursuing their own agendas, although only Churchill and Mountbatten overtly so. Clive Ponting makes a specific point of this in *Churchill* where he records that in 1943 Churchill had even made the remarkable complaint that British casualties were not high enough.[12] Mountbatten was indifferent and totally unrepentant about deaths caused directly by his own irresponsible actions as a destroyer captain and quite insouciant of the enormous losses suffered as a result of his direction of the disastrous 1942 raid on Dieppe, as well as those caused by the 1945 invasion of Malaya.

In similar fashion and to bolster his image, Montgomery would direct operations that were unnecessary, such as the Second Battle of El Alamein, which he claimed as his own triumph, his dithering efforts to take the French city of Caen in 1944 (inflicting huge civilian casualties) and the debacle at Arnhem, which despite being his own invention, he claimed was not his fault. He then topped all these off by distortedly claiming he had almost single-handedly saved the Americans during the Battle of the Bulge in December 1944 and January 1945, causing perfectly justified resentment amongst the Americans, without whose generosity the war could not have been won.

The plaudits for Montgomery seem to have been almost exclusively British, for I have been unable to locate any author, American or German, who had such a high opinion of him. There is plenty of praise from the German side for George S. Patton, Wavell and Auchinleck for instance, or from Britain and America for Erwin Rommel, Heinz Guderian and Erich von Manstein, but there does not appear to be any American or German acclaim for Montgomery—a fact that surely speaks for itself. Certainly there are comments about him from outside Britain, but in every case they are only descriptive of a carefully planned but cautious style. Apart from what Montgomery claimed himself (about himself), it appears his reputation rests on the fact that there was an understandable public need in Britain to find a hero that the nation could celebrate. Besides Wavell and Auchinleck, whom Churchill sacked, there were very few otherwise outstanding generals; and whereas there is now broad acceptance that Lieutenant-General William Slim was Britain's outstanding military leader of World War II, he was stationed far away in Burma and was not the colourful sort of personality that could be so easily promoted.

Churchill's reputation preceded World War II by some 25 years when he was a very young First Lord of the Admiralty. This started with his being implicated in the forced resignation of Mountbatten's father, Prince Louis of Battenberg as First Sea Lord in 1914 and continued as the prime mover of the ill-conceived and disastrous Dardanelles campaign of 1915, which forced his own resignation. Churchill may have had some twinge of conscience about his unjust but politically convenient removal of Prince Louis, so perhaps he tried to balance his guilt through undue patronage of his son.

In the closing chapter of his book *Churchill: The Struggle for Survival 1940/65*, Lord Moran assessed Churchill's image prior to 1940:

> No doubt the eccentricity of his judgment contributed to the lack of confidence of his countrymen. They were bewildered; they did not know what he might do next. They found him quite unaccountable, in a measure irresponsible. It is the tale of a preacher without a text. The fact is that Winston's story before the war is the

chronicle of a self-centred man making his plans in order to win personal renown. In the House of Commons he had few friends. No party wanted him. If he had died before the war he would have been accounted a brilliant failure.[13]

The problem was that leopards do not change their spots—they cannot. Once Churchill had gained power, those around him and who had to work with him, still did not know what he might do next and continued to find him unaccountable; nothing had changed but the circumstances. The fundamental personality characteristics observed by Lord Moran—self-centred, unaccountable and irresponsible—were not likely to disappear overnight, and nor did they do so. The war gave the preacher his text, but beyond his inspiring rhetoric in the early days of the conflict when he was word-perfect Churchill was frequently disturbing because the eccentricity of judgment that Moran had noted was to appear time and time again.

The science of psychological profiling was not developed by the FBI until the 1960s and has subsequently proved a valuable tool in solving crimes by enabling an image of the perpetrator to be produced. Whilst not suggesting that Churchill was a criminal, his own psychological profile, based on the singular characteristics identified by Lord Moran, would seem to indicate a personality that should never have been allowed to have total control; yet apparently, without opposition or question, that was precisely what Churchill made sure he did have. As was to be proved, total power in the hands of such a personality was extremely dangerous.

Lord Moran's book caused something of a controversy, appearing as it did only a year after Churchill's death, and many of his insightful but subsequently accepted views were widely and angrily resented and refuted. However, at the time of his appointment as Churchill's personal physician in 1940 he was already 58 years of age and had a longstanding and very successful private practice. It is reasonable to assume therefore that the personality traits he observed and noted were based on measured and experienced diagnosis.

Mountbatten's name first came to public attention through the overt philandering of his very wealthy wife, Edwina, but his reputation really only started with the war. It continued afterwards with his rushed handling of Indian independence in 1947, the legacy of which is now seen almost every day in the conflicting religious, ethnic, cultural and geographical complexities involving India and Pakistan. The British government had hoped that this very difficult task might be achieved in perhaps 14 months although even that length of time was thought to be optimistic. In the event Mountbatten hurried the whole complex exercise through in a quarter of that time, 14 weeks. To handle the incredibly sensitive establishment of new national boundaries, Mountbatten imported for just 3 weeks a previously unknown boundary drawer, a man who had never before set foot anywhere in Asia let alone India.

Montgomery spent a large amount of his time in the years after World War II satisfying his ongoing craving for fame and glory by criticising the Americans, who had suffered his arrogance during the war with quite remarkable patience, and by writing books telling everyone how he had won the war. In the many books that have appeared on each of Churchill, Montgomery and Mountbatten, these facts have sometimes been mentioned only *en passant* and in others overlooked or deliberately omitted.

It is not the intention of this book to denigrate its three subjects completely, for without doubt there were achievements, nor does it comprise the type of revisionism written by people who seem to specialise in unproven rumour and conspiracy theories. Such books of course tend to attract attention simply because their allegations are in many cases impossible to disprove and, as the saying goes, 'if you throw enough mud some of it will stick'. What is quoted here is either fact or opinion, and in the case of the latter it originates from an unearthed, factually based, authoritative source. Certainly questions are raised, but when unexplained anomalies are uncovered then surely it is only right and logical that they should be questioned. To such a degree was truth a wartime casualty that 50 years ago much of what is written here would have been dismissed as fiction or regarded as heresy. Facts, however, have an uncomfortable habit of leaking out and some balloons should occasionally be deflated.

As a counterpoint to the concealed truths behind the popular images of these three men, the book concludes by examining other concealed truths, the damaging effect of 'class' in officer selection and promotion, how two of Britain's finest generals—Wavell and Auchinleck—were made into political scapegoats and finally the establishment cover-up of the reasons for the dismissal of the inventive and imaginative Major-General Eric Dorman-Smith.

Social class, as such, remains a sensitive subject in Britain, for even in the 21st century there remains an influential element that fervently believes in the entitlements of class system with all its hypocrisies and blatant inefficiencies. Nonetheless it has been a factor so deeply ingrained in Britain and the armed forces in particular that it should be addressed. For the British Army in World War II, officer 'class' was clearly just as important as actual performance or ability and it is examined here because of the manner in which it was responsible for the removal of Dorman-Smith. The burden it imposed in combat conditions naturally also affected the Americans when they came into the war. This prompted specific comment to be made by renowned American historians Murray and Willett in their 2000 Harvard publication *A War to be Won: Fighting the Second World War.*[14] It must have been something of a shock for the Americans to have discovered that they had to fight side-by-side with a social and military system where, even in the 20th century, ancestry was of far greater value than acumen and where parentage was valued more than production. Significantly perhaps, and although they must have been aware of the handicap imposed by this priority, it is never mentioned by any British military historian who himself had a military background. Whether this is also an example of class loyalty, it seems as though this is a no-go area, a cultural minefield whose influence would only be grudgingly conceded and then only if the issue was pressed. It may also be of some significance that for the most part British military historians, when viewing British performance, seem to be reluctant to quote the assessments of various senior German commanders. This may be because from the German perspective only a few emerge with positive reputations. Yet even if the overall subject is a can of worms, it should be opened and exposed to scrutiny, otherwise it will continue to fester to the detriment of effectiveness, efficiency and truth.

Generals Wavell and Auchinleck were men who had performed with distinction at a time when the resources they had available were severely stretched, and yet they were removed on little more than the whim of a prime minister exercising total power and convinced of his own military genius. In so doing he unnecessarily lengthened the war in North Africa by some considerable time and caused the needless deaths of thousands. The quiet achievements of these two self-effacing soldiers are in stark contrast to the acclaim heaped on others who were never slow to grab the limelight and create distorted headlines for their own benefit.

The third, the aforementioned Major-General Eric Dorman-Smith was one of the British Army's most brilliant military thinkers. In the history of World War II he is largely unknown and would probably have remained so were it not for Correlli Barnett in his book *The Desert Generals* and Lavinia Greacon, who wrote Dorman-Smith's life in *Chink: A Biography;*[15] I have drawn extensively on her book for what is written here. Unlike the Germans, Britain had very few individual strategists and innovative tacticians; in spite of this, Dorman-Smith was sacked without reason by Churchill about a month after he had made a huge contribution to the success of the First Battle of El Alamein in 1942. Eighteen months before that he had devised the plan that enabled Wavell and Lieutenant-General Richard O'Connor with a small force to defeat the Italians and capture over 130,000 prisoners. At a time when General Alan Brooke, Chief of the Imperial General Staff, had said that half of his senior commanders were useless, here was one with 30 years' service, proven initiatives and unorthodox ideas and yet he was cast aside without even an iota of vindication. His case brings to light the grim contradiction that existed during World War II between the fictions of the hollow heroes and real heroes that were hidden. It is the story of how snobbery, stupidity and slow-thinking social mores triumphed over intellect and ingenuity. The reason behind the abrupt dismissal of Dorman-Smith has remained permanently suppressed by the official channels; one has to ask why.

Facts are sometimes uncomfortable, unpalatable or unwelcome, especially when they demonstrate that a previously held belief is open to a different interpretation or that in truth a hero had feet of clay. But sometimes they are unavoidable, and if uncovered can lead to a rethink or speculation. It is what is often termed 'cognitive dissonance', a reluctance to accept what is unwelcome. I have quoted widely from the recent—but not necessarily revisionist—authors already mentioned and of course Correlli Barnett, that most analytical, impartial and seemingly inexhaustible writer of military history. For the sake of those who needlessly suffered or lost their lives specifically because of the excesses and contrivances of the individuals mentioned here, a balance should be provided and the record put straight. I hope this book might go some way to achieving that aim.

CHAPTER 1

CLASS AND THE
BRITISH ARMY

*Born into the gentry or the aristocracy, spending
their lives in the last sanctuary of privilege in Europe,
their mental characteristics and morality were not
surprisingly very different from those of the managers,
the scientists and technicians of industry. There was
therefore in the British professional soldier little
identification with the world of twentieth-century
technocracy and little sympathy. They rightly judged
it sordid and barbarous. But this did not help them
prepare for its wars.*
—CORRELLI BARNETT, *The Desert Generals*

*[T]he problem lay in the unwillingness of the British
army to base officer promotion on effectiveness rather
than social class. Too many officers found employment
after failure.*
—MURRAY AND MILLETT, *A War to be Won*

Churchill, Montgomery and Mountbatten were all men who
used war as an instrument for self-promotion; they were 'hollow heroes'. At the end of the war, when everyone else was relieved and happy, Churchill admitted to his doctor that he missed it, for war, as such, had provided him with the stimulus, status and the total control that he had always craved; it had been a drug that gave him a kick. Ei-

19

ther because of their own egos or as a result of their self-promotion, all three had been directly or indirectly responsible for the unnecessary deaths, imprisonment and casualties of thousands of their own people. War is a nasty business, primarily concerned with killing people, for that is how wars are won; but when the losses are needless and are inflicted on one's own side, then those responsible should be identified and exposed.

There was, however, another factor in Britain's struggle to survive before America came to her rescue: the impediment of a system of social class that was evident throughout society and dominated the structure of military command. It resisted change or deviation from the orthodox and impeded innovation, initiative and invention and, as we shall see later, it was the main factor in Britain losing the services during the war of one of her most imaginative strategists, Eric Dorman-Smith.

Probably the most accurate description of the British Army of 1939 can be found in Correlli Barnett's *The Desert Generals,* and it is worth quoting:

It is generally true that an army is an extension of society; military disaster is often national decline exposed by the violence of battle. Examples are Imperial Russia and Austro-Hungary in the First World War, France in the Second. Any army thus reflects in sharp focus the social structure, the state of technological progress and the creative vigour of society. The opposing armies at Crecy illustrate this general rule. However the British army in the Second World War is an exception, perhaps the only one in history. Although the army of a twentieth century social democracy and a first-class industrial power, it was nevertheless spiritually a peasant levy led by the gentry and aristocracy. Its habits of mind and work, its mental and emotional life were those of the social order based on birth and lands that had passed from supremacy in the national life by the end of the nineteenth century. Few poor men of great ability chose the army as a rewarding outlet for their talents—pay for all ranks was less than an income . . . Men of great ability did of course make their careers in the army but, because it was a tradition of their caste and because they enjoyed private means. Therefore in a true sense, most regular officers in the British army were amateurs as well as gentlemen. Born into the gentry or the aristocracy, spending their lives in the last sanctuary of privilege in Europe, their mental characteristics and morality were not surprisingly very different from those of the managers, the scientists and technicians of industry. Cleverness, push, ruthlessness, self-interest and ambition were considerably less prized than modesty, good manners, courage, a sense of duty, chivalry and a certain affectation of easy-going non-professionalism. There was therefore in the British professional soldier little identification with the world of twentieth-century technocracy and little sympathy. They rightly judged it sordid and barbarous. But this did not help them prepare for its wars.[16]

Anyone who served in the British Army during or for some time after World War II would readily recognise the truth of that description. Barnett might have added an affected style of speech, what cricket writer David Frith, when writing about a certain England captain of the 1930s, described as 'strangulated upper-class vowels'. This was a system that hardly 'selected' at all; it merely drew for its ranks from a small social strata, as if background alone would guarantee the required intelligence, ability and initiative. It has been claimed in many quarters that it served Britain well; this is not true—if it served at all it was because that was the established order, but there is no evidence that it served well. It was what veteran journalist Wynford Vaughan-Thomas dryly referred to as 'Eton in Uniform'[17]—accents rather than acumen, breeding instead of brains and inheritance without intellect.

Being a regular army officer in times of peace was rather like being a member of a fashionable cricket club who never made it out of the nets, and therefore was never tested; the style might be there but whether it would function in match conditions was another thing. Indeed the cricket analogy is particularly appropriate when one considers the amateur opposition to league cricket in the south of England before World War II. More than anything else this was because the amateur ethos balked at the prospect of real competition upsetting the comfortable atmosphere of their games. The same could be said of the easy-going and respectable profession in peacetime of what was referred to as the 'officer class'. As if this largely ceremonial environment was not enough of an impediment, there was also a distinct resistance to and dislike of progress and change. Cartoonist David Lowe developed his 1930 character Colonel Blimp after overhearing two military men in a Turkish bath agreeing that cavalry officers should be entitled to wear their spurs inside a tank. That such a notion could have been even a possibility sounds absurd today, but this nostalgic nonsense epitomised the establishment resistance to mechanisation. This attachment to tradition was such that when cavalry regiments were forced to motorise in 1939, some, like the Royal Deccan Horse in India (albeit perhaps an extreme example), found that not one single person in that regiment knew how to even drive a car. Gentlemen either rode horses or took taxis or trains—cars were regarded as a mechanical nuisance.

Occasionally there were outstanding exceptions to this rule: John Harding (later Field Marshal Sir John Harding, 1st Baron Harding of Petherton), whose school was Ilminster Grammar and who started life as a Post Office clerk; and William Slim (later Field Marshal Sir William Viscount Slim of Yarralumla and Bishopston), schooled at St Phillip's Grammar in Birmingham and who was a metal-works clerk before joining the army. So despite it being a socially closed shop, it was still possible for those with ability to be accepted and succeed. Nevertheless, this was only because of the exigencies of war, for both of the above had entered the army in 1914 and had built their careers from then on. At any other time given the prevailing social mores, men of Harding's and Slim's backgrounds could never have been considered. One must ponder therefore just how many others who would have made excellent leaders were passed over because of such a system.

Mention is made at the head of this chapter of the observation by respected American military historians and Harvard professors Williamson Murray and Allan Millett that the British Army did not base promotion on effectiveness but rather on social class. In other words, provided there was the 'right' sort of background a successful army career was assured. A man might have been nondescript but as long as he conformed and 'kept his nose clean', then he could be confident that he would retire at least as a brigadier and perhaps even higher. Murray and Millett's comment was undoubtedly generated by comparing the respective social backgrounds of the American top military with those of the British. This seems to be borne out by looking at a random list of some of the American generals who fought or directed the campaign in Europe: George Catlett Marshall, Dwight D. Eisenhower, Omar Bradley, George S. Patton, Lucian Truscott, Jacob L. Devers, Courtney Hodges, Walter Bedell Smith, James M. Gavin, William H. Simpson,

Leonard T. Gerow, Troy H. Middleton and Anthony C. McAuliffe. It will be found that only two came from backgrounds of some social advantage (Marshall and Patton), the families of the remainder being very ordinary; in fact some, Bradley for instance, came from backgrounds that were distinctly poor. However, unlike the British military, social background does not appear to have been an obstacle to military career prospects in the US Army, it had no effect on discipline and certainly did not influence performance. This does not mean of course that all American generals were outstanding successes any more than that all British generals were failures because there were successes and failures on both sides, but as a general rule it is self-evident that a selection process based on anything other than intelligence and leadership ability is more likely to produce failures.

It may have been this social blend based on merit and performance that made the US military more flexible than the British. Even in this book one only has to look at the differing methods of Patton and Montgomery in Sicily, and Patton's instinctive reaction to the forecast of an impending German break-out in the Ardennes, so rapid a response in fact that it took the Germans by surprise, and was largely responsible for halting them in their first strides.

So, why was the British model so hidebound by class and tradition when common sense required that its leadership should be the best obtainable rather than chosen from a sliver of society? The answer possibly lies in the word 'common' sense; 'common' was a notion that had little place in the thinking of the narrow interests of the landed classes for whom maintaining their position of pre-eminence was totally unrelated to the needs of the nation. One did not require intelligence or need to be effective or even efficient; all that was expected was that one should be conventional, abide by the rules and not make waves.

In this connection it is interesting to note that of all the English-speaking countries who made a major contribution in World War II (i.e. the United States, Britain, Australia, Canada, South Africa and New Zealand), it was only in the British Army that there seems to have been the need for an officer to deliberately differentiate himself through accent and style of speech. This symbolic veneer seems to have been unique to the British Army. In none of the others was there any discernable linguistic difference between general, captain or private.

General Omar Bradley, for instance, spoke just as any other Missouri-born soldier did, so too Bedell Smith from Indiana and Patton from California, and Lieutenant-General Leslie Morshead sounded like any other fellow Australian, and so on. So, the question might be asked, why did the British Army feel that their officers had to *sound* different? Was it believed that their style of speech gave them an authority that they might otherwise have lacked? Was it thought, at that time at least, that a contrived style of speech would immediately be accepted as carrying authority? Or was it because having been selected and promoted because of social background rather than ability, many of them had little else to rely on? A large proportion of Britain's military leaders had, historically, come from the nobility, who in many cases adopted an affected style of speech, so was it a case of a commission carrying with it the obligation to at least sound aristocratic? These are intriguing questions. Only in Britain was there a distinct strata of society recognised as the 'officer class'. Membership of such elites may have conferred social prestige but militarily it was a weakness and was a source of operational problems when reality struck.

Reference has been made earlier to Gordon Corrigan's *The Second World War: A Military History*, and in that book he makes the following interesting statement: 'It is one of the more unfortunate assumptions propounded by British class warriors that, because someone is well bred, has been to a decent school and speaks properly, he is therefore foppish and incompetent.'[18] Corrigan is himself an ex-army officer, but the phrase 'class warrior' is now something of an anachronism; in any event, what does 'decent' mean? Is a school only 'decent' if fees are paid? He also seems to be confusing English that is devoid of regional origin with the heavily affected style of speech that appears to have been de rigueur or adopted by many of those who had emerged from British public schools and/or military academies; there is a world of difference between the two. It seems to have been a cultural idiosyncrasy unique to the British Army, at that time anyway, that many believed such pretentious displays were sufficient in themselves to provide authority and command respect; if so, then it must surely raise valid questions about competence. Such linguistic posturing has now largely died out under the pressures of a more competitive and egalitarian environment, but it is an interesting reflection on the times. As for 'well bred', if that expression means generations of what is loosely called 'breeding', then such a selection process inevitably leads to 'inbreeding' and a shallow gene pool that produces the 'chinless wonders' so often depicted by the standard British caricature of an army officer as an affected dolt. Quite obviously this is not universally true but it must have been based on frequent fact otherwise it would never have existed at all and would not feature as often as it still does today in cartoons and other media outlets.

From about the beginning of the 20th century the British establishment had seen a degree of symmetry between their professed Christian gentlemanly ideals and that most 'English' of games, cricket. Henry Grantland Rice was an American, and although he was writing about American football, his words 'when the last great scorer comes to mark against your name' seemed to be so 'cricket' that they were adopted as though they were British English. Add to that Henry Newbolt's words of about the same time—'Play Up, Play Up, and Play the Game'—and there lay the perfect basis for the 'play' being more important than the 'result'; in other words, proficiency was less valued that attitude. Writing in the mid-1940s, George Orwell stated: 'cricket gives expression to a well-marked trait in the English character, the tendency to value "form" or "style" more highly than success'.[19] This very English priority was in intention and effect little more than a device through which to ensure that despite increasing competition through egalitarianism, the right social class could retain control. Thus, in English County Cricket for instance, every county side was captained by an amateur—a 'gentleman'—who was so different that he required a separate changing room from the professionals as if to ensure that he was not revealed to be exactly the same as anyone else. When in 1926 the *Daily Express* offered the view that a professional captain was necessary if England was to win the Ashes cricket trophy against Australia, it was dismissed as Bolshevism. The 19th century had seen a new word enter the English language—socialism—and its portents threatened the controlling position of those who relied on privileged circumstances of birth rather than ability for their way of life. Thus in exactly the same manner as the British military, English cricket reserved a position of advantage and authority for those of the 'right' social background, and in the same fashion this priority was pursued irrespective of the effect it had on the success of the national team. As in the case of the army it was impossible to produce any actual results to justify the structure, and it certainly could not withstand scrutiny, so uncomfortable questions were either ignored or dismissed.

Britain certainly lacked exceptional military talent during World War II, for although not in any way impugning their undoubted courage or fighting qualities, too many commanders were staid and conformist and few had real ability when put to the test. There were generals and plenty of them, over 200 in fact, many of whom were conventionally competent but little more. It would seem that it was this selection and promotion on the basis of class that was the main reason why, even with Hitler devoting huge resources to the Russian front, Britain could make little impact on a homogeneous and modern German army until the advent of superior numbers and the industrial resources of the United States provided an advantage. On a one-on-one basis with Germany the effect of Britain's class society meant she was unable to compete and such would have been the case even if there had been no war with Japan.

The factor identified by Murray and Millett—social class being of greater importance than effectiveness—has also been one of the basic reasons for Britain's decline as a world industrial power. Britain's position of global strength by the end of the 19th century was due to her Industrial Revolution and this in turn was due to the inventive minds of engineers and scientists and the ingenuity and creativity of foundries and tradesmen, ordinary men all of them. It had been the same imagination and initiative of 'ordinary' men—Robert Clive, Thomas Stamford Raffles and Cecil Rhodes—who had claimed India, Singapore and large tracts of Africa for Britain. It had been entrepreneurial traders such as John Holt and the Lever brothers who opened up West Africa for British business. None of these men felt constrained by ethics but were courageous opportunists spurred on by the vision of profit. The education system of the ruling class was proudly producing what it called 'muscular Christianity'. Industrially and economically Britain might have fared better had it been 'intellectual' or 'commercial' Christianity, but as Correlli Barnett expressed in his book, *The Collapse of British Power*: 'As a consequence of the spiritual revolution English policy ceased to be founded solely on the expedient and opportunistic pursuit of English interests. International relations were no longer seen as being governed primarily by strategy, but by morality.'[20]

It seems to have been the rise and influence of the elitist Christian public (private) schools during the late 19th century that had led to the creation of a belief that boys who had attended such schools had an entitlement to leadership positions. Such schools produced, it was thought, gentlemen, and this, it was also thought, was enough in itself because the product could be relied upon to conform and respect traditions; the 'product' moreover was taught that it was superior. Trade, manufacturing, machinery, mills and mining were not the sort of occupations in which a classically educated gentleman should be interested, and even 'trade' as such was regarded with some distaste. So ingrained was this attitude that even 10 years after World War II an ex-public school and university blue would be refused membership of the elite Band of Brothers Cricket Club because his father was in 'trade'.[21] The inculcation of such values led to a society where the ruling 'class' showed little or no interest in such 'sordid' matters as the efficiency of industrial productivity, improvements in design or the introduction of more profitable manufacturing techniques.

For a 'gentleman' who had nothing in the way of a meaningful inheritance there were three main socially respectable ways of life open to him—the army, the church or the colonial service. Their attitudes encouraged a conceited belief that the Englishman and his culture were supreme and the rest of the world was regarded with some condescension. The very existence of the empire, with its monopoly markets, led to a dilatory attitude towards keeping pace with innovations elsewhere because there was little sense of a need to compete. The consequent decline in efficiency, productivity, competitiveness and innovation could be masked when there were captive markets—the huge Lancashire cotton industry for instance relied almost entirely on British control of India, where tariffs had killed the domestic spinning of cotton (hence the spinning wheel on the Indian independence flag). As a result of this smug condescension the fact that British industry lagged more and more behind other emerging industrial nations was concealed behind an artificial screen and cultural complacency. As the renowned Thomas Arnold of Rugby School stated: 'It is very true that by our distinctness we have gained very much—more than foreigners can understand. A thorough English gentleman—Christian, manly and enlightened—is a finer sentiment of human nature than any other country, I believe, could furnish'[22]

The apogee of the British Empire was probably around the year 1904; as it happens, this was the same year that the GDP of the United States overtook that of Great Britain, but whether anyone was aware of this fact or even regarded it as being of any significance seems doubtful. Instead of investing in the modernisation of British industry at home, massive amounts were speculated overseas in ventures like Argentine railways and Iranian oilfields, such investments subsequently being lost completely when they were nationalised by those countries.

The 'product' of this educational strata did not lack courage or physical bravery, but in being carefully moulded to a certain 'type' the constrictions of the cultural template and instilled reverence for precedent gave little or no room for imagination, invention or initiative. However limiting they may have been, these were the characteristics valued by the military. This self-generating 'system' promoted the belief that a *style* of education was itself of greater value than a *level* of education, and hence intelligence or academic achievement was valued less than social background. Those from this milieu who had achieved positions of influence or authority made sure they accepted or promoted only their own and consequently—irrespective of ability—such a style of education became seen as a passport to success in almost any career.

The influence of this elitism emerged in subtle ways. According to Churchill's last private secretary, Anthony Montague Browne, up until 1940 anyone seeking to enter the Diplomatic/Foreign service would have needed a private income of about £400 a year (roughly £16,000 today).[23] Moreover, it was quite honestly believed by this stratum that it was genuinely in the nation's interests that they should remain in command. It was as though this was an immutable law of nature; dogs were more intelligent than sheep and cheetahs could run faster than bulls, and so it was with the social classes—some were born with or educated to an entitlement to command. Even now, conservative papers in the UK, such as *The Daily Telegraph*, openly champion the continued existence of a 'ruling' class.

Class attitudes have been the root cause of the British establishment's notorious relations with the trade unions. For much of the late 20th century, because of the social stratification of occupations Britain did not used her human resources to the best advantage, and although recognised as an impediment, vested interests, which benefitted from the existing system, resisted any change from the status quo and impeded the necessary moves being made. In an interview in 1975, the Chancellor of what was then West Germany, Helmut Schmidt, said: 'British society, much more than the Scandinavian, German, Austrian and Dutch societies, is characterised by a class-struggle type of society. You have to treat workers as equal members of society. But as long as you maintain the damned class-ridden society of yours, you will never get out of your mess'.[24] Schmidt was Chancellor from 1974 to 1982 and it might be noted that this comment was made just some 30 years after the end of the war and came from a country whose affluence and success was very largely being built on a cohesive society. With virtually no natural resources but due to the efficiency of that society Germany is now even further ahead of Britain than it was in 1975. The 21st century has seen change and greater egalitarianism in Britain, but in World War II a rigid class system held sway and this purist orthodoxy was no more rigorously pursued than in the armed forces. It was rigid to the extent that it was only with the greatest reluctance, and when there was no alternative, that it might be diluted in the interest of efficiency; in fact, protecting it if at all possible seemed to be of greater importance than winning the war.

Having led the FOURTEENTH Army in their largely overlooked campaign to a final and triumphant victory against sizeable Japanese forces in Burma, Lieutenant-General 'Bill' Slim was sacked by Lieutenant-General Sir Oliver Leese in 1945, his stated reason being that he thought Slim was 'tired. Leese had recently been appointed to command the newly formed Allied Land Forces South-East Asia under the overall control of Admiral Mountbatten. Slim's military background had not followed the conventional path. His father ran a small business and Slim had been an elementary schoolteacher and then a clerk in a metal works before being commissioned into The Royal Warwickshire Regiment early in World War I at the age of 23. Old-Etonian Leese by contrast was the son of a baronet and had been commissioned directly into the elite Coldstream Guards, one of the British Army's most formidable regimental tribes. Noting the difference in social origins, American historian Raymond Callahan states in his book *Churchill and his Generals* that Leese had decided 'to put Slim in his place'.[25]

So outraged were Slim's staff and senior commanders that, despite the risk of court martial, a sit-down strike was proposed and several senior officers threatened to resign, with one of them describing Leese as 'an affected silk-handkerchief-waving guardsman'. General Sir Claude Auchinleck, Commander-in-Chief India, intervened through Churchill, and Leese was sent back to Slim by Mountbatten, who instructed him to tell Slim his previous order had been 'a mistake'. Leese was then sacked himself for his action, with Slim replacing him in command of the land forces. Was this a similar military establishment scenario? Was 'class' rearing its head again? There must have been very few military commanders in history who have been removed from their posts immediately after having achieved a spectacular victory.

The practice of 'class' was not limited to the army. In his book *Fighter: The True Story of the Battle of Britain,* military historian Len Deighton recounts that RAF interviewing officers asked candidates if they were fox-hunting men, and that 'social tests' were conducted in which a prospective officer candidate would be given lunch and plied with several glasses of sherry to discover if his language became no longer that of a gentleman.[26] In the Royal Navy it was known that a candidate appearing before an Admiralty Board was likely to be asked the registration number of the taxi he'd used. If this had not been noted it did not really matter, but if he said he had arrived by some form of public transport, then he was clearly 'not the right sort'. Today such trifling trivia sounds like the fiction of P. G. Wodehouse and Bertie Wooster, but in 1940 it was all taken seriously.

The industrial advances being made by other nations could be discounted as merely relative—they did not really concern Britain; after all, Britain had an empire on which the sun never set. There was, however, one scenario where the hollow shell of this comfortable class-ridden complacency would be revealed, where the device of relativism was no shield and where reality would brutally expose it for what it was: war. There are no 'relative' evasions in the stark reality of war—you win or you lose.

The shock of reality can be seen in some performances during the early days of the war. Lieutenant-General Sir Alan Cunningham, a charming fellow, had performed admirably in 1941 when only having to deal with Italian forces in East Africa (most of whom were Ethiopian troops), but when confronted with the real thing in the form of Erwin Rommel in 1942, the stress was such that he suffered a nervous breakdown and had to be relieved of his command. Although he did not sustain the same mental damage, Major-General Neil Ritchie was also replaced because Rommel proved too much for him. In line with Murray and Millett's comment, although having failed, both Cunningham and Ritchie were re-employed elsewhere. In Burma, Lieutenant-General Sir Thomas Hutton had to be removed in 1942 and although having been awarded the Military Cross as a young officer in 1917, the operational demands of top command were beyond him in active service conditions. In other words Hutton was competent in the theory he had learned at staff college but was found wanting when faced with the real thing. In his case he was given a desk job in New Delhi, but then retired completely from the army in 1944, still in the middle of the war against Japan and at the unusually early age of 54. Like many others these three had risen to their ranks through the upward social osmosis of a system where not making waves and being generally regarded as conventional were talents enough to ensure promotion. This was an attractive and comfortable occupation, but in such a non-competitive environment it was impossible to prepare for combat conditions.

As an American might have put it, it was more important to be gentleman than a general. To quote Correlli Barnett once more:

> In this spiritually eighteenth-century army, the cavalry, as the arm of fashion and aristocracy, was the haughty queen. Over its stiff-necked elegance the heroes of the past nodded approval of a military code based not on technical competence, but on high birth, an esoteric way of life, and veneration for the horse. To these lancers and dragoons and hussars was to be given the oily, smelly, clanking product of a technical society: the tank. And with it they were expected to fight a homogenous German panzer arm composed of twentieth-century men of all social classes, who were more interested in sprockets than spurs.[27]

To this problem should be added obstruction of mechanisation from the very top. In 1933, under Lord Milne, Chief of the Imperial General Staff, experiments in motor-driven armour were conducted since this was clearly the way of the future. The move in this direction was checked by his successor, Sir Archibald Montgomery-Messingberd, who said in a newspaper interview that there was a danger of going too fast in mechanisation—prompting military strategist Basil Liddell Hart to point out that emergencies did not wait while changes were slowly made, and hence the Turkish bath conversation overheard by David Lowe.

We shall later explore the strange case of Major-General Dorman-

Smith who seems to have been sacked because he was too forward looking; the British Army appears to have been distinctly uncomfortable with new ideas. It is difficult to imagine the flexible, creative and practical minds of either the Americans or the Germans not recognising an unusual talent and making the most of it. America is the veritable home of innovation and it is not too much of an exaggeration to say that a considerable proportion of the world's inventions have emerged from those two countries, both of them not only willing to embrace change but welcoming it as an opportunity. Just prior to World War I for instance, when Britain's ruling class was struggling to maintain its control, the country had just three technical colleges, whilst Germany had over thirty, an indication that even then Germany had recognised where the future lay. Over and above this the qualifications available through German technical colleges had equal value and prestige compared with any degree obtained through a university.

A classic example of German initiative and ingenuity is the way in which they recognised the potential of their 88mm anti-aircraft gun and converted it into an anti-tank gun, and so created one of the most feared weapons of the war. The British had a similar anti-aircraft weapon and, at 3.7 inches, it was almost identical in calibre to the German model and similar in muzzle velocity, range and rate of fire; but even though lacking effective anti-tank weapons, especially early on in the war, it does not seem to have occurred to the convention-bound British to make similar use of their own ordnance.

The realistic and forward-looking attitude of the Germans flew in the face of the stolid classical priorities of influential figures in Britain, such as philosopher and political economist John Stuart Mill, who in his inaugural address as Rector of St Andrew's University in1867, had pronounced:

> The proper function of a university in national education is tolerably well understood. At least there is tolerably wide agreement about what a university is not. It is not a place of professional education. Universities are not intended to teach the knowledge required to fit men for some special mode for gaining their livelihood. Their object is not to make skilful lawyers, or physicians, or engineers, but capable and cultivated human beings.[28]

In 1939 it had been some seventy years since Mill laid down such archaic and almost Luddite resistance to intellectual progress, but it is not drawing too long a bow to see that the priorities and aims of the British military caste and their military training colleges still followed along similar lines. The gentlemen who entered these hallowed halls were largely men of private means, the necessity for financial independence acting as a social filter, helping to ensure that not too many from the 'wrong sort of background' gained entry. They were to be moulded into an unquestioning product that rigidly conformed in behaviour, appearance (even down to the almost universal small moustache), style of dress (all caps to be worn absolutely straight and never at an angle) and affected speech style, and who could safely be relied upon to respond to a situation in conventional fashion. The analogy would have horrified them but it was a production line not so different from that of Henry Ford, except that four hooves were preferred to four wheels. They were not taught to think for themselves; their training stated that for any given disposition there was an orthodox response. As military historian Mark Urban states: 'drive and brain power were simultaneously indispensable for senior generals and incompatible with the "good chap"/ "good sport" ethos of the officer corps'.[29]

The comparison between the straightjacket of this tradition-bound orthodoxy and the Americans was placed in stark perspective by Erwin Rommel. In the last few pages of his papers he wrote:

> What was astonishing was the speed with which the Americans adapted themselves to modern warfare. In this they were assisted by their extraordinary sense of the practical and material and their complete lack of regard for tradition and worthless theories. The leaders of the American economy and the General Staff have achieved miracles. Starting from scratch an army has been created in the very minimum of time, which, in equipment, armaments and organisation of all arms, surpasses anything the world has yet seen.[30]

The ease with which an enemy could predict the effects of the traditional and established military doctrine of the British was explained to the author in the 1960s by the CEO South-East Asia for the German construction company Hochtief. The individual concerned had been an *Oberst* (colonel) in the German army during the war. He explained that from the rank of about brigadier upwards British reactions to any given situation could be fairly accurately predicted because the Germans knew what had been drummed into them at the staff colleges. Where the Germans did have greater problems, he said, was at lower tactical levels. Forecasting what the reaction might be for anyone of lower rank was more difficult because they might well be only wartime officers who had not been so brainwashed and who would therefore respond according to what their instincts told them at the time rather than being hide-bound by the teachings of regular army indoctrination.

Things have changed dramatically in the last 20 years or so with a completely new set of recruitment standards; the British Army had at last recognised the need to compete with quality. This common-sense change in priorities occasionally produced some odd needs to adapt; there have, for instance, been cases where an officer cadet had to be taught which knife and fork to use in the mess. This necessity would have been quite unthinkable only a few years earlier but the level of intelligence, initiative, leadership and the ability to communicate have improved beyond recognition compared with earlier eras. It took a long time, but eventually it sank in that survival depended on adapting. It was an inability to do just this that caused the extinction of the dinosaurs.

CHAPTER 2

CHURCHILL—
THE BLACK DOG

*Ebullient and self-centred, Churchill had little time
or space for other people and their opinions. That he
was a great man cannot be doubted, but his flaws too
were on the same heroic scale as the rest of the man.*
—JOHN CHARMLEY, *Churchill: The End of Glory*

Winston Churchill was a man with only one ambition in life: to reach the highest position in politics. Yet had it not been for World War II, he would have faded from the scene as a 'might have been'. As biographer Clive Ponting in his book *Churchill* writes: 'His view of politics was clear-cut—he saw it as a field for personal ambition where personality was far more important than policy.' [31]

On being first elected to parliament in 1900 Churchill moved from one constituency to another—Oldham, Dundee, Manchester North-West, Epping and Woodford—and switched political parties on several occasions as and when it suited him. None of these moves concerned any matter of principle, they were all made to suit his own short-term political aims; the ends justified the means. Over the years up to 1939 he held a variety of Cabinet positions including President of the Board of Trade, First Lord of the Admiralty, and Chancellor of the Exchequer. His position at the Admiralty was flawed by his connivance in the forced resignation of the First Sea Lord, Louis Mountbatten's father Prince Louis of Battenberg, in 1914, and his enthusiastic direction of the catastrophic Dardanelles campaign in 1915, which subsequently forced his resignation. This tainted his reputation for some

35

years and although not realised at the time was an omen of things to come and a precursor to his ill-judged and sometimes disastrous interfering in various areas in World War II. As Chancellor of the Exchequer in 1926 he actually opposed expenditure on the defences which, it had been agreed, were vital for the protection of Singapore. Amongst other things he was convinced of the superiority of the white man, was an 'armchair general' and a passionate believer in the glories of the British Empire which, by his own actions and stubbornness during World War II, he eventually helped to break up.

In the early days of the war his use of much-practised rhetoric to create the image of bull-dog defiance provided an inspiration for Britain, but even this was something of a contrivance because despite what he was saying, Churchill knew that unless the United States came to Britain's aid some sort of negotiation with Hitler would be unavoidable. Nonetheless, this in-your-face belligerence was generally to serve Britain well. But behind his reputation as a world statesman there were many facets of his character traits and domineering personality that regularly caused serious problems for his chiefs of staff. Instead of seeking advice where he had little knowledge, he would often give his own imperative orders. In *The Desert Generals* Correlli Barnett refers to 'the ruthless pressure employed by the Prime Minster to get his way in default of rational disposition'[32] and in some cases this feature of his persona led to disasters which he subsequently blamed on others. Clive Ponting described him as 'seemingly convinced of his own military genius and reluctant to allow chiefs of staff to determine details of operations', going on to note that 'he preferred to trust his own instincts and was to have direct access to and control of the joint planning staff who were to work out plans in accordance with his directions.' To quote another close-hand observer, Admiral J. H. Godfrey, Director of Naval Intelligence at the beginning of the war, said of Churchill:

> To get his own way he used every device and brought the whole battery of his ingenious, tireless and highly political mind to bear on the point at issue. His battery of weapons included persuasion, real or simulated anger, mockery, vituperation, tantrums, ridicule, derision, abuse and tears, which he would aim at anyone who opposed him or expressed a view contrary to the one he had already formed, sometimes on quite trivial questions.[33]

During Churchill's political career his dominating self-belief and driving ambition would at times render him very much alone as colleagues left him to his own devices; self-confidence is an asset, a self-opinionated ego quite another. As a backbencher in the 1930s he continuously angled for cabinet posts, positioning and then repositioning himself to his own advantage, and there were numerous episodes during World War II when he refused to listen to others which led to serious problems and disasters that could and should have been avoided. As late as 1937—4 years after the Nazi's widespread public burnings of Jewish literature, 3 years after Hitler murdered some eighty-five political opponents in the Night of the Long Knives and only a year following the reoccupation of the Rhineland by Hitler's troops—Churchill published a book, *Great Contemporaries,*[34] in which and alongside such logical 'greats' as George Bernard Shaw, Franklin D. Roosevelt, Herbert Asquith and T. E. Lawrence (of Arabia), he included Adolph Hitler. In his chapter on Hitler, Churchill wrote admiringly:

> The story of that struggle cannot be read without admiration for the courage, the perseverance, and the vital force which enabled him to challenge, defy, conciliate, or overcome, all the authorities or resistance that barred his path. Those who have met Herr Hitler face-to-face in public business or on social terms have found a highly competent, cool, well-informed functionary with an agreeable manner, a disarming smile, and few have been unaffected by a subtle personal magnetism.

Even as (he himself said) the 'clouds of war were gathering' and while at the same time making pronouncements about the need for rearmament, Churchill the politician was positioning himself politically, still carefully making sure that he could take advantage of any eventuality; there was no principle in this, but simple opportunism. At a meeting of the Anti-Socialist and Anti-Communist Union in Oxford some 4 years before his book was published, he spoke admiringly of Germany's new spirit: 'I think of Germany with its splendid clear-eyed youth marching forward on all the roads of the Reich, singing their ancient songs, demanding to be conscripted into an army; eagerly seeking the most terrible weapons of war; burning to suffer and die for their fatherland.'[35] Not only towards Hitler did he display admiration, but the scope of his opportunism included Mussolini also. In October 1937, in the *News of the World*, he wrote: 'It would be dangerous folly for the British people to underrate the enduring position in world history which Mussolini will hold, or the amazing qualities of courage, comprehension, self-control and perseverance which he exemplifies'.[36]

In 1938 Churchill, a self-appointed expert on a range of military matters, stated: 'the air menace against properly protected ships of war will not be of decisive character, even a single well-armed vessel will hold its own against aircraft.'[37] At about the same time he pronounced that the Maginot Line would prove to be extremely effective and would make it 'very difficult indeed for the other army to break through. The idea that enormous masses of mechanical vehicles and tanks will be able to overrun these fortifications, will probably turn out to be a disappointment.'[38] He was also condescending in his views on the tank, saying, 'the tank has, no doubt, a great part to play, but I personally doubt very much whether it will ever see again the palmy days of 1918.'[39] His pronouncements were to be proven totally wrong on all three counts as even the largest battleships were sunk by aircraft, the Maginot Line was easily outflanked and so important was the tank that over 270,000 were produced during World War II. Given these self-opinionated views and his domineering manner, it is little wonder that Churchill was the cause of so many crises when he assumed total command.

When he became Prime Minister in 1940—and he later wrote in carefully chosen, dramatic words that 'he had felt the hand of fate upon his shoulder'—it is a moot point whether irrespective of the circumstances, or in reality perhaps because of them, he was in fact personally elated at finally making it to the top post which had been his life-long and all-consuming objective. War and power were his overriding passions, he loved them, and whereas many another politician would have baulked at, or with little enthusiasm would have taken over, the job as prime minster in 1940, it was precisely that combination of power at a time of peril and conflict that attracted him. In the midst of the carnage of World War I he is alleged to have written an elated letter to a friend in which he had revealed: 'I think a curse should rest on me—because I love this war. I know it's smashing and shattering the lives of thousands every moment—and yet—I can't help it—I enjoy every second of it'.[40]

Such was the butchery and slaughter in that conflict that in just one day Britain suffered 60,000 casualties, and yet Churchill was writing that he loved it. The question that naturally follows is whether he therefore enjoyed the German bombing raids during the Blitz of 1940, which caused the deaths of British citizens? After all, these were smashing and shattering the lives of thousands.

Becoming Prime Minister was the first big step, but mere leadership was not enough for Churchill: he needed total control and so he made himself Minster of Defence as well. Describing his behaviour once he became Prime Minister, Clive Ponting writes:

> He had always been arrogant and overbearing in his relations with other people, convinced that he was always right and resentful of any criticism. His staff had always been expected to be subservient to his slightest whim. Now that he was head of Government these tendencies were given much freer rein and more people were subjected to them.[41]

Churchill possessed the confidence that was vital for the position of Prime Minister during the war, but he was also the direct cause of a number of decisions that produced disasters. None of this is to diminish his position in history, but his interference, stubbornness and refusal to accept more experienced professional advice resulted in serious consequences. Irrespective of his standing these mistakes should be identified and particularly so in circumstances where he distanced himself from an event which, to use Correlli Barnett's phrase, 'had his fingerprints all over it' and then shifted the responsibility elsewhere. Moreover, because of his domineering attitude and dominating persona, he got away with it. His physician, Lord Moran, recorded:

> Churchill had to school himself not to think about things when they had gone wrong for he found that he could not live with his mistakes and keep his balance. This urge to obliterate had, in the course of time, grown into a cast of mind in which he seemed incapable of seeing that he has been at fault. So insidiously had this refusal to recognise a mistake grown on Winston, that it had become a habit of which he himself was probably not conscious, until it had

affected not only his speech but actually his way of thinking.[42]

Behind this imperious facade there lurked a serious mental condition, little understood at the time, and one that would influence much of his behaviour and many of his actions and decisions during World War II. It has subsequently been established that Churchill was a manic depressive or to use the current more socially acceptable expression for the condition, he was bipolar. Churchill himself called it his 'black dog', an expression that he claimed to be his but which in fact originated in the 19th century. However, there is a difference between periods of depression—maybe his 'black dog'—and the elevated manic phases which also characterise a bipolar condition. When a person who has been depressed suddenly feels the cloud lift it is natural to think that the depression has ended and that the person is finally back to normal. It is therefore quite possible that Churchill was unaware of the exact nature of the condition from which he suffered. He probably thought it was a unipolar disorder—recurrent depression—without realizing the full extent of his problem. His doctor Lord Moran says it was an inherited condition and that many of Churchill's ancestors suffered from what was called severe melancholia. In any event it was little understood at the time, when treatment would have been limited to psychoanalysis and the development of effective medication for mood disorders was yet to arrive.

Symptomatic characteristics of manic episodes are belligerence, grandiosity, a decreased need of sleep, flights of ideas and a belief in having special powers or abilities, all of which may explain many of the highs and lows of his performances during World War II, and all of which describe Churchill to a tee. His hostility in the face of alternative views as a means of getting his own way is well documented, as is his grandiosity and his unwavering belief in himself as a great man, his disdain for others and/or their opinions and the reason why he would come to regard Erwin Rommel as a personal rival and adversary. His massive ego also provides some insight into why he was convinced that he alone was right and why he consistently ignored all the professional warnings about Japan and the Far East. The decreased need of sleep is evidenced from numerous sources who had to endure a working day of such demand that it would start sometimes at 8 a.m. and go on till 3 a.m. the next morning. His flights of disastrous ideas were many, ranging from the already mentioned ill-fated Dardanelles campaign in 1915 to the 1941 Greek operation and then on to the Dodecanese disaster. Churchill is not alone in his struggle with this mental illness and is in good company with Johann Wolfgang von Goethe, Robert Schumann and Leo Tolstoy, who were also sufferers; in most cases it was the highs, the manic phases, which produced their most creative works. However, in Churchill's case although the manic episodes may have been the source of his most inspirational rhetoric, they would also have been the reason for some of his decisions for which the only explanation seems to have been stubborn, self-deluding euphoria. As Anthony Storr wrote in his book *Churchill's Black Dog, Kafka's Mice, and Other Phenomena of the Human Mind*, 'The kind of inspiration with which Churchill sustained the nation is not based on judgment, but on an irrational conviction independent of factual reality'.[43] That maybe so, but when the condition affects an individual who by nature is innately conceited, convinced of his own genius and also a domineering personality, then a dangerous combination emerges whereby logic sometimes just does not exist and no alternative will be tolerated. The truth is that in using those words Churchill was gambling then on the support of the United States because he knew that without such help he would have no alternative but to accommodate Adolph Hitler in one way or another.

So serious was Churchill's psychological problem and so consistent his fear of when it might strike, that Lord Moran recounts Churchill confessing:

> I don't like standing near the edge of a platform when an express is passing through. I like to stand right back and if possible to get a pillar between me and the train. I don't like to stand by the side of a ship and look down into the water. A second's action would end everything. A few drops of desperation.[44]

Such feelings—fear of heights, vertigo, deep water—are not all that uncommon, but it is rare that a person whose image was one of such extrovert ego and self-confidence, a person who loved having his voice heard and being in the public spotlight, should also harbour such private anxieties. Once more it seems to indicate the two conflicting personalities that were emerging from time to time and which would be manifest in some of his directives.

To add to this danger, and as mentioned earlier, immediately upon becoming Prime Minister Churchill had also made himself Minister of Defence, a move that made him a virtual dictator and enabled him almost without opposition to issue military instructions under two hats—what military historian Reginald W. Thompson called 'Generalissimo' Churchill.[45] It is apposite at this point to ask why he did so; was it his inherent ego, or, at only 5 feet 6 inches was this, like Montgomery, a subconscious device to compensate for his lack of physical stature?

This was a very different approach from that adopted by his eventual opposite number (and superior) US President Franklin Roosevelt, who was not exactly short on ego himself. Roosevelt made the political judgements and gave instructions regarding overall strategies but did not interfere with the detailed implementation of those directions or the tactics of his military or naval commanders. This is nicely put in Eliot A. Cohen's book *Supreme Command: Soldiers, Statesmen and Leadership in Wartime,* where he states: 'The Prime Minister had no understanding of operational details nor of logistic constraints and opportunities; but he had a great passion for them. He pestered commanders in the field for information and bombarded them with exhortations that went well beyond his responsibilities.'[46] General Brooke, then Chief of the Imperial General Staff, made this crucial difference clear with his diary entry for 26 June 1942 when he wrote:

> The President had no great military knowledge and was aware of this fact and consequently relied on Marshall and listened to Marshall's advice. Marshall never seemed to have any difficulties in countering any wildish plans which the President might put forward. My position was very different. Winston never had the slightest doubt that he had inherited all the military genius of his great ancestor Marlborough.[47]

An example of Churchill's conviction of his own inspiration was his decision for Mountbatten to head Combined Operations in 1941. Other than doing his best to sink just about every ship he had captained, what had Mountbatten done to justify that position? Perhaps two words would have described Mountbatten's style—impetuous and imperious—and those unfortunately would characterise the manner in which he would direct the disastrous raid on Dieppe in August 1942. But Mountbatten did have, to use modern parlance, the 'gift of the gab', and this along with his vanity and unceasing self-promotion produced a combination that seems to have impressed the Americans. Quiet and experienced wisdom were not qualities for which Churchill had any time and so Mountbatten was handed a job for which he was congenitally unsuited.

Another of Churchill's brainwaves was his promotion of the eccentric Major-General Orde Wingate and his 'Chindit' jungle penetration groups in Burma. It might have been thought wise to have consulted someone with experience in those conditions—perhaps the experienced General Slim who was in charge of the Burma land forces. In his book *Defeat into Victory*[48] Slim later stated merely that Wingate's ideas did not produce results commensurate with the resources required, but Churchill had a bee in his bonnet about Wingate and insisted on taking him to the 1943 Ottawa conference as an example of British ingenuity. Prior to leaving for the Conference, Churchill had issued a directive to the chiefs of staff, stating 'Wingate is a man of genius and audacity. No mere question of seniority must be allowed to obstruct his advancement'.[49] A wiser assessment of Wingate was that made by Major-General Sir John Kennedy, who was the Director of Military Operations at the War Office. In *The Business of War* he described Wingate as 'picturesque but not very important',[50] but then however impractical, the 'picturesque' was always what attracted Churchill, and the more ornate or ostentatious the more allured he would be. The author has discussed Wingate with several officers who served in Burma and the repeated opinion is that he was mentally unstable, a man who would hold meetings with his subordinates whilst sitting in his bath wearing a pith helmet. Churchill's personal physician, Lord Moran, confirmed that assessment: 'He seemed to me hardly sane—in medical jargon a borderline case'.[51] But here again it seems that the bi-polar condition may have been one of the main reasons why Churchill was attracted to colourful personalities. Lord Moran also wrote that Churchill knew the attacks of depression might come on him at any time and without warning, and he avoided anyone or anything that might bring them on. He would not go near a hospital and disliked people of low vitality—hence, probably, the apparent distrust of quiet modesty, however experienced, and the preference for the flamboyant, however shallow that might be.

Over and above the huge industrial resources and the military and material support that came with the decision by the United States to enter the war, Churchill's commanders must have breathed a sigh of relief because he was then largely forced to take a back seat and could no longer interfere in detail. Eliot A. Cohen goes on to relate:

> At the end of the war in Europe, General Hastings Ismay recalled a decade later, Churchill hosted a victory celebration dinner for the Chiefs of Staff at 10 Downing Street. The Prime Minister handed out extravagant praise for the three Chiefs of Staff as having been the architects of victory. Not one of them responded by saying that Winston had also had a little to do with it'.[52]

That surely is a telling comment. Whilst they had admired his nation-rousing rhetoric and the image he had created as a defiant leader early in the war, there were too many of his character traits which they absolutely loathed. To quote General Brooke again, he recorded such feelings succinctly in his dairy in 1942 when he wrote: 'I feel that I can't stick another moment with him, and would give almost anything never to see him again'.[53]

In his book *Blood, Sweat and Arrogance: The Myths of Churchill's War*, Gordon Corrigan explains this further: 'Churchill got rid of generals who would not tell him what he wanted to hear. Churchill had a propensity to sack commanders who were unable to conceal what they thought of the Prime Minister's qualities as a strategist'.[54] Three classic examples of this characteristic were his removal of generals Wavell and Auchinleck from the Middle East and Field Marshal Sir John Dill, Chief of the Imperial General Staff, who was banished to Washington. Wavell, described by military historian Correlli Barnett as one of Britain's greatest generals, and thought by Erwin Rommel to have been the most gifted of all the British commanders in North Africa, had had to stretch his limited resources to the maximum to sort out problems that had arisen in Iraq and Syria. He then had his forces decimated by Churchill's emotional and disastrous foray into Greece in April 1941. He was removed by the impatient and demanding Churchill in July1941 and replaced by the shrewd and quietly determined Auchinleck, who made it clear to Churchill that he was not about to be prematurely hurried into anything, and therefore he in turn was also sacked a year later just as he was turning the tide against Rommel. Both Wavell and Auchinleck were very capable generals who became victims of a Prime Minister who thought himself a military genius and was incapable of comprehending just what they had both in fact achieved. There was an underlying domestic reason for Churchill's interference and impatience: he badly needed a land victory of some sort to save his own political skin. The government had just lost three by-elections and rumours were abundant in Westminster, but Churchill the inveterate politician would pull any rabbit out of the hat to retain the power that was his very lifeblood.

The wise and experienced Dill was very much a thorn in the side of an impatient Churchill, who could not tolerate advice that did not fit in with his own fancies; moreover, if such counter-advice was put to him in writing it was likely to provoke outright rage. In late 1941 Churchill, in his dual capacity as Minister of Defence, removed Dill by sending him to Washington to head up the British Joint Staff Mission. There he was held in such high regard by the top echelons of the United States military that when he died in November 1944 he was accorded the totally unique honour of burial in Arlington National Cemetery, America's most hallowed military burial ground; even today he is the only non-American to be so recognised. In contrast to the sarcasm and contempt his views had consistently received from the abrasive Churchill, on Dill's death the American Joint Chiefs of Staff sent to their British counterparts a message of condolence glowing with admiration of his character, experience and military advice. When Dill was dismissed, General Brooke noted in his diary:

> Winston had never been fond of Dill. They were entirely different types of character, and types that could never have worked harmoniously together. Dill was 'the essence of straightforwardness, blessed with the highest principles and an unassailable integrity of character. I do not believe that any of these characteristics appealed to Winston, on the contrary, I think he disliked them as they accentuated his own shortcomings in this respect.[55]

A withering comment if ever there was one. There does not appear to be any record of what Churchill's reaction was to the news of Dill's death, if indeed he said anything at all. Each one of these talented men possessed a quiet, undemonstrative personality, and none of them had the extrovert attitude so needed by the depression-fearing Churchill.

General Eisenhower commented in his memoirs about an occasion when Churchill showed him a cable he was about to send to a Middle East commander, dealing with specific details of a tactical plan. After reading it Eisenhower told Churchill he would not send such a message to a field commander. Churchill wanted to know why. Eisenhower explained that if as an American commander he received such a message from the President of the United States he would immediately resign. This incident was an illustration of the difference between the American and Churchillian system of command, but Churchill did not seem to understand.[56]

All the chiefs of staff knew that they only continued to serve at Churchill's pleasure because not only had he also appointed himself as Minister of Defence but there was no ministry—just him. In the summer of 1942, the period of the Dieppe disaster and the sacking of Auchinleck, both the First Sea Lord Admiral Sir Dudley Pound and General Brooke had been aware that he was considering replacing them. This had been the earlier fate of Sir John Dill, and was simply due to the fact that they had felt compelled to turn down so many of his impractical 'pet projects'; what they knew from their experience just would not work was regarded by Churchill as simply being 'negative'. Arthur Bryant recounts a meeting when Brooke was patiently trying to explain to Churchill why his plan for the landing of Canadian troops in an out-of-the-way spot like northern Norway in 1942 just would not work.[57] This was nothing more than strategic common sense. As Canadian military historian Jack L. Granatstein notes, it was 'as immensely foolhardy as any of the Prime Minister's self-conceived plans',[58] but it provoked in the petulant Churchill what Bryant describes as 'the most awful outburst of temper',[59] who then slammed his papers together and stomped out of the room, exhibiting again the furious reaction of the manic-depressive.

Clive Ponting, one of Churchill's more perceptive and penetrating biographers, wrote of the disquiet his colleagues felt throughout the war because of Churchill's attitude of total indifference towards casualties and in particular to the orders he had given on Singapore and Egypt. In the same month that Churchill gave the Egyptian order and with the same cool nonchalance towards the loss of lives of his own forces, he ordered that the port of Tripoli be blocked by sinking two Royal Navy capital ships in the harbour. Even manned by skeleton crews this would have involved the loss of hundreds of navy lives, but fortunately Admiral Sir Andrew B. Cunningham (Commander-in-Chief, Mediterranean Station) refused to even consider such an irresponsible instruction—and Sir Andrew was just a little too senior to be cast aside as others had been. Ponting also recounts how, a few months earlier and then totally obsessed with destroying the German battleship *Tirpitz*, Churchill told Bomber Command that the 'loss of a hundred bombers could be accepted if the *Tirpitz* were destroyed'.[60] The *Tirpitz* was the sister ship to the recently sunk *Bismarck*, but once again, fortunately, such recklessness was resisted. The Chief of the Air Staff stood up to him and told him he was not prepared to risk so many planes and their highly trained crews on such an impractical attack. Churchill had used his most colourful language saying 'the whole strategy of the war turns at this point on this ship'. It was palpable nonsense, for in no way was the *Tirpitz* such a pivotal issue for a sacrifice of such magnitude to be even remotely considered. All of these seem, once again, to point to the irrational but self-convinced delusions that occur during a hyper-manic episode.

Churchill adored the sound of his own voice and found listening to other people's conversation quite insufferable. He loved speaking publicly about himself and there are a myriad of such reported comments, one of the most famous being: 'My idea of a good dinner is first to have good food, then discuss good food, and after this good food has been elaborately discussed, to discuss a good topic—with me as chief conversationalist'.

The conceit in this is quite astonishing but it might be noted that this was Churchill talking in a totally unashamed fashion about himself and apparently quite incapable of seeing anything at all unusual in this. His mealtime monologues were of long duration and British television actor and producer Peter Willes recounted his experience when he met Churchill in the south of France in the 1930s:

> At meals he just banged on and on, regardless of anyone else's interest or desires to talk; and if you weren't deeply involved in politics he really was the most dreadful bore. All he seemed to do was smoke cigars, eat, drink and talk far more than anyone else, and never gave a damn what anybody thought of him.[61]

Add to this the comment made by Brian Loring Villa in his book on the Dieppe raid when he said of Churchill: 'He had always enjoyed displaying his rhetorical and didactic skills. As Prime Minister he had often inflicted monologues and soliloquies on his guests long into the early hours of the morning'.[62] Many of these monologues were the classic symptoms of a bipolar disorder, but we should ask ourselves this: if Churchill was unaware of the precise nature of his problem, then was anyone else? He knew he had always suffered from episodes of depression, but was he aware that the periods in between such troughs were not merely a natural relief but were often a violent swing to the other extreme, where the self-doubts of depression became feelings of exuberant self-confidence that were just as irrational as the fears of the depressions?

This 'swinging personality' was certainly noticed and it could hardly have been avoided. General Hastings Ismay was Chief Military Adviser to Churchill throughout World War II and as such was almost in daily contact with him. In April 1942 he wrote to General Auchinleck, saying of Churchill:

> You cannot judge the PM by ordinary standards; he is not in the least like anyone you and I have ever met. He is a mass of contradictions. He is either on the crest of a wave, or in the trough; either highly laudatory or bitterly condemnatory; either in an angelic temper, or a hell of a rage; when he isn't asleep he's a volcano.[63]

'Crest of a wave or in a trough'—what better description of the massive emotional fluctuations of a bipolar condition? Did it not occur to anyone that these huge swings were evidence of a mental disorder, or were they all thinking this was merely 'Churchill being Churchill'? Or was it perhaps a case that, knowing the probable explosive response that even venturing such a possibility would provoke, such questions were never even mooted?

His personal physician, Lord Moran, although frequently mentioning Churchill's 'black moods', in his book on Churchill did not seem to have attributed these to any serious underlying serious psychological condition, or at least if he did, he did not say so. But even the very mention of these periodic 'black' episodes provoked such outraged indignation and resentment, bordering on accusations of treason when his book appeared in 1966, that it was just as well that he did not.

Churchill's position vis-à-vis World War II is neatly summed up by military historian Gordon Corrigan when he writes in conclusion:

> If Churchill was the man who won the war, as election posters in 1945 said he was, then he was also the man who by his political actions between 1919 and 1929 contributed in very large measure to Britain being unready for it, and who by his flights of fancy, his unwillingness to trust professionals and his unshakeable belief that he knew better than anyone else how this nation's efforts should be directed, was very nearly responsible for losing it.[64]

With the benefit of hindsight and placing all events in a purely clinical context an accurate assessment shows that instead of the conventional view of Britain being lucky to have had such a man, in many ways it was fortunate to have survived the war in spite of him, rather than because of him. As Churchill himself confessed to Lord Moran in 1944, 'I have a strong feeling that my work is done. I had a message. I have no message'.[65] On one issue Churchill was absolutely right. In 1940 he certainly did have a message, a message of virtual messianic inspiration, but once that message had been delivered, his functional involvement was incapable of maintaining the same promise.

CHAPTER 3

MONTGOMERY —
MILITARY MESSIAH
OR ARMY ARRIVISTE?

Indomitable in retreat, invincible in advance, insufferable in victory.—WINSTON CHURCHILL on Montgomery

The name, title and honours bestowed upon Field Marshal Bernard Law Montgomery, 1st Viscount Montgomery of Alamein, KG, GCB, DSO, PC, create an image that seems beyond question and not deserving of any scrutiny or post mortem; and thus it was for many years following World War II. A virtual unknown, he was immediately elevated to the realm of military superhero following the Second Battle of El Alamein in 1942. Much of this came from the British press and Prime Minister Winston Churchill, but most of it was orchestrated by Montgomery himself; and since his image rests entirely on El Alamein, it is worth examining the real circumstances of that battle.

One of the biggest problems that Britain's desert commanders had to deal with was not German General Erwin Rommel but their own Prime Minister, Churchill, who convinced of his own inherited military genius was continually badgering them with one fanciful order after another. Impatient with the wise and cautious Sir Archibald Wavell, whose command had been excessively loaded at Churchill's direction with extra responsibilities in East Africa, Iraq and Syria and then seriously weakened by the substantial losses that his forces suffered through Churchill's disastrous foray into Greece. The Prime Minister summarily sacked Wavell in June 1941, accusing him of being 'tired', and replaced him with Claude Auchinleck, Commander-in-Chief, India. This was the same Wavell who, according to Rommel's biographer Charles Douglas-Home, Rommel thought the most gifted of all Britain's desert commanders and who was described by military historian Correlli Barnett as 'one of the very greatest of British soldiers of any age'. But of course, nobody could tell that to Churchill: he was convinced he knew better.

Auchinleck, who many would argue was at least the equal of Wavell, was no more prepared to bow to Churchill's importunate demands than his predecessor—he in fact told Churchill as much during a visit to London—but his 14-month tenure was one of fluctuating successes and he had the misfortune to appoint several commanders who did not perform as expected. Those with the benefit of hindsight have criticised his choices, but as anyone who has operated with a range of subordinates will know, it is not all that unusual for an appointee to appear to have the necessary qualities only to fail when placed in position. Again like Wavell, he was subjected to continuing political interference and had to endure a constant stream of bullying cables from the Prime Minister, in response to which his calm and steadfast refusal to be rushed almost caused apoplexy in Churchill. Both Auchinleck and Wavell had to tolerate an enormous amount of detailed meddling and criticism from Churchill, fussy tactical questions made by someone sitting behind a desk and looking at flags on a map from a distance of over 2,000 miles; this would have tried the patience of a saint, and as Correlli Barnett states, 'Churchill was a man who merely counted numbers.' Their exasperation is totally understandable, for it was, as is shown elsewhere, a situation that would not have been tolerated by any American general.

What Auchinleck did achieve, though (through careful choice of ground and intelligent planning), was to get the better of Rommel in the First Battle of El Alamein in July 1942, the significance of which was either lost on or ignored in London. Assisting Auchinleck in his dispositions had been Major-General Eric Dorman-Smith, one of the few original thinkers in the British Army. But even this was not enough for the impatient Churchill, who one month later discarded both of them. Auchinleck was removed and his responsibilities split between Sir Harold Alexander as Commander-in-Chief Middle East and Lieutenant-General William 'Strafer' Gott to command the Eighth Army. Unfortunately Gott was killed shortly before he took over his new position and so, literally by accident, in came Bernard

Montgomery. Dorman-Smith, who was uncomfortably too brilliant for the status quo mentality of the British top brass, was cast into oblivion. Even in the midst of a war that was then no more than evenly balanced, the British Army remained a very political club where *con*forming was more important than *per*forming.

Churchill and Brooke are reported to have been amazed at the apparent immediate grasp of the overall situation displayed by Montgomery when talking to the two of them in August 1942. What they should have known— but of course what he was not about to tell them—was that only a couple of weeks previously he had received a most detailed exposition of existing deployments and resources plus Rommel's own position and expected moves from Auchinleck and Dorman-Smith. They also told him they had access through Ultra codebreaking to Rommel's signals. So nothing that Montgomery told Churchill and Brooke was in anyway his own summation of the position; it was merely what had been described to him earlier by the original architects of the overall position when he was about to take over. Churchill had no reason to doubt, and Brooke as Montgomery's mentor was not going to ask, whether the concepts were his own. Montgomery explained everything as being his own interpretation, his own thoughts and his own predictions.

At this point Montgomery's further actions and comments come under the microscope. In *The Desert Generals,* Corelli Barnett recounts Montgomery's first action on being appointed:

> In Eighth Army Headquarters on 12th August 1942 he signalled G.H.Q., Cairo that he had assumed command of Eighth Army, two days earlier than he should have done and in complete disobedience of orders. This gesture was of no importance militarily—he did nothing during those two days that he could not have done as army-commander designate but it throws a bleak light on his character as a man. It could serve only to wound Auchinleck in his last two days of command. Sixteen years later his pleasure in his action was undiminished, he made a point in saying in his Memoirs that on 13th August 1942, 'it was with an insubordinate smile that I went to sleep. I was issuing orders to an army which someone else reckoned he commanded.[66]

Even at the very start of Montgomery's desert destiny a childish and ruthless self-promoting deceit was revealing itself. But it was more than that for, having acted deliberately to cause unnecessary insult to Auchinleck, he then went on to brag about having done so in his memoirs as if it was something to be proud of; the action of a small-minded man who was prepared to trample on anyone to achieve his ends.[67]

Montgomery was a short, thin-faced man. He felt he needed a hat that would make him stand out, for unlike the natural leadership personas of Wavell and Auchinleck, Montgomery required some contrivance to provide the sort of image he wanted. As biographer Alun Chalfont describes him in his book *Montgomery of Alamein*, 'He looked more like a Jack Russell terrier than a man born to command.'[68]

His first idea was an Australian-style slouch hat with one side brim turned up, but since it carried no immediate badge he decorated it with up to a dozen different regimental or corps badges and wore it in that style until even he realised it made him look ridiculous. He then switched this millinery Christmas tree for a black beret, but even that hat still carried two badges: his usual general staff badge, plus that of the Royal Tank Regiment. Montgomery needed to look 'different' and to some extent this eccentricity did work because it helped to transform an ordinary looking little man into a 'product' that could be recognised.

In general terms Montgomery and El Alamein can be summed up by the following passage taken from Gordon Corrigan's *Blood, Sweat and Arrogance: The Myths of Churchill's War*:

> National myth has it that Montgomery took over a defeated, demoralised and badly led Eighth Army, and by his own abilities and powers of leadership won the great victory of Alamein and then went on to drive the Germans and Italians out of North Africa in a whirlwind campaign that could not have been achieved by anyone else. We know that because Montgomery has told us so, not only by his masterly grasp of public relations at the time but in one of the most self-serving Memoirs ever foisted on the reading public, and one that did immense harm to Anglo-American relations after the war.
>
> Montgomery and Alamein are also remembered because Second Alamein was a victory and the first British victory lauded to the

British public and the world for a very long time. First Alamein was a victory too, but it was not as dramatic and it was not 'spun', to use the currently fashionable term, by a Prime Minister who badly needed a victory, and a general who craved fame and recognition.

Suffice to say that Lieutenant General Montgomery had what no other Eighth Army commander before him had: a Commander-in-Chief who was able to keep the Prime Minister off his back, time to prepare and train, massive reinforcement and a carefully worked-out plan put in place by Auchinleck and Dorman-Smith. There is nothing wrong with picking other men's flowers, but it is gracious to acknowledge the planters.[69]

And yet shortly before the battle, and having made full use of the plans already drawn up by Auchinleck and Dorman-Smith, Montgomery wrote to a friend in the War Office:

My first encounter with Rommel was of great interest. Luckily I had had time to tidy up the mess (and it was 'some' mess, I can tell you) and to get my plans laid, the situation here when I arrived was really unbelievable; I would never have thought it could be so bad. Auchinleck should never be employed again in any capacity.[70]

This was an astounding comment to have been made by a lieutenant-general about a full general three years his senior. It is interesting to compare Montgomery's arrogant distortions with Auchinleck's measured appreciation two years before when he had taken over from Wavell:

In no sense do I wish to infer that I found an unsatisfactory situation on my arrival—far from it. Not only was I greatly impressed by the solid foundations laid by my predecessor, but I was able the better to appreciate the vastness of the problems with which he had been confronted and the greatness of his achievements, in a command in which some 40 different languages are spoken by the British and Commonwealth Forces.[71]

Auchinleck had been Montgomery's immediate superior a few years earlier in England and quite rightly had insisted that Montgomery go through the proper channels when requesting the transfers of personnel. This was standard procedure and was common sense for movements to be monitored and recorded but it had infuriated Montgomery, who wanted to be allowed his own way; now he was getting his own back. Moreover, very few of the plans made were uniquely those of Montgomery but had been carefully worked out and laid by the Auchinleck/Dorman-Smith team. Montgomery just tinkered here and there, so his comment about 'getting *my* plans laid' is a typical exaggeration.

The actual achievements and morale of the Eighth Army when Montgomery arrived on the scene are well described by General Playfair in his book *The Mediterranean and Middle East*, Volume III, where he states:

> In retrospect the vital importance of the July fighting stands out clearly, and to General Auchinleck stands the credit for turning retreat into counter-attack. His forecast of mid-September as the earliest date for an 'all-out' offensive may not have been popular in London, but it was realistic and reasonable. In the event this offensive began on October 23rd and its success should not be allowed to overshadow the earlier achievements of those who made it possible.[72]

Montgomery said that he kept a photograph of Rommel at his bedside and claimed this enabled him, in his speech defect style where the letter R is sounded as W, to 'wead Wommel's mind'. This was total fiction but a clever ploy to manipulate the truth; the fact was, as mentioned earlier, that the British had broken the German Enigma code through the use of Ultra, and thus Montgomery was receiving complete copies of all German military communications, as well as full details of Rommel's supply problems, and was aware of when and where he was likely to attack. Nobody was 'weading' anyone's mind—least of all Montgomery. A more measured man would have kept such intelligence to himself and his immediate subordinates but even with such sensitive intelligence information Montgomery could not resist the opportunity to brag and self-promote and thus jeopardise a priceless asset. This unwise grandstanding caused the Germans to suspect that the security of their codes might have been broken and as a consequence Montgomery was asked to take more care about what he said in future. As it happened the Germans decided they had nothing to worry about and were so confident of the security of their sophisticated Enigma code that they never discovered it had been broken.

Montgomery had the luxury of this information because under the direction of Auchinleck and Dorman-Smith the interception and interpretation of Enigma intelligence had become so refined and penetrating that, long before El Alamein, Montgomery had in his possession detailed information of Rommel's dispositions, supplies and reserves. General Wilhelm Ritter von Thoma had commanded the Afrika Korps front at El Alamein and was captured when he escaped out of his burning tank. Basil Liddell Hart recounts a conversation in 1948 when von Thoma described to him his astonishment during a later conversation with Montgomery:

> Instead of asking me for information, he said he would tell me the state of our forces, their supplies and their dispositions. I was staggered at the exactness of his knowledge, particularly of our deficiencies and shipping losses. He seemed to know as much about our position as I did myself.[73]

Even after a battle that was almost impossible to lose Montgomery could not help gloating or exercising his congenital urge to rub an opponent's nose in the mud. It was just as well that von Thoma never managed to escape captivity.

There had been building up for some months a massive increase in numbers and resources before Montgomery assumed command and this continued for some time thereafter. For the Second Battle of El Alamein, the date of which was carefully planned (see later), this gave him the previously unknown luxury of 230,000 troops, 1,100 tanks, including for the first time 300 of the new and superior Sherman tanks fresh off the US production line, over 2,300 field and anti-tank guns and overwhelming air supremacy. Against this, Montgomery knew from Ultra that the Afrika Korps could muster only 110,000 men (mostly Italians), 500 tanks (many decrepit Italian models) and 1,300 artillery pieces, was low on ammunition and very short of fuel. From the codebreaking, he also knew that Rommel was not even in Africa but had been away sick in Germany since 23 September. It has been observed by others that this was not the first time that the British, on paper at least, had a numerical advantage and in principle this is true, but rarely before had there been such a massive preponderance of factors and resources in favour of one side. Such was Montgomery's embarrassment of riches that he opened up the battle with a non-stop, five-hour barrage of 1,000 guns over a front of only 10,000 yards. In the open desert such an incessant bombardment meant that with a gun for every 10 yards any defensive positions and/or minefields were totally obliterated. There was however nothing novel or imaginative about such a massive artillery onslaught for it was very much reminiscent of the bludgeoning tactic used so often in World War I.

Rommel was well aware that the dice were increasingly loaded against him. Speaking about the British build-up to his officers shortly after he had failed at First Alamein in July 1942, he said:

> Vast convoys are sailing with powerful escort round the Cape. Already the first of these are in the Red Sea, but that is only the beginning. More and more will arrive. It is obvious that by the middle of September the British 8th Army will be so strong that we shall not be able to deal with it.[74]

As mentioned above, the date for the battle was fixed with some accuracy because Churchill, Alexander and Montgomery were all aware of the coming Operation *Torch*, a joint force of 107,000 British/American troops that were to land at Casablanca, Oran and Algiers and which was scheduled for early in November. They were all, also, fully aware of the fact that once Rommel learnt of this force at his rear, he would be forced to break off any engagement and quickly retire west to protect his base at Tripoli, which was much closer to Algiers than it was to El Alamein. Montgomery had calculated that this battle might last some 12 days, and the date for the launch was therefore cynically fixed for 23 October some *13* days before the expected *Torch* landings, thus making quite sure that his certain victory could not be attributed to the *Torch* invasions. In the event *Torch* was delayed until 8 November but even that was 4 days before the conclusion of what should have been a very one sided affair at El Alamein.

The success of Operation *Torch* in springing a surprise on the Germans is startling given the usual efficiency of their intelligence. It seems remarkable that convoys of over 100 ships could sail from Scotland, past the Bay of Biscay and again past Portugal and Spain, a voyage of two weeks and yet not be detected for the first time until it reached the Strait of Gibraltar. But that was only the eastern section of the *Torch* taskforce, for an equal number of ships comprising the western part sailed in convoy from Virginia across the Atlantic to Casablanca, and this armada arrived unnoticed. Germany had numerous agents in Ireland, Portugal and Spain and yet this massive array of shipping, although noticed at the last moment, was even then and despite its size interpreted as yet another convoy headed for Malta. As historian Correlli Barnett has pointed out:

> it is certain that, even if Montgomery had not fought his battle, Rommel would have been out of Egypt within a month and Tunisia within three. Had Eighth Army held its attack until the moment Rommel had left the shelter of his fixed defences and begun to retreat, it could have completely destroyed the Panzer-armee at small cost. For Rommel would have been helpless, with ninety thousand un-motorised infantry to cover with only two hundred German tanks in the face of British command of the air, one thousand one hundred tanks and a mechanised army of two hundred and twenty thousand men.[75]

In his book *Eastern Epic* yet another renowned author, Sir Compton McKenzie, wrote:

> A legend has grown up that the Eighth Army started its career at the second battle of Alamein, and this legend has been preposterously turned into bad history by those who were responsible for denying to all those who served in it before October 23rd 1942, the numeral 8 on the ribbon of the Africa Star. The only explanation for such denial is the guilty conscience of those who were fundamentally responsible for their ever having been a need for a second battle of Alamein.[76]

So why was the Second Battle of El Alamein fought at all? There is only one possible explanation. Irrespective of what the cost might be in casualties—and this had actually been forecast by Montgomery to be over 13,000—what presented itself was an opportunity that was just too good to miss and in particular a chance for glory that a self-promoter such as Montgomery was not going to pass up. Churchill, as will be shown later, was always indifferent to casualties and was under political pressure, so a totally unnecessary battle was fought. Some 4,600 men lost their lives and 8,900 were wounded for the personal prestige of one man and to save the political skin of another. As an additional comment on this 'great victory', Montgomery still managed to lose 600 tanks as against Rommel's 160.

On the other hand, would a long-sighted and impartial military commander not have said to Churchill something akin to: 'Look, Prime Minister, with the coming "Torch" landings we don't need to launch any attack; we can wait until Rommel retires from Egypt, which we know he must, and then we can chase him. This would involve considerable savings in men and materials and he would be crushed from both east and west.' Such a suggestion would have made much sense, but of course it is almost a certainty that even if such a plan had been put forward, the growling response would have been: 'No, Britain needs to have a battle to win.' What this really would have meant is: 'I must have a victory to hold on to my job.' One can imagine a dictator having such one-eyed priorities, a victory however expensive to crow about, but it is disconcerting to discover that this was the deliberate policy of a democracy.

It has been claimed that the operation was necessary for public morale and British standing after a string of defeats, for which Churchill himself had been largely responsible, but this is a specious argument because a defeat of Rommel could just as easily have been claimed through his forced retreat and pursuit. The truth of the matter was clear to the Americans, who ignored this British posturing, but it was concealed from the general public in Britain because Churchill's position in Parliament was in jeopardy and being able to bask in the reflected glory of what was promoted as a great victory gave him a political lifeline.

But that was not the end of it. Montgomery was again lucky when the experienced General Georg Stumme, to whom Rommel had deputised his command whilst away, died of a heart attack early on the second day of the battle. Once again through breaking the German codes and before the battle commenced, Montgomery knew that Rommel was away in Germany, but he never admitted it. Rommel hurried back as soon as he was able, but for some considerable time his Afrika Korps was without a commander. The Eighth Army had overwhelming superiority in men, tanks, guns and aircraft and could hardly have lost the battle, but because of Montgomery's hesitation, the prospect of a clear-cut and decisive victory hung in the balance for 11 days. No battle goes completely to plan, but as Gordon Corrigan states:

> At one stage the attack was completely stalled, and had Rommel been there the result might have been disastrous for the British. As it was, by the time Rommel returned on the night of 25th October, the immediate crisis for the British had passed and superior forces began to tell.[77]

Having finally come out on top and although proclaiming to the world that he had won a complete and absolute victory, Montgomery then dithered for some time allowing the defeated Rommel to withdraw in remarkable order. There was no immediate pursuit, and to quote Correlli Barnett once more:

> As Clausewitz points out, the fruits of victory are gathered in the pursuit, but no fruits were gathered in the pursuit from Alamein. It was not therefore a 'complete and absolute victory.' In order to gather these fruits, as Clausewitz also points out, the pursuit must be vigorous; Montgomery's pursuit after Alamein showed all the bustling confidence of an arch-deacon entering a *maison close* [brothel].[78]

Niall Barr writes of this in his book, *Pendulum of War: The Three Battles of El Alamein;* the cause was Montgomery's failure before the battle began to plan adequately for pursuit which meant that no unit was given overall priority in the chase.[79] The X Corps had been assigned the job of a *corps de chasse*, a pursuit group, but due to Montgomery's indecision it never got under way in time to achieve anything. For a defeated army, Rommel was able to retire remarkably well organised and without undue haste. Montgomery later excused this debacle on heavy rain saying that it had impeded his movements, but as Correlli Barnett rightly points out the rain fell impartially on Briton and German alike and the Axis retreat was as greatly hampered by it as the British pursuit. In fact the only part of Rommel's Africa Korps that was caught was a panzer division that had run out of fuel, but even then it fought off the pursuers and disappeared again when refuelled.

Rommel himself discussed such a situation when he wrote of Wavell's pursuit of the Italians being curtailed by Churchill:

> When a commander has won a decisive victory it is generally wrong for him to be satisfied with too narrow a strategic aim. For that is the time to exploit success. It is during the pursuit, when the beaten enemy is still dispirited and disorganised, that most prisoners are made and most booty captured. Troops who on one day are flying in a wild panic to the rear, may, unless they are continually harried by the pursuer, very soon stand in battle again, freshly organised as fully effective fighting men.[80]

In spite of Ultra having broken the German codes, so appalling were Montgomery's tactics and indecision following the battle that the scenario is worth quoting direct from another author who makes similar comments. In his book *Armageddon: The Second World War* Clive Ponting wrote:

> As the Germans began to retreat the British knew that the two German Panzer divisions had eleven serviceable tanks between them, a quarter of their normal ammunition stocks and enough fuel for four days. Montgomery's reaction was to sack commanders who showed any initiative in attacking the Germans. By 17 November Ultra showed that the Germans were virtually immobilized in Benghazi for lack of fuel. Montgomery then took twelve days to devise a plan for another crude frontal assault. His failure to attack enabled the Germans to destroy the port at Benghazi. Montgomery repeated this performance at the end of December in front of Tripoli when he waited three weeks before attacking despite the fact that he knew he had 532 front-line tanks and the Germans 37.[81]

Later, in a statement that Auchinleck might have considered defamatory, Montgomery even went so far as to claim that he had been astonished to discover that Auchinleck was planning to retreat if attacked and that it had been he, Montgomery, who had squashed this defeatist strategy. It was a total lie and it was this calumny that specifically prompted Correlli Barnett to write *The Desert Generals,* explicitly commenting there that the allegation 'was a cruel slander without basis of fact.' As Barnett also comments, the Montgomery 'myth' had 'less foundation in fact than in ambition, political convenience and personal spite.'

We must therefore ask whether in fact that 'battle' could and would have been won if anyone else had been in charge; in other words was 'Monty' as brilliant and personally crucial to the outcome as he claims and as he was for some time portrayed? The answer must be an unequivocal 'no'. As mentioned earlier, the massive advantages in planned location, numbers, quality of resources and intelligence on the one side as against practically all the odds stacked against Rommel were such that a British victory was virtually assured whoever was in command. Auchinleck explained in an interview some years later that the reasons for his removal were political and not military and he accepted that at the time.

Montgomery's reputation is based entirely on the fictitious version of El Alamein, and the trap into which so many people naively fall is encapsulated in a 2007 review of Gordon Corrigan's book that appeared in *The Sandhurst Foundation Newsletter*, where in relation to Montgomery the reviewer states: 'Very few other generals seemed to be able to make things happen let alone win.' One might ask, make which things happen? As the above facts demonstrate almost everything was handed to Montgomery on a plate when he arrived in North Africa in 1942. An enlarged and well-trained orchestra had been fully equipped and rehearsed and all Montgomery had to do was pick up the conductor's baton. Had he arrived a year or so earlier and produced the same result then that comment might have had some truth— but he had not, and one of the main reasons why the myth continues that he 'made things happen' is simply because he told us so.

With typical candour Rommel himself put matters into their true perspective via an entry in his diary:

It was a matter of getting the best out of a hopeless situation. Armed with a pitchfork, the finest fighting man can do little against an opponent with a tommy-gun in his hand. There was never any chance of the army achieving success at Alamein.[82]

Given a choice between his good generals and his lucky ones, Napoleon has been quoted as saying that he would always choose his lucky ones. However, he was referring to luck, or chance in battle, a change in the weather, a mistake made by the opposing commander, and so on, but in Montgomery's case El Alamein was cut and dried before anything ever started, and he knew it. The location and dispositions had all been worked out and set in place for him by his predecessor and he knew he was in possession of resources that gave him, well before any battle commenced, one of the most one-sided assembly of advantages ever recorded. Even then and although the Afrika Korps lost their commanding officer, under Montgomery's direction the result still hung in the balance for some time and he failed totally to pursue a defeated enemy. Rommel had been beaten—any other outcome would have been a calamity of monumental proportions—but under Montgomery's cautious and hesitant mismanagement Rommel's army was certainly not in any manner 'destroyed as a fighting force' as it could and should have been. Rommel was allowed time to withdraw in such an orderly manner that the Eighth Army virtually lost all contact with him.

The experienced General Fritz Bayerlein who had accompanied General Guderian in Operation *Barbarossa* (the invasion of Russia in 1941) and later commanded the elite Panzer Lehr Division in Normandy in 1944, had also served in the Afrika Korps, briefly assuming command whilst Rommel was away just prior to the Second Battle of El Alamein. During an interview whilst being debriefed after the war he said he had been amazed at the ease with which Rommel was allowed to escape after that battle, stating 'I do not think General Patton would have let us get away so easily.'[83] He then went on to say that Patton was the equal of Guderian.

To quote Gordon Corrigan once more: 'There is nothing wrong with picking other men's flowers, but it is gracious to acknowledge the planters.' And who did take action to prevent the numeral '8' appearing on the Africa Star for anyone who had served in the Eighth Army prior to the Second Battle of El Alamein? This deprived the '8' from the troops who had fought under O'Connor, Wavell and Auchinleck. One can only speculate but it was a grubby little gesture.

CHAPTER 4

MOUNTBATTEN—PRODUCT OF PROTECTED PATRONAGE

He was a mendacious, intellectually limited hustler,
whose negligence and incompetence resulted in many
unnecessary deaths—the number of which increased
exponentially as his meteoric career progressed.
—ANDREW ROBERTS, *Eminent Churchillians*

The collection of honorifics pertaining to Admiral of the Fleet Louis Francis Albert Victor Nicholas George Mountbatten, 1st Earl Mountbatten of Burma, KG, GCB, OM, GCSI, GCIE, GCVO, DSO, PC, FRS, are even greater than those of Montgomery, producing a conventional reaction that might think the man unassailable. However, Mountbatten was a man of many parts and there is much to show that, for various reasons, he was appointed beyond his capabilities, his huge mistakes were excused or covered up, and moreover that he seems to have been casually indifferent to the consequences and casualties caused by his errors. Again, like Montgomery he would be said to have had 'a good war'.

Mountbatten was born in 1900, the youngest child and second son of Prince Louis of Battenberg who at that time held the rank of captain in the Royal Navy. Prince Louis' mother, Princess Victoria of Hesse, was a granddaughter of Queen Victoria, Hesse itself being one of the fifty odd kingdoms, grand duchies, duchies and principalities that went to make up what ultimately became Germany. Some of these 'regal' entities were no larger than a county in England and occasionally even smaller; Teck, for instance, from which Queen Mary took her title, was nothing more than a single castle in the Kingdom of Württemberg. But like all of Europe's sovereign houses in the 19th century and however quaint it may look today, this almost Ruritanian landscape was taken very seriously.

From an early age the young Louis displayed a remarkable self-confidence that developed into a huge ego. Prior to the outbreak of World War II his naval career showed nothing out of the ordinary for a man born into the aristocracy and the second cousin of King George VI. His father, who had served in the Royal Navy since 1869, had risen to the rank of admiral and First Sea Lord in 1912, but was obliged to resign in October 1914 because of criticisms of his preparation of the Royal Navy for war. In this the unsaid insinuation was that his German ancestry had played a part, but there was no evidence to support this.

The young Louis developed considerable personal charm and successfully served as a midshipman in World War I, anglicising his family name to Mountbatten in 1917. Not unnaturally, the manner in which his father had been treated was a matter of considerable resentment and may well have influenced his later attitude towards authority within the Admiralty; this is a matter of conjecture but seems entirely possible. In 1922 he married Edwina Ashley, the eldest granddaughter of Jewish German-born financier Sir Earnest Cassel. On her grandfather's death Edwina inherited a fortune, at today's values worth some £300 million, which included the 5,000 acre Broadlands Estate on the Test River at Romsey in Hampshire, together with the sixty-room Palladian mansion Broadlands House, as well as a mansion in Park Lane. It was therefore an extremely attractive match and a very opportune catch for a virtually penniless but highly ambitious young aristocrat with close royal connections. For Edwina it was equally profitable, for he provided access to the monarchy that even her money could not buy.

Louis Mountbatten's naval career continued in a fairly conventional fashion and he was given command of his first ship in 1934, but long before that date the state of his marriage to Edwina was the subject of everyday society gossip because of her frequent and very public extra-marital affairs. Whether this was due to inherent nymphomania or deliberate promiscuity is a question that does not appear to have been broached, but she racked up a succession of lovers, one after another—aristocrats (of course), polo players, golfers, film stars, newspaper executives, a prominent symphony orchestra conductor and perhaps the most sensational of all, the bisexual

West Indian cabaret artist Leslie Hutchinson. Rumours of course abounded in London society, with matters coming to a head in 1932 when a Sunday paper, *The People*, published a report of a prominent and extremely wealthy society hostess who was having an affair with a 'coloured man'. Mayfair gossips wasted no time in identifying the lady concerned as Edwina Mountbatten and the paper went on to claim that 'The society woman has been given hints to clear out of England for a couple of years to let the affair blow over and the hints come from a quarter that cannot be ignored.' This was too much for King George V, who ordered Mountbatten to return immediately from his posting in the Mediterranean and sue for libel. The individual widely but wrongly thought to be the 'coloured man' was American singer Paul Robeson. Edwina was awarded costs but declined damages. The establishment closed ranks and the Mountbattens gleefully celebrated by throwing a party that night at London's Café de Paris, followed by lunch the next day at Buckingham Palace and then a day or so later yet another party, hosted by Edward VIII, Prince of Wales.

Mountbatten however, had no private means other than his naval salary and was dependent on Edwina for the lavish lifestyle that her affluence could provide; this plus his naval ambitions and a brazen and impervious ego were probably the reasons why he endured her outrageous behaviour and the humiliations consequent upon these scandals. Certainly her money came in handy. In *Eminent Churchillians* Andrew Roberts recounts an episode in Malta in 1937 when Mountbatten ran his destroyer into another destroyer during an unauthorised race.[84] For any other officer this would have been a matter for demotion, a severe dressing down or at least an embarrassment, but Mountbatten, with access to Edwina's money, paid for the repairs privately without the Admiralty getting to hear about the episode. He did however respond to his wife's affairs by having several quiet flings of his own, but compared with her extraordinary conduct they were very discreet. It is not difficult to imagine the comments that must have gone on behind his back, but all previous authors on Mountbatten seem to have skated around this as if they might be opening a can of worms. In various Royal Navy wardrooms Mountbatten must have been a laughing stock.

The Mountbattens' strange marital relationship has been glossed over on the questionable rationale that 'they understood each other', but it seems far more likely that irrespective of public embarrassment Louis shrugged this off because he was materially much better off with Edwina than without her. All this was at a time when people of royal rank or lineage, however remote, just did not go in for divorce with the same abandon as they do now, and no doubt Buckingham Palace was grateful; and Edwina continued her indiscriminate and overt philandering without further censure. If any other naval officer's wife had behaved in such a scandalous manner, it would have ruined her husband's career or at least resulted in a dead-end posting, so why did the lords of the Admiralty turn a blind eye to such public sexual arrogance that, if nothing else, reflected very badly on the Senior Service? Why were such antics apparently dismissed as some sort of transient peccadilloes? Did the Admiralty not feel this demeaned the navy, and if not, then why? It does look as though these lurid episodes were just the start of a career where Louis Mountbatten would be forgiven almost anything because of his royal connections; it seems he was untouchable.

Mountbatten greeted World War II with great excitement, for he felt it would provide him with a stage on which he could be seen to perform. In 1939 he was put in command of a destroyer flotilla from aboard his ship, the newly launched 2,400-ton HMS *Kelly,* and it was then that certain other character traits began to emerge. He exhibited a propensity for reckless and foolhardy decisions accompanied by an apparent insouciance concerning the consequences, and never missed an opportunity for self-promotion. Official 'spin' has transformed these episodes to such an extent that online sources refer to the HMS *Kelly* as being 'famous for its many daring exploits'. Nothing could be further from the truth. *Kelly* was involved in the usual wartime duties within a destroyer flotilla but as the following will show the 'exploits' were in fact acts of glory-seeking stupidity and irresponsibility rather than 'daring'.

The first example occurred in October 1939 when the *Kelly* was ordered to recapture a 5,000-ton American freighter that had been taken by the German navy. This ship was en route to Germany under a prize crew and was also carrying the captured crews of various ships sunk by a German raider. It was sailing down the Norwegian coast towards Germany and success would have meant the award of a DSO for the captain of the *Kelly*. Although the freighter's position was known, a basic navigational error by Mountbatten resulted in the *Kelly* completely missing her quarry. The standard procedure would have been to aim at the furthest likely position for the target and then patiently work back to waylay the target vessel, but Mountbatten had wanted to make a 'splash' by aiming full speed for a direct interception; as a result the freighter got clean away and slipped into Norwegian territorial waters. When challenged by a Norwegian gunboat, Mountbatten's flippant response was to use his loudhailer and say, in German, 'Please give my compliments to my cousin, Crown Prince Olaf.'[85]

As if this poor judgement and showing off was not enough, irritated by his failure to capture the slow and unarmed freighter Mountbatten then turned and headed for Scotland at a speed of 28 knots, an unnecessary and excessive pace in gale-force winds and heavy seas and conditions that would normally have demanded no more than half that speed. For reasons that are clouded in mystery, at one point and whilst proceeding at this excessive speed, he suddenly made an 80-degree turn to port; this abrupt change in direction caused the ship to heel 50 degrees to starboard. Guardrails, davits and lifeboats on that side were stripped away and all disappeared leaving a tangled mess the whole length of the starboard side of the ship. Also needlessly lost was a luckless stoker who was swept overboard to his death. Yet despite having no excuse for failing to capture the freighter, the totally unnecessary loss of life and significant damage to his ship, the powers within the Admiralty appeared to be protecting Mountbatten, for he came out of this bizarre and irresponsible episode relatively unscathed.

But this was only the first of a succession of 'mishaps' where Mountbatten's style of command exposed *Kelly* to unnecessary peril. During a blizzard and shortly after having been repaired, a terrifying grinding and jarring was felt aboard the ship. Perhaps with a degree of prescience Mountbatten had given prior instructions to his radio operator to react to any exceptional sound by immediately sending a signal reading, 'Have been struck by mine or torpedo, am uncertain which.' What had actually happened was explained by the taciturn reply from the vessel in front, which signalled 'That was not mine but me.' HMS *Kelly* had run into the stern of another British destroyer, HMS *Gurkha,* whose propellers had torn a huge gash in the bows of *Kelly*. Again this required a number of weeks in the repair yard.

And yet there was more to come, comprising perhaps one of Mountbatten's most ham-fisted displays of wilful irresponsibility. A few months after the propeller fiasco, *Kelly* was accompanying the cruiser *Birmingham* on a mission to disrupt German minelayers operating off the Dutch coast.

Whilst conducting this operation a report was received that a U-boat was operating in the area. Nothing was detected and although an absolute blackout was vital so close to the Dutch coast, *Kelly* signalled the *Birmingham* with an Aldis lamp; amongst the messages one read, 'How are the muskets? Let battle commence.' The maximum speed at which Aldis lamp Morse messages could be transmitted was fourteen words per minute, and since the above is only part of what was sent it may be safely assumed the total transmission length of time was at least one minute. A 20-inch Aldis lamp is visible to the horizon and so for the whole of that transmission time the location of HMS *Kelly* was brightly broadcast for all to see. It was the height of irresponsibility to have advertised his position in such an obvious fashion and the consequence was virtually inevitable. Almost immediately a torpedo from an undetected E-boat (a motor torpedo boat) hit the *Kelly* on the starboard side under the bridge; it blew a 50-foot hole in her hull and ripped open the boiler room, immediately killing twenty-seven men and seriously injuring countless more. Apparently Mountbatten had spotted the wake of the approaching torpedo and according to Ziegler had thought to himself, 'That's going to kill an awful lot of chaps'.[86]

Whether he also considered that the imminent death of the 'chaps' would be entirely his fault has not been recorded. Fortunately, too, there does not appear to be any record of the reaction of the Admiral aboard the *Birmingham,* but it is not difficult to imagine what that might have been. The *Kelly* was kept afloat and towed to a shipyard on the Tyne for repairs thus avoiding any further unnecessary loss of life. It seems to have been at least an impertinence, almost bordering on insubordination, for a mere destroyer captain to have sent such an open and importunate message to an Admiral aboard the cruiser. As in the matter of his wife's very public affairs, was this yet another case where Mountbatten could behave differently from any other naval officer of equivalent rank?

In a final twist, rather than being reprimanded for his foolish and unauthorised action, the fact that the *Kelly* was successfully towed back for repairs was hailed as an act of heroism on the part of Mountbatten, whereas the basic reason for the *Kelly's* survival was her design and the seamanship of the towing vessel, the destroyer HMS *Bulldog*. The episode caught the eye of Churchill, who suggested that the gallant captain should be awarded a DSO for this 'courageous achievement', totally ignoring the fact that it had been Mountbatten's reckless folly that had caused the damage and loss of life in the first place. Churchill's request went to the Admiralty where the Commander-in-Chief, Home Fleet tersely replied that there were many other destroyer captains more worthy of the decoration. Nevertheless, Mountbatten felt that he was entitled to a decoration and enlisted the help of another second cousin, Prince George, the Duke of Kent (although knowing that man's indiscrete proclivities, it might be thought better to have avoided him), who then also tried to intervene but achieved nothing. Bitterly disappointed, Mountbatten wrote to Edwina: 'If the King's brother cannot get his cousin the same decoration as every other destroyer captain has been given then the powers working against me must be very strong indeed'.[87] If ever there was evidence that he lived in a world of his own, this was surely it—never mind the lives quite needlessly sacrificed.

There was, however, even more of the same to come. This time it was to take 6 months for the *Kelly* to be repaired and during this period Mountbatten was put in charge of another destroyer flotilla from aboard HMS *Javelin*. At night in November 1940 they encountered a group of German destroyers crossing ahead from right to left at the mouth of the English Channel. As was his style, Mountbatten was sailing at full speed but efficient radar gave the Germans plenty of warning of his imminent arrival. The accepted and intelligent naval strategy in a situation of this sort, at night and at close range, was to approach straight ahead and open fire thus providing the enemy with the minimum target. In his book *Destroyer Man*, the commander of the *Javelin*, Commander (later Rear Admiral) Alan Pugsley, described it thus:

> 'Straight at 'em I presume Sir?' To my dismay he replied 'No, no we must turn to a parallel course at once or they will get away from us.' Our turn to port was disastrous—it offered the enemy a perfect target for his torpedos. In a long range daylight encounter, the manoeuvre would have been a wise one, but in a night action, such as this, with ranges almost point blank, the first few salvos could be decisive.[88]

Pugsley does not elaborate or say whether he remonstrated with Mountbatten, but his book clearly describes how approaching an enemy directly is a far more secure position and one that the ships should have maintained, compared with the known and obvious perils of the course ordered by Mountbatten. The manoeuvre was an irresponsible act of madness. The side-on position provided the Germans with a perfect target for their torpedos. In quick succession three torpedos struck the *Javelin*, blowing off her bow and stern and causing massive damage amidships, which resulted in the deaths of forty-six of the ship's crew together with a large number of wounded. Further loss of life was averted by *Javelin* managing to stay afloat and being towed back to Plymouth. This time Mountbatten was not hailed in the press as such a courageous hero.

According to his biographer Philip Ziegler, Mountbatten's diary entry was slightly testy but totally self-centred: 'Maddening to be put out of action but lucky to escape with 50 killed [in fact 46] and bow and stern blown off.'[89] Maddening? Most irritating for someone positioned safely on the bridge and probably bent on obtaining his DSO. 'Lucky'? Lucky for whom? After all, shells might land on the bridge, but torpedos tend to strike a little lower down—where the 'chaps' were. An investigation concluded that Mountbatten had blundered but such was the desperate need for good news at this point in the war that Churchill invited Mountbatten to Chequers and congratulated him, although it is not clear what it was that warranted any congratulations. This was perhaps just another of Churchill's flights of fancy because it is difficult to see just what Mountbatten had achieved other than causing the loss of yet another destroyer. There was no evidence at all of any damage having been inflicted on the Germans whilst the Royal Navy had very nearly lost a ship and a further forty-six seamen had needlessly gone to their deaths. Despite this Mountbatten yet again escaped official censure and vigorously denied that he bore any responsibility. As another of Mountbatten's biographers, Adrian Smith, dryly commented:

> One can only wonder why no further action was taken, and yet the answer is obvious. Mountbatten was a high profile naval hero at a time when Britain needed every hero she could muster—even the slightest reprimand might undermine national morale should news leak out, whilst just the slightest hint of an enquiry could guarantee a torrent of indignation from both the 'old man' (Churchill) and from his sovereign.[90]

With such a succession of disasters behind him it might be thought that matters would improve when Mountbatten returned to the repaired *Kelly* in December 1940, but even that was not the case. On her first day at sea *Kelly* rammed into the old trawler SS *Scorpion*, and had to return to shore for further repairs to her bow. The event was described by Ziegler as 'a fleeting if familiar setback', but the view of other naval officers was different. Terrence Healey, the younger brother of post-war British politician Denis Healey, was a naval officer during the war; he told his brother of Mountbatten's royal arrogance and that it was only his birth that saved him from the court martial that any other officer would have faced. And so it seemed, for at the end of that month it was announced that Mountbatten had finally been awarded his long coveted DSO. According to Ziegler this was in recognition of 'action seen and dangers survived', but if so, why was he more deserving of the honour than all the other destroyer captains who had faced and come through similar perils, and who had managed to do so without unnecessarily losing the lives of seventy-four crewmen and disabling their ships? The answer is of course uncomfortably obvious and it must have stuck in the throats of so many others whose only rank was within the Royal Navy.

In March 1941 Mountbatten decided his flotilla would intercept and destroy the two German battlecruisers *Scharnhorst* and *Gneisenau*, which together with four cruisers and a destroyer screen were believed to be making their way from the Atlantic and into the French port of Saint-Nazaire. Fortunately for Mountbatten his flotilla completely failed to make any contact with the German ships, which had instead slipped into Brest—'fortunately' because the chances of his flotilla of five destroyers surviving against the overwhelming firepower of such an array of capital ships would have been distinctly remote to say the least. As it happened, Mountbatten had predicted the German fleet would head for Brest rather than Saint-Nazaire and he used this to claim vindication of his action, conveniently ignoring the fact that he had in fact only narrowly missed the decimation that would otherwise have been the result of his gung-ho decision. A consistent pattern of conduct seems to have emerged: act irresponsibly and take unnecessary risks and if by chance it comes off, bask in glory; and conversely, when such ill-advised and irregular tactics result in the loss of ships and lives then rely on the protection of royal connections to avoid the censure that would befall any other officer. All of this had about it the unhealthy miasma of an unstated but accepted insulation, for whenever his actions were criticised by his superiors in the Admiralty, Mountbatten frequently had the temerity to argue that he had been right. There was nothing self-righteous about this—rather the flamboyant behaviour of a protected species. He was untouchable.

According to Ziegler, and as if to confirm this assessment, shortly after HMS *Kelly* was sunk by enemy aircraft a few months later in the Mediterranean, the commander-in-chief of that theatre, the very competent Admiral Sir Andrew Cunningham, confided to one of the remaining of the flotilla captains, 'The trouble with your flotilla, boy, is that it was thoroughly badly led.'[91] Ziegler goes on to suggest that Cunningham's comment was prompted by jealousy of Mountbatten's wealth and royal connections, but it seems more likely that rather than envy it was the justified annoyance and frustration of a very senior and experienced naval officer who had been lumbered with a headline-seeking dilettante whom he knew he had to handle with kid gloves.

In his book *Engage the Enemy More Closely: The Royal Navy in the Second World War,* the 58-year-old Cunningham was described by historian Correlli Barnett as 'the embodiment of the Royal Navy's best tradition of fighting sailors'[92] so it seems unlikely that his dismissive comment was anything other than a factual assessment. Even Ziegler, who obviously admired Mountbatten, was forced to concede:

> He seemed to regard himself as the equal of men far senior to him. Mountbatten was not a good flotilla leader or wartime commander of destroyers. Mountbatten was impetuous. He pushed the ship too fast for little reason except his love of speed and imposed unnecessary strain on his own officers and the other ships in the flotilla and among all his peers who have expressed an opinion the unanimous feeling is that, by the highest standards, he was no better than second-rate.[93]

Rather than 'daring exploits' therefore, it may be said with total accuracy that considering the impetuous and devil-may-care manner in which she was skippered by her glory seeking captain, the *Kelly* and those aboard her were lucky to survive as long as they did. Bravery is one thing, but without intelligence it can be little more than exhibitionism that endangers others.

But HMS *Kelly* did not disappear beneath the waves, for Mountbatten persuaded Noel Coward to salvage her as HMS *Torrin* in his film *In Which We Serve*. Inspired by Mountbatten's super-heroic version of tragic events and casting himself as a thinly disguised Mountbatten, Coward's plot was refused by the Ministry of Information on the understandable grounds that for public morale at that time in the war, a film about the sinking of a British warship by the Luftwaffe was not exactly what they had in mind. Furious that the film that he and Coward had concocted was not going to proceed, Mountbatten resorted to his informal lines of influence and went straight to Buckingham Palace. In her book *Indian Summer: The Secret History of the End of an Empire* Alex von Tunzelmann described the events as follows:

> Coward 'phoned Mountbatten; Mountbatten took the script directly to the King and Queen; something unknown occurred; the Ministry's support was mysteriously reinstated. All the opposition that came up during filming was dealt with according to a similar protocol.[94]

There were also accepted 'protocols' within the Admiralty and the government, but it does not require too much reading between the lines to perceive that Mountbatten would have bypassed anyone to obtain what he wanted or what he felt he deserved. It must be remembered too that whereas today the royal family are looked on with affection and maybe curiosity, 1941 was a time when 'royalty' was still regarded with reverence and awe and it was prepared to wield a clout that would now, rightly, be unthinkable.

As it happened the film was a resounding success and received a 1943 Academy award. It could therefore be said that Mountbatten had been right, but as was so often with the man, it was not only what he did but the way he did it; there were other more conventional channels that were open to him that would probably have achieved the same result without causing resentment. Why did he have to choose this method, or was this his way of demonstrating what he could do if he wanted to? If so, even though it had worked, it was a tasteless and ham-fisted exhibition of aristocratic in-fluence. By the time the film was released Mountbatten had moved on from destroyers and was working in a completely different area, but he put in an appearance at so many of the early screenings of the film that it prompted biographer Adrian Smith to ask 'why someone carrying so much rank and responsibility should—and could—invest so much time and effort in such a peripheral project?'[95] The question has to be asked: was this self-promotion, with Mountbatten saying in effect, 'This is all about me, so here I am'? Was it all about reflected glory and autographs in the foyer?

CHAPTER 5

CHURCHILL AND
SINGAPORE

If we wait until an emergency arises
in the Far East, we shall be too late.
—GENERAL SIR JOHN DILL,
   memo to Churchill, April 1941

Sir John Dill's 1941 forewarning was the sort of experienced advice that Churchill hated. He could not tolerate any opinion that ran counter to his own views, and particularly when it was in writing. When he issued his warning, General Dill was Chief of the Imperial General Staff. Six months later he was dismissed by Churchill, and six weeks after that his timely warning proved to be correct.

In 1941 the regular British Army forces in Malaya and Singapore numbered about 76,000 of which some 37,000 (over 48 per cent) were Indian. For some years there had been political agitation for independence in India, largely through peaceful protests lead by Mahatma Gandhi, and yet when the Viceroy of India, Lord Linlithgow, declared in September 1939 that India was 'at war', he did so without any consultation with India. It was autocratic and hardly conducive to gaining the wholehearted support that Britain so badly needed yet when, as a soothing gesture, Linlithgow suggested inviting some members of the Congress Party to join his Executive Committee, it was Churchill who violently opposed such a move saying that he would 'never consult with Indians.' As a result, the Congress Party resigned from those provincial governments it had controlled, and British governors resumed powers. Churchill's outspoken obsession with British control of India had got the British government off on completely the wrong foot at a time when Indian support was most needed. Immediately following the fall of Singapore, Churchill realised his mistake and launched a diplomatic initiative to win the support of the Congress Party. He sent Sir Richard Stafford Cripps, the left-wing Leader of the House of Commons, to India to lead the mission. It failed largely because he was not allowed under his terms of reference to offer what the Indians wanted, which was a promise of independence and a date to be set for it. In this Churchill had connived to ensure the Cripps mission would be a failure in order to remove him as a political threat, and it is remarkable that despite the subsequent jailing of Jawaharlal Nehru and Gandhi, loyal and effective Indian troops still continued to fight for Britain in various theatres of war.

Several years earlier, Churchill had offensively described the dignified Gandhi as a 'malevolent fanatic' and a 'seditious Middle Temple lawyer now posing as a fakir of a type well known in the East'[96] and yet this offensive description came from the same man who, as Prime Minister, now expected the full support of the Indian Army. If many in the Indian Army were somewhat less than enthusiastic about assisting Britain, it should have come as no surprise and it must have helped those like another Indian independence leader, Subhas Chandra Bose, whose Indian National Army were recruiting disaffected elements of the army to join their cause. There would seem to be little doubt that news of these events filtered through to the Indian troops in Malaya and must have caused them to pause and think. As Wavell was to remark to the Secretary of State for India, Leo Amery: 'Winston knows as much of the Indian problem as George III did of the American colonies'.[97]

There was a long-standing plan that a fleet would be dispatched to Singapore within 70 days should hostilities break out in the Far East, and this was drawn up at a time when changes in warfare did not appear to have registered with the British chiefs of staff. The 'fleet' was to consist of eight capital ships, a number smaller than it was thought the Japanese could muster, but probably just enough to get by. The effectiveness of air power was barely taken seriously at the time even though in 1921 American aviator Billy Mitchell had demonstrated that an aircraft could sink a battleship with bombs. For reasons of self-interest, this achievement was played down at the time by the American and British navies as a failure, although it had in fact been quite the opposite and was a spectacular success. It appears that even though 20 years had passed, neither of the navies still wanted to concede the effectiveness of air power in an area of warfare where they had always been the predominant service.

As previously noted, immediately upon becoming Prime Minister Churchill also made himself Minister of Defence, a move that made him a virtual dictator and enabled him to issue military instructions under two hats. In addition to his own convictions on military strategy and weapons, the imperialist Churchill considered it unthinkable that a small Asian country like Japan would even countenance attacking the British Empire. Some time before the war he said: 'I do not believe Japan has any idea of attacking the British Empire or that there is any danger of her doing so for at least a generation to come'.[98] That prediction was made in 1925 so perhaps it might be excused because of the time factor involved; but according to one of his biographers, Clive Ponting, in his book *Churchill,* even as late as mid-1941 when surely the writing was on the wall, 'Churchill consistently refused to regard developments in the Far East as a serious threat to British interests.'[99] He was convinced, as he had been for the previous 15 years that 'the Japanese would not dare to attack white powers'.[100] Obviously his racist convictions continued to dominate his thinking. In March 1939 he had comforted Neville Chamberlain saying:

> Consider how vain is the menace that Japan will send a fleet and army to conquer Singapore, it will never commend itself to them until England has been decisively beaten. You may be sure that provided Singapore is fully armed, garrisoned and supplied, there will be no attack in any period which our foresight can measure.[101]

A defence conference was held in Singapore in October 1940 attended by the local chiefs of staff, plus observers from Australia, New Zealand, India, Burma and the American naval attaché from Bangkok. The conference recommendations sent to London were for substantial reinforcements and yet in his book *Singapore: the Pregnable Fortress: A Study in Deception, Discord and Desertion,* Peter Elphick states:

> in December 1940 Churchill categorically rejected the idea of

sending the Australian 7th Division to Malaya. He decided that it must go to the Middle East as originally planned. He maintained that the principle defence of Singapore must be the fleet and that the idea of attempting to defend the whole of the Malayan peninsula had no merit.[102]

Churchill, convinced that Singapore was a fortress still did not rate the Japanese threat highly. Writing to the First Lord of the Admiralty, Albert V. Alexander, three months previously he stated: 'the Naval Intelligence Division are very much inclined to exaggerate Japanese strength and efficiency.' This was a classic example of Churchill making policy decisions based largely on his own preconceived ideas and prejudices. To revert to Peter Elphick once more, he quotes a 'Most Secret' directive from Churchill, dated 28 April 1941:

DIRECTIVE FROM PRIME MINISTER
AND MINISTER OF DEFENCE

Japan is unlikely to enter the war unless the Germans make a successful invasion of Great Britain, and even a major disaster like the loss of the Middle East would not necessarily make her come in, because the liberation of the British Mediterranean Fleet which might be expected, and also any troops evacuated from the Middle East to Singapore would not weaken the British war-making strength in Malaya. It is very unlikely, moreover, that Japan will enter the war either if the United States have come in, or if Japan thinks that they would come in consequent upon a declaration of war. Finally, it may be taken as almost certain that the entry of Japan into the war would be followed by the immediate entry of the United States on our side.

These conditions are to be accepted by the Service Departments as a guide for all plans and actions. Should they cease to hold good it will be the responsibility of Ministers to notify the Service Staffs in good time. There is no need at the present time to make any further dispositions for the defence of Malaya and Singapore, beyond those modest arrangements which are in progress, until or unless the conditions set out (above) are modified.[103]

Most of this document is quite out of touch with reality and is grim evidence of Britain's war effort being directed by a domineering personality who would brook no alternative to his own views. Apparently this document was marked 'Most Secret, War Cabinet, To Be Kept Under Lock and Key' and was further endorsed 'It is requested that special care be taken to ensure the Secrecy of this Document.' In view of what was to transpire these requests were a wise precaution, but the peremptory tone should be noted: 'These conditions *are* to be accepted by the Service Department' (author's emphasis). In other words the self-appointed supremo—Churchill—was speaking and no alternative view would be tolerated.

At the time of Churchill's directive Major-General Sir John Kennedy was Director of Military Operations and Plans at the War Office, and he recorded his views later:

> It seems to me quite wrong that a Strategic Directive of this kind should be issued by the Prime Minister without the advice of the Chiefs of Staff. The last sentence in the first paragraph is quite unacceptable from a military point of view. It takes some three months to dispatch and install additional defences in Malaya.[104]

In his *History of the Second World War*, Liddell Hart recounts a paper submitted by (the then) General Sir John Dill to Churchill in May 1941 in which he wrote:

> The loss of Egypt would be a calamity which I do not regard as likely. A successful invasion alone spells our defeat. It is the United Kingdom therefore and not Egypt that is vital and the defence of the United Kingdom must take first place. Egypt is not even second in order of priority, for it has been an accepted principle in our strategy that in the last resort the security of Singapore comes before that of Egypt. Yet the defences of Singapore are still considerably below standard. Risks must of course be taken in war, but they must be calculated risks. We must not fall into the error of whittling away the security of vital points.[105]

The one senior British commander who could clearly see the looming problem in the Far East was Sir John Dill, but his persistent advice and warnings are well documented. This very able soldier, whose quiet cerebral counsel about Singapore was not to the taste of the abrasive and emotional Churchill, was removed by him as Chief of the Imperial General Staff in late 1941 and sent to Washington as Chief of the British Joint Staff Mission. There, as already noted, and in contrast to the denigration he had suffered at Churchill's hands, he was held in high esteem by the perceptive top echelons of the United States military. That Dill was held in such high regard in Washington is demonstrated by the message of condolence sent by the American Joint Chiefs of Staff to their British colleagues:

> We feel we share equally with you the loss to our combined war effort resulting from the death of Field Marshal Sir John Dill. His character and wisdom, his selfless devotion to the Allied cause, made his contribution to the combined British-American war effort of outstanding importance. It is not too much to say that probably no other individual was more responsible for the achievement of complete co-operation in the work of the Combined Chiefs of Staff. We have looked to him with complete confidence as a leader in our combined deliberations. He has been a great personal friend of all of us. We mourn with you the passing of a great and wise soldier, and a great gentleman. His task in this war has been well done.

It was later discovered that Dill had suffered from undiagnosed aplastic anaemia. The Americans could recognise experience and wisdom, which the impatient Churchill dismissed as 'dilly-dally'—an obstacle to his own views. Dill's assessment was supported by General Kennedy.

It might be noted that Churchill was admitting that anything provided for Malaya and Singapore was only 'modest' and seemingly he considered that to be sufficient. However, even as late as September 1941 Churchill was still stubbornly resisting any warnings, saying to the Chiefs of Staff, 'Malaya can wait.'

Irrespective of experienced military logic no alternative view would move Churchill, who rode roughshod over anything that did not fit in with his thinking. Things had changed since his advice to Chamberlain in March 1939 but even in 1941 he apparently knew more about the navy than the

Admiralty, for to quote Ponting once more, and at about the same time as the Greek catastrophe was taking place, he was telling the admirals: 'The Japanese Navy is not likely to venture far from its home bases so long as a superior battle-fleet is maintained at Singapore or at Honolulu. The Japanese would never attempt a siege of Singapore with a hostile superior fleet in the Pacific'.[106]

This attitude is all the more difficult to comprehend when Churchill must have known by then that a detailed and highly pessimistic top secret assessment of Britain's Far East preparedness for war had been captured by a German raider in November 1940. The report was carried on board the SS *Automedon* en route from Liverpool to Singapore when she was captured and sunk by the raider. Before the sinking, however, the captain of the raider found the top secret report and had it sent it on to Tokyo, giving the Japanese a veritable gold mine of information.

It did not seem to occur to Churchill that there was no fleet at all in Singapore let alone a battle fleet and there was 12,000km of ocean between Singapore and Hawaii. By comparison London to New York is about 6,000km, but as was so often the case, Churchill was not seeking the views of his experienced chiefs of staff but was dictating to them how they should do their jobs. Making even more of a mockery of this prediction and known to British intelligence was the fact that located almost midway between Hawaii and Singapore and 2,800km south of Tokyo was the island of Saipan, where the Japanese had already built up a substantial garrison. This shows that Churchill either lived in a world of self-delusion and conveniently ignored facts or never consulted a map, for his naval prediction was made some time after he knew that the all-revealing secret assessment of Britain's Far East military capabilities had been discovered on board the *Automedon* and was now in enemy hands. In August 1941 Churchill was to meet President Roosevelt for the first time at Placentia Bay in Newfoundland but there is no evidence he told Roosevelt that the highly sensitive report had been lost from the *Automedon* some 9 months earlier. It is clear that his predictions about the Japanese navy were made with little knowledge of or consultations with the Americans about their plans for the Pacific. This again was indicative of Churchill being Churchill.

Following Hitler's invasion of Russia in July 1941 an all-out trade embargo against Japan was imposed by the United States and supported by

Britain. Churchill pressured the Dutch government in exile, based in London, to follow suit. Churchill's advisers recognised that this might well lead to war but he was unconcerned at what his colleagues viewed with some anxiety as an overexposed position. This apparently was because of his long-held conviction that the Japanese were an inferior race and would not dare challenge white powers, describing them to newspapers as the 'wops of the East' who he said would 'shout and threaten but would not move.'[107] As mentioned earlier, Churchill maintained that the principal defence of Singapore must be the British fleet, but when that proved difficult to muster he insisted that a small force should be sent as what he called 'a deterrent.'

The recently commissioned aircraft carrier HMS *Indomitable* had been intended to provide air protection for the new battleship HMS *Prince of Wales* and the older cruiser HMS *Repulse,* in their three-ship mission to Singapore. The *Indomitable* was damaged during a proving cruise in the West Indies and was temporarily out of commission, but Churchill insisted that *The Prince of Wales* and *Repulse* should nonetheless proceed to Singapore without any seaborne air support. It was well known that the quality and numbers of RAF resources in Singapore and Malaya were far below what was necessary but, Churchill, having only recently stated that 'a single well armed vessel will hold its own against aircraft', appears to have been dismissive of the threat of any air attack.

This obstinate conviction is all the more absurd because it was only a few months earlier that an even larger battleship, the German *Bismarck,* had been sunk following a torpedo attack launched from a Swordfish aircraft. A torpedo fired from the aircraft struck the battleship's rudder, which immobilised her by totally disabling her steering mechanism. On another occasion it had been a Swordfish, a biplane aircraft with a maximum speed of only 140mph, that had decimated the Italian fleet at Taranto in November 1940, both episodes proving that battleships were distinctly vulnerable to air attack. It had also been the lack of air cover that caused the loss of nine capital ships during the battle of Crete in May 1941 but the stark reality that air cover was essential for shipping failed to sway Churchill, who was determined to make a heroic gesture of support for Greek resistance to Nazi occupation. His ill-conceived Greek fiasco resulted in the serious weakening of Britain's position in the Mediterranean and the summary loss of valuable lives and equipment.

When both *The Prince of Wales* and *Repulse* were, inevitably, sunk by Japanese air attack, Churchill tried to distance himself from the disaster by making the bizarre comment that his idea had been that after they had made their deterrent effect felt in Singapore the ships should then disappear into the immense archipelago. To do what it might be asked? Was Churchill saying that having 'popped' into Singapore and saying 'Here we are', *The Prince of Wales* (draught 36 feet) and *Repulse* should then have hidden themselves amongst the surrounding collection of low-lying islands and swampy inlets? Fortunately for Churchill too many other events were unfolding at the time so that his mindless comments were allowed to pass without question. Even after the Japanese had successfully landed in Malaya in December 1941, and to quote Ponting once more:

> Churchill thought that the Navy should be concentrated in the Indian Ocean to protect the supply lane to the Middle East and not in the Far East, and that reinforcements from the Army should be sent to India and secondly to Singapore but not to Malaya. He was convinced, *against all military advice* [author's emphasis], that there was no need to defend Malaya and that Singapore was a fortress that could withstand a siege for probably six months . . . Altogether Churchill demonstrated an arrogant and wilful under-estimation of the Japanese, at a time when others did see the dangers.[108]

It is also as a result of his dealings with President Roosevelt that Churchill is culpable. Knowing that Britain could not possibly win the war without American intervention and despite being aware of the opposition in Congress and the American public to US involvement in the European conflict, Churchill kept egging Roosevelt on to provoke a Japanese attack. He colluded with Roosevelt in implementing the total embargo of all raw materials for Japan in July 1941 and encouraged him to refuse to offer the Japanese any compromises. He knew the embargo would provoke Japan into a hostile attack to obtain relief for her depleted oil and other vital resources and supplies denied her, which would almost certainly lead to a Japanese move on Borneo and the Dutch East Indies. Malaya and Singapore stood in the way of any such Japanese move to the south-west and would therefore be the target of an invasion, and he also knew, as did Roosevelt, that any Japanese attack must come by December 1941 or thereabouts, otherwise she would run out of the oil and other supplies she so desperately needed.

So obvious was the threat and so irrational was Churchill's stubborn refusal to strengthen Singapore that it prompted Basil Liddell Hart to make the following comment in his book *Strategy: The Indirect Approach*:

> It had always been recognised that such a paralysing stroke would force Japan to fight, as the only alternative to collapse or the abandonment of her policy. No Government, least of all the Japanese, could be expected to swallow such humiliating conditions, and utter loss of face. There was every reason to expect war in the Pacific at any moment, from the last week in July onwards. In these circumstances the Americans and British were lucky to be allowed four months' grace before the Japanese struck. But little advantage was taken of this interval for defensive preparation.[109]

What makes Churchill's blind stubbornness even more incomprehensible is that once Hitler had launched his massive attack on Russia on 22 June 1941, the concentration of his forces to the east meant that there was no longer any threat of a German invasion of Britain, as Germany did not have the capacity or resources to undertake substantial offensives on two fronts at the same time. Churchill must have known that. However, in the 6 months prior to the German move on Russia and before the invasion threat was lifted, he insisted that huge supplies of men and materials be made available for the Middle East. With Hitler's attention being concentrated towards Moscow, the United Kingdom was now free from the menace of a German attack. What might have been a reason to withhold resources for home defence purposes no longer applied and at least some of these resources could have been released for the Far East. The only conclusion that can be drawn as to why these resources were not sent was because of some weird personal prejudice or a mental block. It could not even be argued that a shortage of available shipping was the problem because shortly before Singapore fell General Wavell had stated that if the garrison could hold on for a few weeks longer it would give time for necessary reinforcements to arrive. However, by that time Japanese control of the surrounding seas and air would have made any relief virtually impossible;

unfortunately it could have been achieved months earlier; the opportunity was there, but it was ignored.

Ignoring for the moment the position of the troops making up the woefully inadequate defence resources in Malaya and Singapore, why were European civilians such as women and children not given the option of being evacuated much earlier than they were, say, to Australia or New Zealand? There is no doubt that such an evacuation might have caused alarm and may have been interpreted as a sign that the defences of Malaya and Singapore were not all that they had been held out to be, but the evacuation of civilians from a possible danger zone would no more have indicated an expectation of defeat than the evacuation of children from London meant an imminent German invasion. It could have been explained as a precautionary measure against bombing attacks and infinitely preferable than allowing people to be sacrificed and with women and children out of the way it would have made it that much easier for the British ground forces to operate. There were plenty of similar bombing evacuations out of London into the British countryside and to Canada, so why not out of Singapore? Japan had stated on a number of occasions that Asia should be free from European domination and that they were their targets and not the local Asian population. Corelli Barnett makes a similar point in *Engage the Enemy More Closely*: 'The cool strategic brain of a Moltke or Wellington would have recognised this and begun to evacuate British civilians and military "useless mouths" in good time, and even to thin down the fighting troops to a rearguard'.[110] Barnett goes on to state: 'Had Malaya and Singapore been evacuated in time like Greece and Crete, Britain would still have sustained—as in those cases—a disastrous defeat. As it was, by insisting that Singapore be reinforced and defended to the uttermost, Churchill inflated defeat into a highly dramatised catastrophe.' From 1977 to 1993 Corelli Barnett was keeper of the Churchill Archives at Churchill College, Cambridge. His opinions are therefore based on unrivalled access to detailed material regarding Churchill.

On 10 February 1942, when reality did finally hit home and Churchill woke up to the fact that the loss of Singapore was staring him in the face, he sent a cable to Singapore stating:

There must at this stage be no thought of saving the troops or sparing the population. The battle must be fought to the bitter end at all costs. The 18th Division has a chance to make its name in history. Commanders and senior officers should die with their troops. The honour of the British Empire and of the British Army is at stake.[111]

This was almost identical to what he had said about Egypt some 10 months earlier in April 1941, when he stated:

It is to be impressed upon all ranks, especially the highest, that the life and honour of Great Britain depends on the successful defence of Egypt. No surrenders by officers and men will be considered tolerable unless at least 50% casualties are sustained by the Unit or force in question.[112]

Both of these directives were little more than imperial bombast and dramatic rhetoric, and one can only imagine the top commanders in the Middle East and Singapore shaking their heads in disbelief. The order regarding the troops on and population of Singapore indicates an inhuman and callous disregard for the welfare of civilians that was almost Stalin-like. It was at Churchill's personal insistence that the 18th Division be sent to Singapore, where it arrived only a few days before the surrender and immediately sacrificed its men as prisoners of war. His instruction for commanders to die with their troops could have been convenient had it been carried out, for there would then have been no one left to tell the truth afterwards.

Perhaps one of the most revealing comments made by Churchill about his thinking at this time was in a letter to his wife in December 1941 whilst he was on his way once more to meet Roosevelt shortly after the Japanese attacks on Pearl Harbor and Malaya. In his book *Road to Victory, 1941–1945* Martin Gilbert quotes from that letter as follows:

We must expect to suffer heavily in this war with Japan, and it is no use the critics saying 'Why were we not prepared' when everything we had was fully engaged. *The entry of the United States is worth all the losses sustained in the East many times over* [author's emphasis].[113]

It was of course just not true to claim that 'everything we had was fully engaged' when what had happened was that, against all military advice, Churchill had decided to allocate considerable resources to the Middle East and ignore the Far East. Was this a tacit and perhaps unintentional admission that any sacrifice including Singapore was worth the candle as long as he had Roosevelt and the United States alongside? Or was he attempting to rationalise what had happened as if this had always been part of his long-term strategy?

Churchill, who twenty-five years earlier had himself masterminded the Dardanelles disaster, was still convinced of his own genius, a man much admired from afar but frequently detested at close quarters. In any event it was quite untrue to claim that the entry of the United States into the war inevitably caused Britain to lose Singapore. The Japanese were induced to attack but there was no reason, other than Churchill himself, why Singapore could not have been held. And there is one additional point in all of this: following Pearl Harbor, the United States participation in the war would probably have been limited to the Pacific if Hitler had not stupidly declared war on them. This was luck, pure and simple—Churchill had no hand in this.

In a geographical position that was strategically important because of the sea routes that it straddled, Singapore was militarily significant; and even with the fall of Hong Kong and the American Philippines, a peninsular such as Malaya was defendable and could have been held. Hong Kong, surrounded by Japanese-occupied mainland China, was virtually incapable of being defended for long. The Dutch East Indies could never have been defended given the fact that the colonial power Holland itself was under Nazi Germany occupation and holding them was beyond the capability of British resources. If the Japanese had not been able to take Malaya and Singapore, they would have had to bypass them in their south-western move, and if they could have been kept resupplied, that area would have remained a considerable thorn in the side of the Japanese strategy. This would have required the necessary resources which had been repeatedly recommended and persistently requested by the various service chiefs but just as consistently denied by Churchill in his capacity of military overlord. The tragedy is that these resources were available, for one only has to look at the massive investment of men and material that was poured into North Africa and wasted on Greece but withheld from Singapore because of Churchill's obsession with Erwin Rommel and the Middle East that eclipsed everything else. In a letter to Singapore's *The Straits Times* in April 1997, Corelli Barnett wrote:

> The thing about Winston was that he was a romantic, seized by romantic words and symbols. He was not an analytical thinker. But if the campaign in Africa had not been given greater priority than the Far East, aircraft and weapons could have been found to hold the airfields in Malaya. When General Percival arrived to take command he found he had already lost. Percival was a sound and intelligent soldier. He assessed the situation correctly, for it was cut and dried. He had no choice but to surrender. He had to, to save untold lives and suffering. The casualties would have been enormous, especially among the peoples of Singapore, and he could not accept that. Winston had a remarkable capacity for distancing himself from mistakes and disasters that had his name all over them.[114]

Need we say more?

CHAPTER 6

THE MONTY MYTH

His self-regard was almost comical and the Americans were not alone in believing that his reputation had been inflated by an adoring British press. 'Monty', observed Basil Liddell Hart 'is perhaps much more popular with civilians than with soldiers.'
—ANTONY BEEVOR

Montgomery was widely known in the British army as 'the nasty little shit'.
—JACK L. GRANATSTEIN

One might ask how could an abrasive, cocky, and ambitious character like Montgomery fit into the establishment scenario of 'nice chaps'? Surely this sort of persona would not sit comfortably with his peers? He seemed to qualify from the outer rings of the social strata requirement since his grandfather owned a small estate in County Donegal and he went to the 'right sort' of school, although St Paul's School, London did not perhaps have quite the 'pull' that would have come from the higher ranking military public schools such as Eton, Harrow, Winchester or Wellington. At Sandhurst he only distinguished himself by nearly being expelled for almost setting fire to a fellow cadet during a fight with fire pokers; perhaps the first indication of a 'prickly' personality. Wounded in World War I when he was awarded a DSO, he later served in County Cork in the early 1920s where there emerged in him the first signs of a self-centred, merciless streak. On combatting the Irish independence movement, he wrote:

My whole attention was given to defeating the rebels but it never bothered me a bit how many houses were burnt. My own view is that to win a war of this sort you must be ruthless. Oliver Cromwell or the Germans would have settled it in a very short time.[115]

Montgomery held the rank of brigade-major whilst in Ireland, but with such callous indifference to the loss of civilian lives from a relatively senior position it is little wonder that the rank and file of the Black and Tans developed such an appalling reputation both in Ireland and mainland Britain. It should be added here that it was in Cork that the most alarming atrocities were inflicted by the British forces against Irish independence fighters, with twenty-four towns being torched in the month of December 1920. Whether or not Montgomery was in any way involved in these operations is obscure, but he was in charge of that area when a British patrol was attacked by the IRA. In retaliation, the previously loyal city of Cork was looted and numerous buildings burned on the night of 11/12 December 1920. It may be significant that out of some 500 pages in his *Memoirs,* Montgomery, a man who was never reticent about his exploits, devotes only one very brief paragraph to the whole of his time in Ireland; his biographers are equally vague. Some 24 years later Montgomery would demonstrate the same offhand attitude towards the deaths of thousands of ordinary French citizens caused by his stubborn and flawed attempts to capture the city of Caen some weeks after D-Day, by bombing it to pieces because his military effort at a frontal assault had proved futile. Shortly thereafter he would be responsible for the deaths of thousands of Dutch civilians as a result of his disastrous but determined plan to capture a bridge at Arnhem.

Up to 1940 Montgomery's career was unremarkable. He had performed effectively but without distinction in various postings, although the rudeness and abrasiveness of his personality no doubt hindered his prospects of promotion. That he prospered when war came along is perhaps more a reflection on the mediocre quality of many of his peers than on any outstanding talent on his part. As mentioned in the chapter on *Class and the British Army,* after the withdrawal from Dunkirk, Montgomery found himself subordinate to Auchinleck in Southern Command and it was there that another unpleasant facet of his personality emerged. As one of his biographers, Alun Chalfont, describes in his book *Montgomery of Alamein:*

During 1940 Auchinleck was Montgomery's immediate superior as GOC Southern Command. In the BEF (British Expeditionary Force), Montgomery had given his corps commander, Brooke, wholehearted support and approval. This he consciously and in a most unprofessional way withheld from his new chief. He allowed his personality to intrude into the chain of military command to such an astonishing extent that it is not difficult to understand why the officers of the Selection Board in 1939 had been so reluctant to take responsibility for him, and it seems clear that only in the grave wartime situation could he have achieved the pinnacle of his career. For in his attitude to Auchinleck there often seems to have been a sustained attempt to humiliate and anger.

This was precisely what Correlli Barnett described when he wrote about the myth Montgomery had created about himself: 'It had less foundation in fact than in ambition, political convenience and personal spite.'[116]

It might be said that the requirements of a wartime environment sorts out the men from the boys and that ability and performance are more likely to emerge under the reality of hostilities. The characteristics of 'cleverness, push, ruthlessness, self-interest and ambition' which Barnett has described as making a peacetime army somewhat uncomfortable, would in principle be precisely what would be sought in wartime conditions. However, the essence here is 'in principle', because although those traits could be attributes when actually having to deal with an enemy, they can become a distinct hindrance within an overall command structure if used for the pursuit of power-hungry careerism. If, in addition, downright dishonesty and distortion of facts are also added, then there is likely to emerge the sort of unnecessarily uncomfortable atmosphere that would always colour Montgomery's relationships with colleagues and Allied commanders. To that should be added a propensity to stab another in the back, as he did when he took over from Auchinleck, and unfortunately you then have a fairly accurate description of Montgomery's personality.

This problem is of course not all that unusual, for the pressures and demands of wartime do tend to throw up the sorts of people 'who get things done' but who are rapidly discarded when peace returns. Prima donnas such as Douglas MacArthur spring to mind and he, in some ways like

Montgomery, was allowed considerable latitude by Roosevelt during the needs of war, only to run into a brick wall when President Truman eventually ran out of patience with his imperious attitude during the Korean War. In the Pacific War however, MacArthur, had for some years successfully conducted a long and bloody campaign over a massive area against a fanatical and totally ruthless enemy. Following the Japanese surrender he had been virtual sole supremo in Japan and his sense of omnipotence, although misguided, was perhaps understandable. Montgomery never once had anything like this level of responsibility, but his consistent self-promotion as a superstar, although swallowed by an eager British press, was very largely a self-contrived myth.

Some talent, of course was present, but outstanding ability or military genius? Almost certainly not, and what was there was sullied by the character traits of the man as a whole. Surely it should be the complete persona we should be looking at, for if we do not, then we are allowing ourselves to be guided too much by what he said himself, about himself. Even the most ardent of admirers could not deny that Montgomery appeared on the stage only when the balance of power, the supply of men and materials, had shifted decidedly in favour of Britain. He performed as well as might have been expected at Dunkirk in 1940, but no better than a number of others. He was fortunate to have operated there under Brooke, who was later to become Chief of the Imperial General Staff, in which capacity he had not only selected Montgomery for command of the Eighth Army but stuck with him when the problems he caused were such that he should have been relieved. It could therefore be said with total validity that had his corps commander in 1940 been anyone other than Brooke, then some other general was just as likely to have got the job in Egypt; and given the overwhelming strength of the war machine that had been built up there, another commander would probably have been equally successful, or perhaps even more so, for the Second Battle of El Alamein.

Military historian R. W. Thompson makes the same point about 'competence' in his book *Churchill and the Montgomery Myth*, when he writes:

> Montgomery who feared the unpredictable, who relied upon the textbook and training, and an assessment of the factors, denied himself the possibility to rise above competence. The vital factor

of the human spirit eluded him. He imposed the strait-jacket of his severe limitation upon his army.[117]

We shall later come to the manner of his performance and relationships in Sicily, Italy and Europe, but it is because of what one might, to be kind, call his 'idiosyncrasies' that a deeply flawed character is revealed. Another historian, Anthony Beevor, has said that he feels Montgomery may have suffered from an inferiority complex and the defensive and prickly personality was developed as a defensive mechanism, a need to compensate for this;[118] his biographer Nigel Hamilton describes him as a man 'tormented by inner insecurity, an emotional cripple.'[119] Insecurity and a sense of inferiority are similar conditions and could also explain why, irrespective of any evidence to the contrary, he would always insist that everything had gone according to his plan and that whatever had occurred had been exactly what he had intended. In other words, there was not sufficient strength of character to concede that he might, ever, have been wrong. This is a fault that can be concealed or ignored when in the ascendant, as one way or another Montgomery was for some time after Alamein, but one that would have come back to bite him had he ever been forced to deal with a situation of overwhelming enemy advantage that some of his predecessors had been obliged to handle. His apparent 'self-confidence' may well have concealed quite the opposite.

Some of his mannerisms border on imperious defiance and a complete disregard of the feelings of others. It seems that once he had obtained prominence and because of the impetus of wartime events, he felt secure in his position and he then did just as he wanted in the belief that he could get away with almost anything, which he did. However, one has to ask whether many of these traits were not those of a confident personality but one that was concerned with needing to continually prove himself, to unnecessarily demonstrate who was in charge, and irrespective of his obvious standing, an underlying anxiety caused by personal insecurity.

A factor that might have contributed to these traits may have been his lack of physical stature. He was probably smaller than most other generals in the British Army, Correlli Barnett describing Montgomery's chin as being about the same height as Auchinleck's decorations. Admiral Sir Tom Phillips, an even smaller man than Montgomery, was renowned in the navy for his pugnacious personality and was referred to by Admiral Sir James Somerville as 'the West's pocket Napoleon', and it was largely because of his arrogance and bellicose attitude that HMS *Prince of Wales* and HMS *Renown* were lost to the Japanese in December 1941. Like Montgomery, he had a haughty disdain for the views of others but in Phillips' case he paid for his opinions with his life when he went down with his ship. Generals do not have ships to go down with, but whereas Phillips' conceit exposed his ships to the attack of over 350 bombers and torpedo bombers, in Montgomery's case he never had anything less than a distinct over-abundance and superiority of resources at his disposal.

From the moment he arrived in Egypt, Montgomery always had everything he needed or wanted, and moreover, despite seemingly going out of his way to annoy them, he could operate with the huge support provided by the American forces, which had entered the European theatre in November 1942. He had appeared on the scene as the tide was inexorably turning and, with ever increasing force and speed, all Montgomery had to do was ride the crest of the wave. Writing what would become his memoirs in 1944, Rommel observed:

> Montgomery was in a position to profit by the bitter experience of his predecessors. Moreover, while supplies on our side had been cut to a trickle, American and British ships were bringing vast quantities of material to North Africa, many times greater than Wavell or Auchinleck ever had. His principle was to fight no battle unless he knew for certain he could win. Of course that is a method which will only work given material superiority; but that he had.[120]

It is important to bear in mind that Montgomery himself realised this, hence his constant need to proclaim his own personal genius in what was achieved. Had he not done so, his role would, quite rightly, have been subsumed within the successes of the overall Allied command structure and strategies of which he was, in reality, just a part. Montgomery could not allow this; he had to stand alone and be seen to be doing so, because if he did not, he feared he might not be noticed.

The snide side of Montgomery's personality comes unpleasantly to light in the timing of the offensive comments he made about various colleagues. Of Field Marshal Sir Harold Alexander, an outstanding British general who had been his superior in both the desert, Sicily and mainland Italy, he later said: 'First-class general, Alex—did everything I told him to do'.[121] This was a remark he made after Alexander had retired from the army and was in Canada, where he had been invited to be governor-general—and was a very popular and successful one. Alexander was the very antithesis of Montgomery in style and personality, was admired by and got on well with the Americans and had he not been approached by the Canadians, would probably have been Chief of the Imperial General Staff in 1946. Montgomery knew this, hence the knife in the back from a safe distance of 3,000 miles.

Another cheap shot made by Montgomery about his erstwhile superior Eisenhower, once peace had removed the threat of repercussions, was: 'Nice chap. No soldier.'[122] In 1963 military author Cornelius Ryan was talking to Eisenhower to obtain material for one of his books when he happened to mention Montgomery's name, causing the normally mild-mannered Eisenhower to explode:

> First of all he's a psychopath. Don't forget that. He is such an egocentric that everything he has ever done is perfect—he has never made a mistake in his life. He even says that all of the Operations after we landed on D-Day went absolutely according to plan![123]

We have already noted Montgomery's spiteful comment about Auchinleck, which stated that he 'should never be employed again in any capacity'. It was a totally unnecessary and contemptuous statement made about a senior colleague who had just been removed for solely political reasons, but a situation that the gloating Montgomery just could not resist. If nothing else it was a mean and petty gesture. Moreover, the arrogance in saying 'in any capacity' is quite mind-numbing, coming from a junior officer. As mentioned earlier Montgomery had crossed swords with Auchinleck whilst serving under him in Southern Command in 1940, when Montgomery decided to short-cut established procedures to obtain the officer transfers he wanted. An examination of the correspondence that took place reveals from Auchinleck a most understanding and gentle explanation of the necessary procedure, but it seems to have been the very fact that he was corrected, however charmingly, that caused such fury in Montgomery. So, was this spiteful comment just another example of someone with an inferiority complex obtaining what he felt was retribution against another whom he knew, in every sense of the word, was his superior?

There is another even less attractive explanation, that in each of the above men, Auchinleck and Eisenhower, Montgomery knew he was dealing with people of gentle dispositions, men who were unlikely to publicly put him in his place and he felt that, even as a subordinate, he could get away with such bullying behaviour without danger to himself. This seems quite possible, but if so it adds just one more piece to a jigsaw of highly unattractive characteristics. In so many situations, and quite unnecessarily, Montgomery seems to have behaved with all the viciousness of a cornered rat.

Another facet that suggests the existence of insecurity and an inferiority complex was Montgomery's habit of seeking the company of younger men—his chosen chief of staff, Major Francis de Guingand, was 13 years his junior—indicating that he felt more confident when he knew he was the eldest one in a group and therefore more likely to be deferred to. Biographer Alun Chalfont relates:

> There was always something disturbingly equivocal about his attitude towards boys and young men. In their company he often seemed to display a heightened awareness and an almost febrile gaiety. His tactical headquarters in the desert, with its entourage of gilded youth and its cloying atmosphere of hero-worship, suggests that he had a predilection for the company of younger men and found a contentment there which he was unable to find with women or with older men.[124]

This is a description that is perhaps heightened by understatement. It would have been a circle that he could dominate with ease, one where his views would not be questioned, where he would feel there to be no threat, either socially or professionally. He would have felt more secure in the company of his juniors for there would have been none of the innate fear that he probably felt amongst his peers and which he then attempted to overcome by behaving in an unnecessarily aggressive fashion. On the contrary, he would have been surrounded by a collection of adoring young officers hanging on his every word, young men who would have been quite flattered that he even spoke to them.

Yet again this is a characteristic that points towards the inferiority complex discussed earlier, for even ignoring the possible implications of Chalfont's words 'disturbingly equivocal', when he was amongst younger people, Montgomery's views would go unchallenged. His inner doubts seem to have been such that wherever he was and whatever he was doing, he not only tried to subjugate but perhaps more importantly for his mental well-being, he also needed to be seen to dominate. Reginald W. Thompson makes the same observation:

> Montgomery preferred only the company of young men. He had constructed a personal hierarchy in which he had his place, a kind of House-Master, subordinate to the High-Master, and of course to the Board of Governors and The Lord Mighty in Battle. But in his House he was unchallenged. He heard only those things he wished to hear, and it is in the nature of young men to please their seniors of exalted rank. Montgomery's young men were not sycophants, but they were lieutenants and captains sitting at the feet of the commander of an army.[125]

This type of personality would also explain the need for a style of dress that was different, theatrics to compensate for a lack of confidence, artifices that someone more balanced and assured would not have needed. In *The Business of War*, Major-General Sir John Kennedy specifically mentions the fact that when films of the 1943 Sicily landings appeared, Montgomery's appearances on the beaches were so theatrical that they provoked considerable adverse comment in London, but Kennedy says he got away with this on the grounds that he could win battles.[126] After all, if the man is winning, why worry about the fact that he looked so comical? In truth it was probable that with the momentum of a war that was steadily going the Allies' way, the significance of such exhibitionism was ignored as a mere eccentricity and the British press would have promoted this as an example of their commander's colourful panache. He won battles, but as this book so frequently demonstrates, with all the advantages that Montgomery had, virtually any other general would have done just as well.

Compare this with the demeanour of Slim in Burma. Against the Japanese and in a steeply undulating terrain of dense jungle or tropical rainforest bisected by raging rivers, Slim was fighting a far more fanatical and tenacious enemy than Montgomery ever faced, and his eventual success with an army that was 75 per cent Asian was indeed a direct reflection of his calm but natural authority. It was not for nothing that his army referred to him as 'Uncle Bill' and his own account of that contest, *Defeat into Victory*, is marked by a distinctly self-effacing modesty compared with the self-serving distortions and exaggerations with which Montgomery coloured his own memoirs.

British parliamentarian and Labour minister Sir Denis Healey was commissioned in the Royal Artillery during World War II. In his autobiography *The Time of My Life* he recounts being singularly unimpressed when he heard Montgomery speak in Tunisia. He described the experience thus:

> We were drawn up in a square to hear an inspirational speech from General Montgomery. He did not impress us with his sharp, ferret-like face and pale grey-green eyes, wearing his vanity like a foulard. When he told the veterans of 78 Division, who had almost taken Tunis within three days of landing in Algiers, that they should feel proud of joining the Eighth Army the temperature dropped below freezing in a second.[127]

Healey would not have recalled the event were it not for the appalling impression produced on the troops by the Montgomery ego. But thus, unfortunately, did Montgomery continue to tell everyone how lucky they were to be joining *him* and *his* army, all part of the myth he fabricated that the Eighth Army was only created at the Second Battle of El Alamein. When it came to self-promotion or public relations Montgomery was always the great schemer, displaying a speed of opportunism or reaction that he rarely showed on the field of battle, where he was noted for extreme caution and slowness of decision. Many people will believe anything, provided those with an agenda tell them stridently and frequently enough. This Montgomery did from the moment he took over in Egypt. As is often attributed to Nazi propaganda Minister Joseph Goebbels, 'If the lie is big enough then the more likely it is that people will believe it.' And did Montgomery perhaps actually mislead himself as well? Alun Chalfont recounts a conversational question: 'Who do you think were the three greatest commanders in history?' To which, he says, Montgomery replied: 'The other two were Alexander the Great and Napoleon.' Chalfont then adds that it was not intended as a joke.[128] Once more the vanity and conceit is astonishing.

But, a thought—was this yet another manoeuvre in an effort to stamp his authority, an authority that he doubted and therefore felt a constant need to assert and exaggerate? For if one makes a seemingly outlandish statement like that, 'in your face' to use a current expression, it is unlikely that anyone will argue.

On another occasion Chalfont describes that when talking to a small schoolboy at a school he was visiting Montgomery asked: 'Do they teach you about Marlborough? Do they teach you about Wellington? Do they teach you about *me* [author's emphasis]?' A further example perhaps of a little man who knew inside himself that he did not rate those comparisons, and it was for that reason that he kept demanding them—and especially perhaps when talking to little boys? Both Marlborough and Wellington were singular military commanders who had considerable influence in shaping both British and European history by blunting French expansionist ambitions through defeating firstly Louis XIV and then Napoleon. These successes had been achieved in campaigns taking place over a number of years and prior to that Wellington had also secured British India by defeating the superior forces of the Maratha Confederacy. Both of them were frequently outnumbered and had very unpredictable and unreliable allies. Montgomery had to contend with none of these difficulties. His good fortune was to have been caught up in the momentum of an Allied coalition, a wave of huge numerical and equipment advantage on land, at sea and in the air, bankrolled by the vast industrial capacity of the United States. As an individual Montgomery had shaped nothing but his own reputation, and as such it is difficult to see how there could be any rational comparison with Marlborough or Wellington. He knew this, but it seems he could not tolerate being seen to be a support player, however important the role; hence the constant need to exaggerate his contribution.

Even after the Word War II Montgomery's penchant for continual backstabbing emerged once more when he paid a 48-hour visit to India in 1947. At that time Auchinleck was in the midst of the painful and complex task of breaking up, regiment by regiment, the 200-year-old Indian Army. Totally insensible to the strains this imposed on tradition and caste, and even after 5 years still attempting to denigrate the modest but highly capable Auchinleck, Montgomery's inspection report stated: 'It seemed to me that Auchinleck was wrapped up entirely in the Indian Army and appeared to be paying little heed to the welfare of the British soldiers in India'.[129] And yet this was the man, as he was then Chief of the Imperial General Staff, who was making the most ignorant and insensitive comments about one of the oldest and proudest armies in British military history. That army was being torn asunder by Mountbatten, his rushed Indian independence and the politics of the moment. In those most complex, difficult and sensitive of circumstances Auchinleck was doing his utmost to make sure that the ultimate fracture was as painless as possible. To say that Auchinleck was 'wrapped up entirely with the Indian Army' was rather like criticising a surgeon for paying to much attention to his patient. But this was Montgomery; despite the passing of 5 years since he had taken over in North Africa, he could never pass up the slightest opportunity to stick the knife into anyone, and especially if it was Auchinleck.

In 1995 Jack L. Granatstein, an established and admired Canadian military historian, examined the performance of his country's military leaders in his book *The Generals: The Canadian Army's Senior Commanders in the Second World War*.[130] In doing so he also naturally touched on their relations with various Allied commanders such as Eisenhower, Bradley, Horrocks, Paget, and the like, but it is interesting that he also makes a general comment on Montgomery. Granatstein says that in the British Army Montgomery was widely known as 'the nasty little shit'. Given all of the above, that reputation is not surprising, but perhaps it took a Canadian to have the guts to say so.

CHAPTER 7

MOUNTBATTEN—
DISASTER AT DIEPPE

Only a foolhardy commander launches a frontal
attack with untried troops, unsupported, in daylight
against veterans dug in and prepared behind
concrete, wired and mined approaches, and enemy
with every psychological advantage. It was bad
plan and had no chance of success.
—LORD LOVAT, commander,
  No. 4 Commando

Combined Operations was a department of the War Office originally established by Churchill in 1940 to harass the Germans. After Germany attacked Russia in June 1941, its aims were also to reassure Stalin that the West was serious in making a contribution in the war against Hitler. This was in some ways indirectly successful; for instance, commando attacks in Norway so convinced Hitler of an impending invasion that by 1944 Germany had 370,000 troops stationed there. Another success was Operation *Chariot* in March 1942, which totally disabled the important dry dock at Saint-Nazaire on the Atlantic coast of France for the remainder of the war. This meant that large German battleships like the *Tirpitz* would have to return to a German shipyard for any servicing or repairs.

The first director of Combined Operations was Admiral Sir Roger Keyes, but by November 1941 he was 69 and although he had performed well, it was decided to replace him with a younger man. To the surprise of many and virtually out of the blue Churchill picked for the job the youthful

102

Louis Mountbatten, then merely a destroyer captain in the Royal Navy. As previously revealed, up to that point in the war Mountbatten's career had been chequered to say the least, his two commands, HMS *Kelly* and HMS *Javelin,* having both suffered considerable damage due to reckless and foolhardy decisions on his part. The *Kelly* in particular had almost continuously run into one scrape after another where crew were lost and the ship had to be laid up for some time for repairs.

Remarkably, not one of these stupid and irresponsible escapades, which would have ruined or seriously hampered the career of any other officer, seems to have caused any undue concern at a higher level. Quite the opposite in fact, for after one episode when the *Javelin* was very nearly lost as a result of Mountbatten going completely against accepted engagement procedures, instead of being censured for his lack of sense of responsibility he was invited to Chequers to be greeted by Churchill as if he was some sort of hero. By clever wartime manipulation of the facts, what had been a near idiotic disaster was transformed for the media into a Royal Navy triumph.

Mountbatten was then only 41, he had no experience in the type of warfare that he was about to undertake and moreover even at that youthful age and for no apparent reason—certainly not for performance—he had just been elevated to the rank of commodore and then further up to vice admiral. There was therefore no logic in his appointment, merely a matter of personal favouritism. In his book *Blood, Sweat and Arrogance: The Myths of Churchill's War,* Gordon Corrigan wryly observes that 'Although some in the Royal Navy considered him a rash and flamboyant mountebank, he appealed to Churchill', and in truth there could have been no other rational explanation for his elevation.[131] This sort of 'appeal' was in line with Churchill's enthusiasm for the eccentric Orde Wingate in Burma, who for some time he had even thought should replace Slim. It did not seem to matter just how loony or outlandish the idea might be, it would probably attract Churchill's support, at least until such time as his chiefs of staff managed to bring him back to the real world; sometimes they could not. These decisions, it would seem, were all symptomatic of his manic phases where the greater the unfavourable odds, the greater the attraction for Churchill. Such operations were also part and parcel of Churchill's personal determination to keep chipping away at Hitler, whatever the cost.

In the case of Dieppe, Churchill's domineering decision making was to lead to one of Britain's greatest disasters of World War II, and as usual he would then distance himself from all responsibility. Casting around for possible locations for his special forces after their success at Saint-Nazaire, Mountbatten had for some time been considering Dieppe as a target because it seemed to offer, in principle, the possibility to gain experience in seizing and holding a major and well-defended port for a short period, with tanks, artillery and landing craft. These objectives were nebulous in the extreme and speak of straw-grasping because the tangible benefits, other than just showing what could be done, seem to have been non-existent. There was an obvious difference between this Dieppe scheme and that of Saint-Nazaire, for at the latter there had been a definite and intelligent objective—to put out of use the dry-dock facilities needed by the Germans to service their large battleships for operation in the Atlantic—and in this they succeeded. However, even without the advantage of hindsight it should have been obvious to all except perhaps the most pig-headed that the plan was in fact a stupid idea, for surely the admitted fact that Dieppe was a 'well-defended port' should have been sufficient deterrent? So how, one might ask, did this venture ever get to be launched when the odds against its success were so obvious, and why has there never been any clear explanation of who, ultimately, was responsible? Or was all this thought of but not mentioned because of protection from on high?

Investigations into the concept started on 4 April 1942 when Mountbatten gave orders for the plan to commence and a committee was established. But as the various planners started to assemble the separate but necessary components for a successful attack, it became clear that there would be too many simultaneous assaults in the Dieppe area, which would produce massive congestion. Also there were large German artillery batteries, colourfully named 'Goebbels' and 'Hesse', well positioned on the headlands either side that completely covered the entrance to the harbour, and these had to be silenced first if a frontal assault was to have any chance of success. However, it was then realised that if these guns were to be put out of action, they would have to be attacked about half an hour before the main assault fleet arrived, and if this occurred then the vital factor of surprise would be lost. One would have thought that this element alone would have been enough for caution to be exercised even if no one realised that the plan was not going to work.

On 18 April 1942 the committee decided that further planning should commence with the main frontal assault being preceded by a barrage from navy battleships to eliminate the coastal batteries. The operation was to be called *Rutter* and was scheduled to be launched early in July when tides would be favourable. Later in May, and because they were afraid of losing a capital ship to Luftwaffe attack so close to shore, the navy suggested instead firepower from destroyers. This would obviously not have the same strike power as the guns of a battleship, and therefore the help of the RAF was requested to bomb the gun emplacements. After some further consideration this plan too was discarded because the RAF could not guarantee the accuracy of their bombing, which was vital in order to protect the invading forces; so an airborne assault on the guns was considered instead. This too was dropped in favour of commando attacks on the German batteries. The planners were back to square one because the commandos would have to be seaborne causing enormous congestion of landing craft, but nonetheless the project went ahead. The lack of any meaningful bombardment of the two coastal batteries was to prove disastrous for the landing parties. This was just part of an overall patchwork of ideas that were not properly thought out but were pushed through by a command impatient for personal accolades. It is little wonder that military historian John Keegan was later to comment that in retrospect Dieppe 'looks so recklessly hare-brained an enterprise that it is difficult to reconstruct the official state of mind which gave it birth and drove it forward.'[132] Since there was no official authorisation there was of course no 'official state of mind', but the driving force was there: Mountbatten.

Practice landings were organised for some weeks on the Isle of Wight, which was sealed off for the purpose. However, when the time came for the raid to be launched the period of favourable tides coincided with very unsettled weather and as a result the order to sail was delayed; and as if to prove that the operation was ill-fated, the assembled fleet of ships in the Yarmouth Roads was observed by German reconnaissance planes, which then bombed them on 7 July 1942. The resulting damage was not serious but the weather got even worse, and worried that the German bombing attack might indicate the element of surprise had been lost, the operation was cancelled.

With this development most felt that Operation *Rutter* was finished, and indeed that seemed to be the most sensible decision—but not for Mount-batten, who was not to be denied his glorious raid, and so he pressed on re-gardless with a parallel scheme to be called *Jubilee*. Following cancellation of the *Rutter* raid, the servicemen who had been involved—some 6,000 with varying degrees of knowledge of what had been planned—were returned to their barracks, and naturally enough it became a talking point in local pubs and messes. One would have thought this security breach would be suffi-cient for the whole plan to be abandoned. Relief that an operation regarded as very risky at the best had been cancelled came from a number of quarters. The Naval Force commander, Rear Admiral Harold Baillie-Grohman, and the commander of the Canadian 2nd Division, Major-General John H. Roberts, co-signed a letter to Mountbatten pointing out that there had never been an overall military assessment of the operation to explain how the var-ious parts of the plan were to be integrated, and this had unfortunate effects on subsequent planning.

Mountbatten would have none of this and rather than taking into con-sideration these valid arguments from a man of such seniority and experi-ence as the 54-year-old Baillie-Grohman, he was simply transferred elsewhere, a move that was completely in line with the Churchillian phi-losophy of not listening but just removing anyone who did not agree with him. This in turn of course meant that Mountbatten would have to find a replacement at fairly short notice if he intended to relaunch his project in mid-August. Such a move would usually have required a replacement of similar rank, but the ever resourceful Mountbatten decided on Captain John Hughes-Hallett, who had been one of his chief planners for the op-eration; this choice also had the advantage of keeping everything under wraps. Hughes-Hallett was forever afterwards protesting that he had no idea that the raid had no official authorisation. Another factor that Mount-batten may have regarded as a benefit was that Hughes-Hallett was a year younger than him.

It is astonishing that Mountbatten proceeded with his own plans for the operation to be relaunched using unofficial channels despite the dis-approval of the chiefs of staff. Even Churchill, who was away in Egypt and Moscow for most of the month of August 1942, had not been told, for the simple reason that his chiefs of staff did not know either. A search through Cabinet files also failed to reveal the decision to remount the operation.

How Mountbatten got away with this is a mystery. Canadian historian Brian Loring Villa puts this succinctly in his most detailed book *Unauthorised Action: Mountbatten and the Dieppe Raid*:

> If, as now seems certain, Mountbatten was acting without authorization, we can also explain so many aspects of the raid that have always looked incriminating to those who have nursed dark suspicions. They have been particularly troubled by the fact that there was no cover plan, that the Intelligence Services did not render the assistance they should have given this operation. But this failure can be explained, most easily, by their not having been informed by Mountbatten, who was keeping the secret of the actual decision even from his own deputy as well as from his own chief of staff.[133]

But of course it goes far beyond that, because having kept the intelligence services out of his picture also meant that he was denying himself the up-to-date intelligence that the services could have provided. So, not only was this 'keeping his cards close to his chest' a deliberate deception, it was also, and in keeping with other actions of his during the war when pursuing his own agenda, professionally negligent and recklessly indifferent to the safety of others. Mountbatten's methodology also suggests that he feared his plan would be stopped if too many people got to know about it; after all, if not, then why the secrecy?

Some months later when they discovered what had happened, the chiefs of staff issued directives that in future no operation of this sort of magnitude would be allowed to proceed without first having obtained clearance from the Inter-Service Security Board. That was for the future, but the fact that so many officers did not at that time apparently even question their orders is an indication of the aura of personal authority that Mountbatten had built up. It all looks as though this was intended to be a Mountbatten tour de force—'I did it my way'—but because of his lack of experience and conceit what he had intended as a personal triumph unfolded into one of the greatest tragedies of the war.

In the aftermath of the disaster and despite a total lack of evidence to support him, Mountbatten was vehemently arguing that he had the necessary official approval, as he has done ever since. However, Brian Loring

Villa's detailed and thorough investigations have revealed an almost Machiavellian network of intrigue designed to put everyone of seniority off the scent. He states:

> What really happened can be pieced together from the well-scattered evidence. In Hughes-Hallett's papers there is a note from him to Mountbatten dated 17 July, suggesting that he send to the 'Most Secret' distribution list—i.e. the top officers of COHQ—a 'draft information' chit informing them that an Operation Jubilee was to be mounted (without mentioning what the destination or objective would be). The explanation for the raid to be offered was that the 'Chiefs of Staff have directed that if possible an emergency operation is to be carried out during August to fill the gap caused by the cancellation of Rutter.' There is no evidence the Chiefs had ordered anything of the sort when Hughes-Hallett distributed his information chit. So Mountbatten had either already begun the deception, or he and Hughes-Hallett were anticipating they would get approval. In any case the note implied that the top staffs were to be told that their services would not be required for Jubilee because everything would be left to the Force Commanders. This directive clearly indicates an attempt to restrict knowledge of Jubilee to the fewest people.[134]

Other than No. 4 Commando, commanded by Lord Lovat, which successfully landed at dawn, climbed the cliffs, silenced the German guns and withdrew as planned, all the other areas of the operation were just one disaster after another. At the very start and almost as the fleet was leaving Portsmouth, intelligence warning that a German convoy would be encountered was ignored. In fact this avoidable encounter, although it caused serious delays, did not involve much in the way of damage or losses but it did alert the German forces ashore. Thus the vital element of surprise was gone, although it is difficult to accept that it was seriously believed the approach of a force the size of 237 ships and landing craft, including eight destroyers, could be kept secret. Surely this was wishful thinking and the demonstration of a self-deluding attitude so frequently evident in Mountbatten.

On all other sectors, timing, coordination and the lack of surprise—crucial factors that others had pointed out would be almost impossible to achieve—became critical issues combining to produce almost widespread chaos. Delays caused smoke screens to have lifted by the time troops reached shore, exposing them to machine-gun and artillery fire. Of the 556 men of the Royal Regiment of Canada either killed or captured, only 92 survived.

Although preceded by a barrage from destroyers and bombing of the town by the RAF, the landings for the main frontal assault immediately ran into trouble due to coordination difficulties. Infantry should have been supported by tanks but they arrived late, leaving the infantry without armour support and exposed to heavy machine-gun fire which decimated their ranks. When the tanks did eventually arrive many either sank in deep water or became bogged in the shingle beach; the few that did get through found that tank obstacles prevented them from entering the town. Not one tank returned to England and all tank crews were either killed or captured. Two reserve units sent in shortly afterwards were blinded to what had occurred by a destroyer-laid smokescreen, and on landing were also devastated by heavy machine-gun, mortar and grenade fire. Many landing craft of Royal Marines sent in to support them were destroyed or disabled and all the Marines were either killed or captured. Some sort of escape from this carnage and confusion was eventually managed by withdrawal under heavy fire at about 11 a.m.

So, what was the final toll for this ill-advised and illicit enterprise? Around 6,000 troops, mostly Canadian, had been involved. Of these 3,642 were killed, wounded or captured, a casualty rate of 60 per cent that is almost unsurpassed. The navy lost 1 destroyer, 33 landing craft and 550 dead and wounded, and the RAF, which should have been providing support to keep the skies clear of the Luftwaffe, lost 100 aircraft resulting in the deaths of 62 airmen plus 30 wounded and 17 captured. Dieppe was Canada's first action in the war against Germany and of the 4,963 men who took part in the ill-fated exercise, only 2,210 returned safely. It was the most appalling slaughter, and to achieve what? Just what was accomplished, what information was obtained that could not have been acquired by any other means? This question has never been answered. As Gordon Corrigan states in his already quoted book:

Many a commander had been sacked for less, but Mountbatten always maintained that Dieppe was an essential rehearsal for Overlord, the D-Day landings in Normandy in June 1944. It is difficult to give credence to that assertion. The tactical lessons of Dieppe—that very heavy fire support was essential to and after landing, that contemporary tanks could not cross sea walls, that sappers with demolition kit needed to be well forward, and that reliable communications were vital—could surely have been learned without the deaths and imprisonment of so many men.[135]

If every single point that Corrigan makes is examined, it is clear they could all have been worked out by intelligent trial beforehand. An issue he does not mention, that a large number of the tanks became completely bogged down in the shingle beaches, is a classic example of a factor that should have been seen as a possible problem, and if so there were plenty of shingle beaches around Britain's coastline where the performance of tanks could easily have been trialled. It is not exaggerating too much to suggest that Mountbatten's attitude seems to have been one of 'shouldn't cost too many lives but let's try it and see if it works'—and of course, the bigger the project then the greater the fame for the overall commander who had launched such a brilliant scheme. Quite clearly not only was Mountbatten too immature and inexperienced to be put in charge of the operation where he had such authority, but to heighten this danger, and like Churchill whose protégé he was, he appears to have been totally convinced that whatever he did was right.

Mountbatten would calmly rationalise *ex post facto* not only about Dieppe, but about other incidents and events where huge questions should have been asked but where it seems he was regarded and thought of himself as untouchable. Granted, he was the second cousin of the king, as he was wont to remind those around him, and at that time Buckingham Palace had rather more influence in such matters than it does today, but even so his survival and further promotion at top level is remarkable considering the trail of debris and death that he left in his wake.

The Germans were handed a propaganda scoop which they naturally exploited to the fullest, but at the same time they were puzzled. The German interrogator of one Canadian officer asked him: 'It was too big for a raid, too small for an invasion—what were you trying to do?'[136] What indeed? One can only imagine the dilemma of the poor officer concerned, for even if he had wanted to he probably would not have been able to provide any intelligent explanation. Liddell Hart says that one of the basic military maxims, overwhelmingly supported by the evidence of history, is that no general is justified in launching his troops to direct an attack upon an enemy firmly in position. That was precisely what Mountbatten had done, and it is therefore little wonder that the Germans were so perplexed. One of the senior German officers at Dieppe later commented that it was 'incomprehensible that a single division was expected to be able to over-run a German regiment that was supported by artillery. The strength of the naval and air forces was entirely insufficient to suppress the defenders during the landings'[137]

The whole debacle was 'spun' as a display of heroism to obtain badly needed information and necessary data. 'It succeeded,' said Mountbatten, 'in providing experience and priceless information that would prove invaluable for future operations and that would not otherwise have been obtainable'. It was nonsense, but in other words don't make the same mistake again!

However, apart from totally incompetent direction and planning what makes the whole scenario very odd is why, as an exercise in invasion planning, attack a well-defended position? There was no way, when the invasion of Europe came, that the Allied plans would ever have envisaged a direct assault on such a strongly protected port; and of course so it proved when the D-Day landings were made on the Normandy coast between Le Havre and Cherbourg. That much must have been a given, so why attempt it just to see what would happen? It all had the odour of swashbuckling bravado—on the part of those who stayed in England that is.

Even in friendly surroundings serious military rehearsals can result in heavy loss of life when things go wrong, and this was revealed some two years later. Late in 1943 the Americans sequestered a large area of land around Slapton Sands on the south Devon coast in south-west England for invasion training and rehearsals. By that time Normandy had been decided as the invasion area for D-Day, and Slapton Sands provided as near as possible a replica of what would be encountered on the French beaches. In April 1944 Exercise *Tiger* was a disaster involving the loss of 749 American lives. This was largely due to German E-boats reading an unusual volume of radio traffic and deciding to 'have a look'; their arrival amongst the fleet on the rehearsal scene caused chaos. But even that was not the only reason for the high death toll, for a number of Sherman tanks found that their intended flotation skirts did not work and when launched from their landing craft they went straight to the bottom. Exercise *Tiger* is quoted here to show that even in what were regarded as non-hazardous surroundings, and despite careful planning and earlier practice, disasters could still happen. There was nothing new in this; even in peacetime military manoeuvres do involve danger—otherwise they would not be of any value—but it does highlight Mountbatten's gung-ho attitude in hostile waters in wartime conditions.

As he had made clear in his devil-may-care destroyer theatrics in the quest for personal kudos, Mountbatten cared little, if at all, about the lives of others. It might have been expected that he had learned a chastening lesson from the catastrophe of Dieppe, but only 4 months later in December 1942 he launched yet another of his madcap schemes, one where the rehearsal was such a disaster that yet again common sense should have dictated the project be dropped.

Operation *Frankton,* later presented for popular consumption as the film *Cockleshell Heroes*, was a scheme to launch a small fleet of two-man canoes to damage enemy merchant vessels found in the port of Bordeaux. This was to be achieved by launching the canoes from a submarine offshore and then paddling, in winter conditions, some 90km up the estuary of the Gironde, a waterway renowned for very strong tidal currents, indeed almost tidal bores, and if Bordeaux was successfully reached without detection then to attach limpet mines onto the hulls of whichever ships they might find there. In distance this was roughly the equivalent of paddling along the south coast of England from Southampton to Brighton and was hardly the sort of voyage or location for canoes in enemy territory; and yet when predictably the final trial was a complete shambles, instead of cancelling the operation Mountbatten's only reaction was: 'Splendid, you must have learnt a great deal, and you'll be able to avoid making the same mistakes on the operation'.[138]

As far as possible consequences were concerned, it was an answer of the most dangerous indifference and irresponsibility. Even without enemy interference, the fiasco when attempting to reproduce the real thing did not in the least suggest to Mountbatten that it might, just possibly, be wise to cancel an operation that was clearly suicidal, but he ordered it to go ahead. Out of ten men who actually took part in the mission only two survived, a small number perhaps but a combat fatality rate of 80 per cent and, since they had no prior intelligence, all for the scant reward of slightly damaging four unimportant cargo ships. The operation was stupid and irresponsible, and yet as in Mountbatten's previous foolhardy acts the operation was 'spun' as a triumph of British initiative and heroism; his initiative, but other people's heroism.

What also emerges from the overall circumstances of Dieppe and Operation *Frankton* is a clear behavioural pattern pointing towards the fact that Mountbatten had clear psychopathic tendencies'.

Amongst the accepted psychopathic symptoms are a lack of empathy or remorse, and behaviour that is callous, selfish, dishonest, impulsive, irresponsible and often superficially charming. Even ignoring the psychological implications, every one of these characteristics describes Mountbatten with unerring accuracy, and looking at the man from this angle, his dangerous and reckless actions when he was a destroyer captain come into a different focus.

Protected as he seemed to have been by royal and prime ministerial patronage, there would unfortunately be more occasions when his disturbing personality weaknesses would be on display.

CHAPTER 8

CHURCHILL—MEDDLING
IN THE MIDDLE EAST

Rommel! Rommel! Rommel! Rommel! What else
matters but beating him?
—WINSTON CHURCHILL, 1942

Italy had obtained a foothold in Africa in 1888 with the founding establishment of a protectorate on the Horn of Africa at the southern end of the Red Sea which was called Italian Somaliland; the country's influence was further extended in that region a year later with the military occupation and colonisation of neighbouring Eritrea, also on the Red Sea. On the Mediterranean coast of Africa the territories ceded to Italy following the Italo-Turkish War of 1912 were the provinces of Tripolitania and Cyrenaica, which became known as Libya in 1934. Following his successful 1935 invasion and occupation of Abyssinia, Mussolini proclaimed the province of Italian East Africa in 1936, which consisted of Abyssinia plus the adjoining territories of Eritrea and Italian Somaliland. Italy's presence in the region was therefore quite substantial, and fearing an Italian invasion King Farouk of Egypt signed the Anglo-Egyptian Treaty in 1936, which required the United Kingdom to withdraw all troops except those necessary to protect the Suez Canal and to provide training for Egypt's army and assistance in its defence in the event of war. That was the overall position in the region in 1940 when in June of that year France, Britain's largest ally, collapsed against Nazi Germany and nearly all the French navy, the fourth largest in the world, either fell into German hands or was no longer operational.

It was at this point, just one week after the British escape from Dunkirk and with typical political opportunism, that Italian dictator Benito Mussolini declared war on Britain. His grandiose plans were to expand his African territories into a neo-Roman Empire, which threatened to turn the Mediterranean into an Axis lake. Hitler does not appear to have shown much interest in Mussolini's venture, nor does the Suez Canal itself seem to have been a strategic objective of the Italians but simply the prestige of acquiring territory. Following the French surrender and feeling sure he was onto a good thing in Africa, Mussolini launched attacks into Egypt from Libya and the Sudan from Italian Somaliland. Sudan had been administered by the British from Egypt and although large in area it was of no strategic or geographical importance, which only emphasised the fact that as far as Mussolini was concerned it was the glory of territorial conquest that he was seeking; Britain's North Africa campaign had to thwart these plans. Despite his army and air force equipment being largely obsolete, Mussolini's forces met with some initial successes, on paper at least, for he had vastly superior numbers; but his tactics, which had proved successful against desert tribesmen in other areas of Africa, were soon shown to be wanting against smaller but better trained and equipped forces under the direction of General Sir Archibald Wavell, the British commander in the Middle East. A number of significant battle reversals ensued and by December 1940 there loomed the complete loss of all Mussolini's north and east African territories, which would have brought the whole of the African Mediterranean under British control.

In April 1941 an anti-British coup in Baghdad led by Prime Minster Rashid Ali, also threatened Britain's interests in the region. Churchill decided that the revolt in Baghdad must be stamped out immediately; as overall commander Middle East, Wavell was instructed to get the place under control. A brigade of the Indian 10th Division that was en route to Malaya was diverted and landed at Basra at the end of April 1941, and several days later Wellington bombers and a few Gladiator fighters from Egypt plus troops were airlifted into the RAF air base just outside Baghdad. This action prevented the revolt from gaining momentum. However, the British Ultra codebreaker had in the meantime intercepted urgent Iraqi requests for Axis support that had been furtively channelled through the Italian embassy in Baghdad, and to forestall any possible German intervention, Wavell was directed to reduce his forces by an invasion and occupation of Iraq. A 5,800-strong British force was hastily assembled in Palestine for this purpose, and supported by about 200 aircraft it proved far too strong for the Iraqis.

By 1 June the revolt had been completely put down and Prime Minister Rashid Ali had fled to Persia. Iraq was now under British control but only a week or so later yet another possible threat arose. Vichy France, collaborating with and actively assisting Nazi Germany, offered the latter the use of French air bases in Syria, which could provide the Germans with an ideal springboard for attacks on Egypt and the Suez Canal from the immediate north. Damascus was only some 440km from the canal, the same distance as Paris to London, and within easy range of German bombers. So fixated was Churchill with the control and security of the whole Middle East that yet another forestalling action had to be mounted in the area by the already overstretched resources at Wavell's disposal, and almost immediately following the Iraqi campaign he was ordered to invade and occupy Lebanon and Syria. This was achieved after 6 weeks of heavy fighting against the Vichy French forces.

The Iraqi insurrection had been sorted out and the Levant occupied to prevent Luftwaffe use, but as if these were not enough for Wavell to have to contend with, Churchill's next bright idea was Greece. At his insistence, in April 1941 58,000 men and their equipment were dispatched on a futile foray into Greece to forestall expected German reinforcements for Mussolini's deteriorating Greek invasion. This British expedition was in fact little more than a limp political gesture but Churchill persisted with this half-baked scheme against odds that had been forecast to be overwhelming, in spite of serious misgivings voiced by his military advisers. The Director of Military Operations at the War Office, Major-General Sir John Kennedy, had warned that at least twenty divisions would be required for the operation to be successful, roughly double the number that were sent, and (the then) General Sir John Dill, Chief of the Imperial General Staff, advised Churchill that the troop strengths in the Middle East were insufficient for any to be spared for such an undertaking. Earlier Wavell had also told Churchill:

> Nothing, repeat nothing we can do from here is likely to be in time
> to stop German advance if really intended, it will lead to most dan-

gerous dispersion of force. I am desperately anxious lest we play enemy's game and expose ourselves to defeat in detail.[139]

But Churchill would have none of this; irrespective of the military realities protested by his generals, heroic political gestures were of greater importance, were demanded for Britain's Greek allies and were needed to impress Roosevelt with Britain's resolve to fight. With typical imperial gravitas he replied to Wavell:

> Destruction of Greece would eclipse victories you have gained in Libya and might affect decisively Turkish attitude, especially if we had shown ourselves callous of fate of Allies. You must therefore conform your plans to larger interests at stake. We expect and require prompt and active compliance with our decisions for which we accept full responsibility.[140]

Just how the loss of Greece could in any way be of greater strategic importance than the fact that practically the whole of Libya was within Wavell's reach was never explained, but Wavell knew better than to question such a peremptory order. Churchill's political grandstanding made no impression on Roosevelt, at least not the one that Churchill had in mind, and there was never a chance that Turkey might enter a war in which she could see no benefit for herself. This was just another of Churchill's flights of historical fancy, and watching from the sidelines Roosevelt must have been singularly unimpressed by the military theatrics of a leader who was asking for his help.

The Middle Eastern theatre was seriously weakened by this senseless escapade just as Wavell's forces were about to take Tripoli. Within a week the invasion of Greece was in disarray, and forces had to be withdrawn to the island of Crete, which itself then also fell to the Germans. The overall result of this ill-conceived folly was the loss of 31,000 men killed, wounded, missing or taken prisoner; and the loss of 8,000 trucks, 200 aircraft, plus 100 tanks and all stores. On top of this, the navy lost 3 cruisers, 6 destroyers and 2,000 men; 5 of these vessels were sunk by Luftwaffe bombing attacks due to there being virtually no British air cover. Many of the troops were Australian or New Zealanders and their experience of being thrown into a situation without air support was to understandably colour many of their attitudes towards the British top brass for some time to come. This tragic waste of men and materials occurred very largely because of the self-convictions of one man, Winston Churchill, who had earlier told his chiefs of staff that because of the naval base at Suda Bay, the island of Crete should be transformed into a fortress, which would then immensely improve Britain's position in the eastern Mediterranean. With an unrealistic rhetoric that was a horrible foretaste of what was to come some 9 months later in Singapore, Churchill then ordered that the 'fortress' of Crete 'must be stubbornly defended'. As Corelli Barnett writes in *The Desert Generals,* 'This Greek episode lengthened the campaign in North Africa by two years—a campaign that sucked in the major ground efforts of the British Commonwealth, and left the Far East almost undefended against the Japanese.'[141]

The 'episode' concerned may have contributed to the length of the North African campaign but the point should be made that in Churchill's judgment, such a quantity of men and equipment quite clearly could be spared otherwise he would not have ordered their deployment to Greece, and therefore they could have been sent instead to Malaya where they would have made a decisive difference—58,000 troops would have increased the forces at Lieutenant-General Arthur Percival's disposal by some 76 per cent. This was precisely what General Dill had said to Churchill in May 1941, when he pointed out that 'the small addition required to the garrison of Singapore would scarcely affect the strength of the Middle East defences.' He also warned that if Britain were to wait until an emergency did arise in the Far East, it would then be too late. Events were to prove Dill to be absolutely right but Churchill ignored this professional advice and instead continued to pour reinforcements into the Middle East. Churchill's acolytes might well say that such criticism is only made in retrospect, but the truth is that from several authoritative quarters he was warned at the time but decided that his inspired political vision carried priority. To quote Corelli Barnet once more:

> The Greek question was a major crisis in grand strategy; by his decision to intervene, the Prime Minister showed for the first time in the war that although he was a Churchill, he was not a Marlborough. Instead of his ancestor's cold and long-sighted sagacity, he

displayed emotional impulse; some times generous, some times ruthless, always overwhelming. Greece was the first occasion in the war that these impulses had worked disastrously.

In his biography of Marlborough, Barnett takes the comparison even further, saying of his subject: 'His judgment, moreover, was cool, far-sighted, sagacious; there could be no greater contrast to the hot-blooded and hasty opportunism of his descendant Winston Churchill'.[142] To satisfy criticism Churchill did direct that a court of inquiry be mounted to investigate the Greek debacle. The findings of the court were completed by early July 1941 but made such inconvenient reading that Churchill decided to suppress publication. After all, why publish the results of an investigation if that would only identify you as the culprit?

Whilst Wavell was scraping together the remnants of Churchill's Greek debacle, little notice appears to have been given to the arrival in North Africa a few weeks earlier of a virtually unknown German general by the name of Erwin Johannes Eugen Rommel. Adolf Hitler had always promised Mussolini that he would never forget his support when he launched his Austrian Anschluss in 1938 and he was now concerned on two fronts: one, to prevent the humiliation of his Italian ally being totally evicted from Africa, and two, for fear that unless he was given some German support, Mussolini might decide to change sides yet again. To achieve this, Hitler directed General Rommel to North Africa, where he arrived with his two-division Afrika Korps in February 1941. In North Africa Rommel was to become a legend and according to historian Correlli Barnett displayed the brilliance of a Marlborough or a Napoleon. He became the most highly respected German general of World War II and has earned a permanent place in the history of warfare. Due to his adaptation of German panzer tactics for the terrain of the open desert, his uncanny ability to anticipate his opponent's moves and his genius in handling massed formations of armour, which the British did not yet understand, he became known as 'the Desert Fox'.

Rommel was a 49-year-old lieutenant-general when he arrived in North Africa. He saw considerable action as a young officer in World War I, was awarded the Iron Cross and had performed with distinction and initiative in command of the 7th Panzer Division in the German blitzkrieg of 1940. He made a reputation for himself as a commander who led from the front, but the German military hierarchy did not seem to have regarded him as particularly exceptional. He was never a member of the Nazi Party and did not have to accommodate either the political interference of the Gestapo nor the brutality of the SS in his Afrika Korps. As a consequence of this the North African campaign was fought as one of the cleanest and most honourable theatres of World War II, fought under Rommel's own dictum of *Krieg ohne Hass*—war without hate. Although a brilliant and charismatic leader, Rommel was hampered during most of his North African campaign by inadequate supplies. Whilst Churchill regarded the area as being one of crucial strategic and seemingly emotional importance, the Germans never intended Rommel's role to be anything more than a holding operation to prevent an Italian collapse and were concentrating all their planning and materials on the impending attack on Russia. Once he had launched that attack in June 1941, Hitler had little more than peripheral interest in North Africa.

Later in 1942, Rommel's deficiency in men and materials was the reason for the British victory at El Alamein. So overwhelming was the British advantage having twice the number of men, tanks and guns plus a three to one superiority in the air, that they could hardly have lost the battle. One of Rommel's oft-quoted military maxims was, 'In a man-to-man fight the winner is the one who has one more round in his magazine'—and Montgomery had thousands more rounds in his magazines. Had Rommel been able to face the 8th Army on an equal footing, it is a virtual certainty that Montgomery would have made no impression, but although this swing of the pendulum could not have been foreseen in 1941, the breaking of the German codes plus the sinking of many of Rommel's supplies meant that Churchill and his commanders already knew that North Africa was no longer a priority for Hitler and they were in the ascendant. Intelligence sources indicated that Hitler had lost interest in North Africa, but still Churchill persisted in maintaining that the security of the Middle East was more important than diverting urgently needed resources to Singapore irrespective of the depletion in the forces he had caused by his futile and costly foray into Greece. The then Chief of the Imperial General Staff General Dill wrote to Churchill stating that the security of Singapore was more important than Egypt, and he went on to state that the loss of the Middle East would not lead to defeat so long as Britain and Singapore remained intact.

In his *History of the Second World War,* Basil Liddell Hart states that Churchill was upset by this paper because it was the reverse of his dreams of a decisive victory in North Africa. He goes on to state: 'Thus Rommel indirectly produced the fall of Singapore—and as much by the personal impression he made on a personality-minded Prime Minister as by his potential threat to the Nile Valley and the Suez Canal.'[143] Liddell Hart seems to have felt that, psychologically, Winston Churchill had come to regard the North African campaign as some sort of personal crusade, a duel between himself and Erwin Rommel. This view is supported by Rommel's biographer, Charles Douglas-Home; in his book *Rommel*, he reports Churchill stomping around the bedroom of his Cairo hotel, thunderously fulminating:'Rommel! Rommel! Rommel! Rommel! What else matters but beating him?'[144] Correlli Barnett also speaks of the Prime Minster being obsessed with beating the legendary German general; everything was concentrated on building up the strength of the forces to conquer Rommel, as Barnett comments:

> between January and July 1941 no fewer than 239,000 soldiers and over a million tons of vehicles, fuel and stores had arrived by sea to be unloaded in Egypt. Yet the object of this colossal and ever-increasing effort was to defeat a German expeditionary force of just under two under-strength panzer divisions and a trucked infantry division; hardly a hundredth part of the army of the one power, Germany, which threatened the United Kingdom's own survival— barely a fiftieth of the army with which Hitler invaded Soviet Russia.[145]

Barnett goes on to ask: 'Did the swelling of British military investment in the Middle East represent the rational pursuit of strategy or a growing obsession?' In addition to this concentration of resources and refusal to listen to any other advice, in July 1941 Churchill sacked Wavell and replaced him with General Sir Claude Auchinleck. Wavell was sent to India to take over Auchinleck's job as Commander-in-Chief, India. There was no logic in this at all, the only explanation being that, like Montgomery, Churchill thought he was Marlborough reincarnate. Although he rationalised his decision by alleging that Wavell was 'tired', this excuse was refuted by Auchinleck when he arrived in Cairo, saying: 'Wavell showed no signs of tiredness at all. He was always the same. I think he was first class; in spite of his silences, he made a tremendous impact on the troops. I have a very great admiration for him but he was given impossible tasks'.[146]

Such was this massive concentration of resources that when Montgomery eventually launched his attack at El Alamein at the end of October 1942, Churchill made sure, at the expense of almost everything and anywhere else, that he would be able to proclaim a victory. Indeed, even the battle itself was a political artifice for Churchill's benefit rather than one of military strategy, for he had known for many months that only a few days after the date decided for El Alamein an American-led force of some 107,000 troops under the overall command of General Eisenhower was due to land at Casablanca, Oran and Algiers. These landings were supported by a fleet of 3 naval task forces numbering over 130 ships under Admiral Sir Andrew B. Cunningham, plus sizeable American and British air forces, the whole armada operating under the banner of Operation *Torch*.

As Correlli Barnett has written, the British did not need to attack but could easily have waited until the *Torch* invasion occurred in the knowledge that with such a sizeable force now threatening his rear, Rommel would be forced to abandon his Alamein dispositions and quickly withdraw to protect his base at Tripoli. All Montgomery would have had to do then would have been to pursue rather than to attack, thus risking far fewer combat casualties. Churchill, Alexander and Montgomery were all aware of this through the breaking of the German codes and all three men were also aware that their prey, the legendary Rommel, for whose personal defeat this massive force of men and materials had been assembled, was away in Germany on sick leave for some weeks; they could therefore launch their attack in the knowledge that he was not there.

The loss of Singapore, for which Churchill was responsible, followed by three by-election defeats, made Churchill's political position at Westminster extremely precarious and he was desperate to somehow contrive some good news in order to stay in power. He admits this himself in Volume IV of his *History of the Second World War, The Hinge of Fate*, where he states that during the month of July 1942 'I was politically at my weakest, and without a gleam of military success'. He was aware that the concentration of men and materials had made the position in North Africa secure but again he wanted to put his personal stamp on things; to achieve this he travelled to Cairo in August 1942, shortly after the successful First Battle of El Alamein and contrived to portray Auchinleck as defeatist. During a meeting shortly after he arrived in Egypt, he asked for an outline of the current position, which Auchinleck provided, explaining that an offensive was planned for about 6 weeks later. This would not satisfy Churchill, who demanded immediate action, as Brooke recorded in his diary: 'I could see that he didn't approve of his replies. He is again pressing for an attack before Auchinleck can possibly get ready. I find him almost impossible to argue with on this point'.[147] Churchill then turned to Major-General Dorman-Smith, who along with Auchinleck had devised the victory that Churchill was ignoring, and asked if he agreed. Dorman-Smith said he was in complete agreement with Auchinleck and explained that the division that Churchill angrily demanded be immediately sent into action was not ready.

Auchinleck's mature and experienced philosophy in such a situation was revealed some years later when he was interviewed by David Dimbleby. He said then:

> For a man in command to start a major offensive with what he thought was inadequate means, was little short of murder, really, and the general had to consider the men under his command first, before he considered anything else. There are occasions when he has to ask them to do the impossible because he is forced to do so by the enemy.[148]

Auchinleck was right, but as we have seen Churchill was always quite indifferent to casualties and he would have seen such an argument, however valid, as little more than a semantic distraction from what he wanted. The scene is vividly described by John Connell in his book *Auchinleck*: 'Such home-truths as Churchill heard he scorned. Corbett explained the large, apparently non-combatant "tail" of the army: Churchill lost his temper. Auchinleck, supported by Dorman-Smith, refused to commit Eighth Army to a premature offensive: Churchill stood and raged in the desert'.[149]

Churchill sacked both Auchinleck and Dorman-Smith and replaced them with Alexander and Montgomery. Having done so, he then sent a report to the Cabinet rationalising the steps he had taken by saying that disaster was imminent 'under the former regime' and he had discovered that a retreat to the Nile was planned when Rommel next attacked. As a matter of urgency, Montgomery had insisted on taking over the Eighth Army immediately and this had resulted in an almost instantaneous uplifting of morale amongst all of the troops. He then stated that on his orders Montgomery was to prepare to take the offensive.

No doubt, those back in London were impressed and relieved at such good news, except for the fact that practically all of it was a lie. There was not even the slightest indication of any disaster, in fact rather the reverse, after Rommel had been rolled back at the First Battle of El Alamein. There was no plan to retreat to the Nile, Montgomery had seized control with unnecessary haste for no other reason than to demonstrate who was in command, and far from being immediately uplifted, the atmosphere in the army was one of puzzlement at the removal of a respected commander who had just led them to victory. As John Connell perceptively states, 'The ritual smearing of the scapegoat had begun with gusto'.[150] He further comments: 'Because these two officers acted as they did that morning, a division was not squandered and many men's lives were saved, but they set the seal on their own professional doom.'

But there were others who knew the truth and were not afraid to put pen to paper. Almost immediately Auchinleck received a succession of letters from army commanders who did not fall under the control of Montgomery and who could make their views known without fear of repercussion. Without exception, they all said they were shocked at his dismissal because they were so well aware of what he had achieved. Amongst these, letters came from (the then) Major-General Leslie Morshead, commander of the Australian troops; Lieutenant-General Jozef Zajac, Commander of Polish Forces, Middle East; Free French General Georges Catroux; and (the then) Major-General Andrew Galloway at the War Office. They all knew the true lie of the land.

Another letter came from the man who would become Montgomery's chief of staff, Brigadier 'Freddie' de Guingand, who had worked closely with Auchinleck as his Director of Military Intelligence, and it is worth quoting from what he wrote:

It was a very great shock to hear your news this evening. The injustice of it all is difficult to believe. As you must realize I am utterly sorry that it should have happened, and I am convinced that they will regret the decision—a decision obviously arrived at so as to turn aside criticism from its rightful target. I'm afraid it is also a victory for the old privileged school. You will be missed by many from this arid land.[151]

This letter has been quoted here because when in 1947 de Guingand came to write his memoirs, *Operation Victory*, there was only the most fleeting reference to the fact that he had written any letter to Auchinleck, whereas correspondence he had with Montgomery is quoted in full.[152] It seems the facts of de Guingand's honest views at the time would have been something of an embarrassment after the war because the contents of this letter only came to light in 1959 when John Connell wrote his book *Auchinleck*. Here were professional opinions from a variety of sources, but facts had never been an obstacle for the willful Churchill. The latter revealed, albeit unintentionally, just how theatrically and emotionally he had over-dramatised the situation in his own mind when he wrote in his book *The Second World War*, whilst sitting in the Residency garden in Cairo:

> During the last days of my visit all my thoughts rested on the impending battle. At any moment Rommel might attack with a devastating surge of armour. He could come in by the pyramids with hardly a check except a single canal until he reached the Nile.[153]

This was quite absurd, but revealed yet again Churchill's emotional and unbalanced dramatic obsession with Rommel. From intelligence sources he was well aware of Rommel's shortage of armour and his critical supply problems, and the one direction from which Rommel could not approach Cairo was up from the south through the pyramids unless he made the virtually impossible diversion of going round the salt marshes of the 20,000km² Qattara Depression and the Great Sand Sea. Churchill seems to have attributed Rommel with almost supernatural ability, as though he was likely to appear out of the blue and strike like some Scarlet Pimpernel, and it says something about his fanatical preoccupation that he should have written this some 10 years after the event. It was an all-consuming and stubborn fixation for which too many Allied troops unnecessarily paid with their lives.

However, so desperate was Churchill to save his political skin by ensuring a victory for Montgomery that he cabled Roosevelt urgently requesting him to send 300 Sherman tanks, and 100 105mm self-propelled anti-tank guns round the Cape of Good Hope to bolster his forces even further. When the Battle of El Alamein came in October these new Shermans would increase Montgomery's tank number by nearly 40 per cent. It might be noted here that Montgomery already had 750 tanks whereas only 12 months earlier, and because of Churchill's intransigence, not one single tank or anti-tank gun could be found for Percival's flimsy force in Singapore; Churchill was learning.

One might have thought that Churchill would have been satisfied with his intemperate actions, but with his impatience for attack the new top brass in Egypt were still under pressure 'to do something.' As a result, and having apparently learned nothing from the recent Dieppe disaster, a similar but smaller assault on the port of Tobruk was launched on 13 September 1942, codenamed Operation *Agreement*. The apparent objectives were to destroy harbour facilities, ships, vehicles and airfields. With an almost grizzly inevitability, it was a debacle on a scale similar to Dieppe, with the Royal Marines sustaining losses of 75 per cent and the army 83 per cent, and the Royal Navy sustained 300 killed plus the loss of one cruiser, two destroyers and seven motor torpedo boats; 746 men died for the destruction of just 30 aircraft. This 'operation' was quite unnecessary for two reasons: firstly, Rommel had a larger port at his disposal further down the coast at Benghazi, and secondly, Churchill was well aware that the *Torch* landings aimed at Rommel's rear were shortly to arrive. However, again being driven by emotion rather than rational judgement, he was obsessed with regaining Tobruk, which to him had a symbolism way beyond its strategic importance. Just 8 weeks later, on 12 November, Tobruk was peacefully reoccupied by the Eighth Army following Rommel's westward withdrawal. So what had it all been about? This was just another tragic example of the human cost of Churchill's commanders having to cope with his deluge of unreal demands for aggression.

Accordingly, El Alamein was launched before the arrival of the Americans because this could cause an inconvenient distraction, and as a result

13,500 dead, wounded or missing were sacrificed for purely domestic political reasons so that Churchill could triumphantly announce his 'British' victory. The Americans did not swallow this, but the British public, in ignorance, basked in Churchill's reflected glow as he had indeed intended they should. In a speech at London's Mansion House shortly after El Alamein, Churchill proclaimed:

> General Alexander, with his brilliant comrade and lieutenant, General Montgomery, has made a glorious and decisive victory in what I think should be called the Battle for Egypt. Rommel's army has been defeated. It has been routed. It has been very largely destroyed as a fighting force.[154]

Like his distorted communiqué from Cairo, this was blatantly untrue. In fact as we have seen in the chapter *Churchill—The Black Dog*, so badly did Montgomery direct the follow-up to the battle that far from being 'destroyed as a fighting force', Rommel's Afrika Korps was allowed to withdraw in an orderly manner; in the words of Correlli Barnett, 'the Eighth Army moved so slowly that it lost all contact with the enemy, who was retiring in no haste'.[155]

It is not taking anything away from the men of the Eighth Army to say that the 'glorious and decisive victory' had in fact been an unnecessary and almost a foregone conclusion and was launched for propaganda rather than military reasons. Of course, neither Alexander nor Montgomery was ever likely to concede this, and if asked would probably say they had just been obeying orders. Montgomery in particular was not the sort of man to pass up the opportunity of grabbing the limelight for himself, which he did ever after.

Churchill had made quite sure of the victory he could proclaim and this saved his political position until the end of the war, but the British public did not realise the underlying truth, and at what price? Were wartime propaganda and the political position of any man worth the lives of 4,600? For a ruthless politician, interested primarily in his own survival, apparently they were. In another calumny to enhance his stature Churchill had claimed that there had been no victory before the Second Battle of El Alamein and no defeat thereafter. There had in fact been two victories before that battle—Richard O'Connor's Beda Fomm against overwhelming odds in February 1941, and Auchinleck's First El Alamein, which halted Rommel in July 1942—but these were downplayed so that Second El Alamein could be trumpeted.

And the overall effect of these political musical chairs? Writing whilst he was recuperating from wounds in 1944, Rommel was to observe:

> It was a great mistake for the British to be continually replacing their Commander-in-Chief, and this forcing the new man to learn the same bitter tactics all over again. The British commanders were capable soldiers; it was merely that some of them had pre-conceived ideas—like those which many German generals brought with them to Africa—which they would certainly have discarded after their first reverses. But they were always relieved of their command before they had a chance.[156]

As a footnote to this unsavoury episode, it appears that although Auchinleck was interviewed a number of times after he retired from the army in 1947, and two biographies were written, he was apparently never asked whether, had he not been removed, he would have advocated attacking Rommel after he became aware of the coming *Torch* landings at Rommel's rear? In posing this question we should remember that Rommel, with considerable fuel and other material problems, was some 1,600km from his base at Tripoli whereas Algiers, where some of the *Torch* troops attacked, was only about half of that distance. The consideration would have been a military one, whereas Churchill's imperative was political survival. We shall never know the answer.

CHAPTER 9

MONTGOMERY — PRETENTIOUS PLODDER

For your most secret and confidential information
I will give you my opinion of Montgomery which is
that he is so proud of his successes to date that he
will never willingly make a single move until he is
absolutely certain of success—in other words, until
he has concentrated enough resources so that anybody
could practically guarantee the outcome.
—EISENHOWER, letter to George Marshall, 1943

L et us look, in principle, at what characteristics and/or achieve-ments go to make a *great* general and ask whether, in truth Montgomery could even stand comparison with the likes of Alexander, Hannibal, Marlborough, Napoleon, Wellington, Manstein, Gud-erian or Rommel. They were not all British but even if the list is limited to the British, is there really a place for Montgomery when one considers the huge problems that Marlborough and Wellington had to overcome over much longer periods? This question is not asked because he has been fa-vourably compared with Marlborough and Wellington but because Mont-gomery himself has claimed that he was at least their equal.

Marlborough's campaigns were spread over a period of some years dur-ing the War of the Spanish Succession (1701–14) where England, with the help of the Dutch Republic, variously faced the combined forces of France, Spain and Bavaria and ranged over the ground of present-day Belgium, Bavaria and northern France. Involved were important victories at Blenheim

(1704), Ramillies (1706), Oudenaarde (1708) and Malplaquet (1709). At no time did Marlborough ever enjoy the same overwhelming advantage in numbers and armaments as Montgomery; in fact his opponents' resources were mostly evenly matched with his own and, moreover, the allies on whom he could rely on for support were unpredictable.

Any comparison with Wellington reveals an even greater disparity as against Montgomery. Wellington's campaigns stretched over a period of more than sixteen years from the Mysore and Maratha Wars in India from 1798 to 1803, the Peninsular War from 1808 to 1813, and culminating in the deciding Battle of Waterloo in 1815; and like Marlborough, Wellington never had the same material and logistical advantages that Montgomery could always call on. Compared with the achievements of these two, Montgomery's own individual contributions in World War II were piecemeal and prosaic.

What did Montgomery accomplish that could be regarded as outstanding? When did he ever perform with brilliance and éclat? Greatness in the field is not a question of success following cautious planning when there is a huge advantage in numbers, supplies and logistics, but the ability to overcome such a handicap and still emerge victorious. This was a situation that Montgomery never, ever, had to face—he was given command when the tide of war, in all senses, was turning inexorably in favour of the Allies. Greatness in battlefield command is also demonstrated where initial defeat and retreat is reversed and turned into victory. There were several examples of this in World War II, the outstanding one being Slim in Burma and then Macarthur in the Pacific. To these two should be added the triumphs achieved by the Russian high command in driving the Germans back after so many initial retreats. As the title of his book indicates, Slim's was indeed a case of *Defeat into Victory*: a long and difficult withdrawal, culminating in stopping the Japanese advances on Indian soil at the desperate battles of Kohima and Imphal and then turning the tide and driving them out of Burma—an exceedingly tough campaign that took 3 years over very difficult terrain and in very trying climatic conditions. This involved rebuilding an army that was largely Asian and one-third the size of the Japanese. It was an outstanding achievement and against this standard Montgomery is nowhere to be seen; competent, yes, fairly efficient, yes—great, no.

The position of massive advantage that he took over in Egypt in 1942 has already been detailed in the chapter *Montgomery—Military Messiah or Army*

Arriviste? but the question has to be asked whether, were it not for El Alamein, the world would ever have heard anything much about a British general by the name of Montgomery? The clear answer is 'probably not'. Going on from that question, after El Alamein when was there ever a single outstanding achievement of note on the part of Montgomery? The answer has to be 'never' because he became just part of an Allied team of ever increasing and overpowering strength and confidence. As Correlli Barnett, already quoted in the *Introduction* of this book, wrote of Montgomery, he was little more than 'a Plumer rather than a Wellington'. Herbert Plumer was one of the more effective British generals of World War I, but no one would have called him another Wellington; and so it was with Montgomery—technically competent but no brilliant, risk-taking leader à la George Patton. One only has to look into the writings of the great military authority Karl von Clausewitz to see that Montgomery fails two of his basic precepts. Firstly, 'It is even better to act quickly and err than to hesitate until the time of action is past'; here is a description of an attribute that Montgomery never had, for he was renowned for caution, indecision and deliberation rather than action. He failed to act and pursue Rommel immediately after the Second Battle of El Alamein when the Afrika Korps could have been destroyed but was allowed to escape; he waffled in Sicily; and as we shall see he dithered for several weeks over the battle for Caen in June/July 1944. Secondly, 'Never forget that no military leader has ever become great without audacity'; if there was one attribute that Montgomery completely lacked it was audacity. Of course it may be said, with some validity, that since he was always part of a force of overwhelming strength he did not need speed of reaction or daring but in any event neither of those characteristics were in his make-up. To draw a comparison with Patton again, the latter always kept at the front of his mind the words of Frederick the Great: *'l'audace, l'audace, toujours l'audace'*. Montgomery's dithering following El Alamein, despite intelligence that surely said he should move quickly, and as described by Clive Ponting in his book *Armageddon: The Second World War,* has already been quoted in the chapter *Montgomery—Military Messiah or Army Arriviste?*, and it is a litany of missed opportunities.

Having followed, rather than pursued, the retreating Rommel westwards across North Africa, Montgomery then became bogged down in a succession of encounters, and although the combination of the Eighth

Army and the forces of Operation *Torch* that came from the west eventually proved too much, it was not until 12 May 1943 that the German forces in Tunisia surrendered. Admittedly the Afrika Korps in Tunisia had been reinforced, but Rommel had long since left for Europe and after the much-vaunted victory at El Alamein it had taken another 6 months to finally overcome an army that Churchill claimed had been 'defeated, routed and largely destroyed as a fighting force.'

In any case, credit for the strategic plan that brought final victory in Tunisia must go to Operation *Torch*'s Lieutenant-General Kenneth Anderson and not the Eighth Army's Montgomery. However, and true to the way he would forever distort and dissemble for his own benefit, Montgomery claimed it had been his own brainchild. This lie caused fury amongst those there and so annoyed Eisenhower, who was getting just his first taste of what it was like to deal with Montgomery, that he called a press conference to correct matters; but the British media had already been manipulated. Montgomery persisted with this lie in his *Memoirs,* provoking Alexander to unearth the original correspondence amongst his papers, proving that the plan had entirely belonged to Anderson.

Two months later Montgomery became part of the Allied team under the overall command of generals Alexander and Eisenhower for Operation *Husky,* the invasion of Sicily. Here overwhelming numbers came into play once more: the full strength of the Allied invading force was some 470,000 as against a defending army of 230,000 Italian and 60,000 German troops, the Allies had a three to one advantage in the number of tanks, plus 1,800 guns, 14,000 vehicles, over 2,500 ships from various navies and massive air support. Montgomery was one of the two ground commanders, the other being Patton; although Montgomery and his Eighth Army were given the shorter and dominant role, instead of taking advantage of this his performance was a strange mixture of attack, unnecessary caution and changing plans. Patton on the other hand, although in reality playing a subsidiary role, performed as described by Eisenhower in his book *Crusade in Europe*:

> Patton was a shrewd student of warfare who always clearly appreciated the value of speed in the conduct of operations. Speed of movement often enables troops to minimize any advantage the enemy may temporarily gain but, more important, speed makes

possible the full exploitation of every favourable opportunity and prevents the enemy from readjusting his forces to meet successive attacks. Speed requires training, fitness, confidence, morale, suitable transport and skilful leadership. Patton employed these tactics relentlessly, and thus not only minimised casualties but shook the whole Italian Government so forcibly that Mussolini toppled from his position of power in late July.[157]

In quoting Eisenhower it should be noted that although he knew Patton could be impulsive and insubordinate, he was also aware that Patton was one of the most brilliant field commanders he had.

Having been proclaimed as the inspired mastermind of the El Alamein victory, Montgomery had contributed to the planning for Operation *Husky*. In so doing he had assigned for himself and his Eighth Army the most direct route to capture the political prize of Messina, the major port facing the Italian mainland, by going directly up the east coast of Sicily. His force landed at the southernmost point of the island giving him a distance of about 180km to his goal. In the event it was Patton, landing to the east of Montgomery and who had been given a role that was really just to protect Montgomery's left flank, whose drive and imagination enabled him to cover twice that distance, including the capture of the Sicilian capital Palermo in the north-west, and still get to Messina ahead of Montgomery. As had been the case in Tunisia, too often Montgomery became bogged down, and instead of maintaining his drive he hesitated and seemed to become dogged by introspective caution before coming to a decision.

In his book *Bitter Victory: The Battle for Sicily, 1943,* noted military historian Carlo D'Este succinctly states: 'Sicily will not rank as one of Montgomery's memorable campaigns'.[158] That is perhaps an understatement and both Eisenhower and Bradley in their respective memoirs make the same point in a diplomatic way. In reality, Sicily had revealed Montgomery in his true light, competent but plodding, and frequently allowing himself to be too rigidly tied down by preconceived plans and ideas. As was always to be his good fortune, he had not lacked for men or materials and was superior in all areas to his opponents; and although he did eventually break through, it was success by attrition rather than dash and elan—and this would be the Montgomery style. Having said that, it must in fairness be admitted that he did succeed; as Eisenhower himself said, generals tend to be judged by their overall record of victories against defeats, and so by this somewhat clinical and detached criterion it has to be admitted that Montgomery did achieve success—but—in the manner of the Plumers of military history rather than the great leaders.

In spite of a distinctly lacklustre performance in Sicily, Montgomery still managed to emerge as the darling of the British media. He played the media as consummately as he had in Africa, avoiding facts, providing his own perspectives, insisting that everything had gone according to his plan. Always available for a photo opportunity and a newsworthy comment with the press on his side he emerged with his reputation nothing like as diminished as it might have been. His performance had been adequate, but nothing more; the ultimate objective had eventually been achieved and if analysed in that factual context, it can be seen that Montgomery, as nothing more than a part of the overall team for Operation *Husky*, was not in any manner exceptional. He had played the part assigned to him, or to be honest the role he had selected for himself, and had managed to emerge with his image just about intact even if some of the shine was missing.

Early in September 1943, Montgomery along with his Eighth Army took part in the Operation *Baytown* landings in Calabria as part of the Allies' invasions of southern Italy. He was there only until the end of December when he was transferred to England, where he was to join in the planning for *Overlord*, the D-Day invasion of 6 June 1944. However, in those 4 months and despite very little opposition to begin with his forces had moved only 480km to the Sangro River, a rate of advance of about 4km per day; in Sicily it had taken him 40 days to move 180km—almost exactly the same measured pace.

Judging advance rates on a simplistic overall per day basis can be quite misleading but it is a useful rule of thumb. Along with the other Allied commanders there he became bogged down, as he had been in Tunisia and Sicily. So where was the super-performer of El Alamein repute? Where was the master tactician of the set-piece? The truth was that when Montgomery was forced to perform as a general alongside other generals, rather than being able to continue the fiction of the great and individual military leader that he had fashioned for himself in the deserts of North Africa, it became increasingly clear that he was no genius and he was no more likely 'to make things happen' than any other mortal—in fact, if anything he was less likely. Carlo D'Este has made his comments about Montgomery's performance in Sicily and one of his own biographers, Alun Chalfont, was to observe about Italy:

> Montgomery later criticised almost every aspect of the campaign except his own part in it. If the planning and conduct of the campaign in Sicily were bad, the preparations for the invasion of Italy and the subsequent campaign in that country were worse still. He accused his superiors of having no master plan and no clear idea of how they expected the operational situation to develop. No attempt, he alleged, had been made to co-ordinate his own operations with those of the Fifth Army.[159]

As Chalfont also commented, Montgomery criticised planning as though he had had no part in it, whereas he had been heavily involved, which of course was typical Montgomery—'everyone is wrong except me'. For both the Sicilian and Italian campaigns Montgomery had played an integral part in the planning and execution—he had insisted that he should—but when his self-polished star was brought down in the mud of reality, it was not his fault. In line with D'Este's assessment about Montgomery's performance in Sicily, Chalfont went on to make a similar understated comment about the two campaigns: 'Whoever was fundamentally to blame, the Sicilian and Italian campaigns were not the most glorious episodes in Montgomery's career'.[160]

This is an appropriate point to have a look at what Montgomery had actually achieved, as opposed to what he claimed to have done, since his arrival in Egypt in July 1942. We know now that the Second Battle of El Alamein was not the great and unexpected victory that was trumpeted by both Montgomery and Churchill and there is little to be gained by repeating the facts already demonstrated in this respect. Thereafter it is also clear that his performances, although ultimately successful, were always backed by hugely superior numbers and were mostly cautious and sometimes uncertain. But where there was caution of military planning and pedantry of execution there was always a public relations operation, photo opportunities and press conferences that never missed a beat in the unscrupulous manipulation of events to present whatever had happened as having been exactly as he had planned, or if it had not, then the fault lay elsewhere. Military historian Reginald W. Thompson puts this aspect of Montgomery's persona nicely in his book *Churchill and the Montgomery Myth* when he writes: 'He found it increasingly easy to believe that what had happened was what he wanted to happen, and since he could not lose, events could always be fitted into a time framework to reassure him of his infallibility'.[161]

And so Montgomery continued his upward climb of a ladder whose first steps came to him when he was gifted a golden opportunity in Egypt, and once he had hoisted himself up and grabbed the initial rungs, he was determined never to let go. This was the dizzy ascent of a competent general, an army officer of unexceptional military ability, but an opportunist of quite extraordinary ruthlessness, who once given the chance clung to it with singular intent; Montgomery was the *arriviste extraordinaire*. As Thompson stated in his aforementioned book:

> He was on the road to a success of which he had never even dared to dream. He began to expand, and his inner zest boiled over into words. Does he really believe what he says? Or is he making some kind of personal noise, as a lion roars or a hyena screams? Is it a form of gamesmanship cunningly thought out; or is it the spontaneous shout of the barker drawing exaggerated attention to his prowess?

Thomson goes on to comment: 'Churchill had recognised Montgomery at once as a "man on the make"'; the dictionary definition of the latter being a person greedy of gain, in modern parlance a 'hustler' or 'con-man'. In repudiation of Montgomery's version of events, he was not as he claimed, automatically selected as one of the subordinates to Eisenhower for the invasion of Europe. Feeling that he might have difficulties in handling him, an intimation of some prescience given what transpired later, Eisenhower has said he would have much preferred Alexander, as would all of the Americans. The decision in favour of Montgomery was very much a close-run thing but in the final hour it was made by Brooke, who something of a plodder himself, had championed Montgomery from early on. (Brooke's prejudice in favour of the conformist as against the brilliant had emerged earlier in his part in the dismissal into obscurity of the very talented but unconventional Major-General Dorman-Smith, which will be examined later.)

Montgomery arrived in Normandy on the morning of 7 June and in a odd example of posturing eccentricity, Chalfont reports that virtually the first thing he did was to order a Russian major to obtain a budgerigar for his caravan, and he was instructed to obtain it by 4 p.m. that afternoon or he would be sacked. Chalfont and others have merely reported this event without further comment but as in other aspects of Montgomery's behaviour one has to ask just what was it he thought he was achieving by such an unnecessarily peremptory demand? Was this, as in so many other instances, just another case of Montgomery needing to act the part of the total supremo to such an extent that even for such a trivial matter he had to turn a simple request into a stipulation carrying dramatic consequences? As Gordon Corrigan observed, today Montgomery would be a psychiatrist's delight and the question that was raised in the chapter *The Monty Myth* comes up again: was this caused by some pathological urge to continually demonstrate who was in charge? It seems to indicate insecurity or maybe even an underlying inferiority complex that was balanced by being seen to issue such an order.

But in summation, were all these behavioural patterns—apparently conceited but over-cautious, obsessive insistence on set-piece operations, slow to adapt to changed circumstances, inability to accept criticism, preference for the company of younger men, readiness to blame others—symptomatic of a man who knew he was little more than average but who continually tried to overcome and compensate, not through performance on the field of battle, because he knew he could not, but by overtly acting out a part? These are thoughts to keep in mind as we look at the invasion of Europe.

The first of Montgomery's disguised failures came within a day or so of the D-Day landings. In his master plan the city of Caen, just 9 miles from the coast, would, he said, be taken within 2 days; at that time Caen was about the present size of the English town of Tunbridge Wells. The beaches were predicted to be weakly defended and would provide an excellent base for building up a fortified centre of operations. As Gordon Corrigan states, this plan was unreasonably optimistic in any case, and because German resistance was stronger than expected, Caen was not eventually taken until 10 July, by which time the lovely, 800-year-old city had been virtually obliterated by 2 days of aerial bombing and some 300,000 shells fired from over 700 naval and land-based heavy artillery pieces. The German resistance was not of course Montgomery's fault but his refusal to quickly adapt his original plan to adjust to a different situation allowed the Germans plenty of time to bring in more reinforcements and resulted in a totally unnecessary slogging match. Corrigan also states:

> Montgomery should have known better, but this was a time to throw caution to the winds and crack on. As it was defensive-mindedness, caution and reluctance—fear almost—to depart from pre-arranged plans and orders held everyone back and the opportunity was lost.[162]

This savage assault caused the needless deaths of over 2,000 civilians and reduced the city's population from about 55,000 to a mere 17,000, provoking considerable and justified resentment for many years to come. Reconstruction of the ancient city would take another 17 years, with very few of the original buildings remaining. In his 1983 book, *Decision in Normandy*, veteran military historian Carlo D'Este provides a succinct account:

> The British press trumpeted the seizure of Caen as a great victory; had it been captured early in June it would indeed have been a significant one, but by now the capture of this once great city was largely a hollow victory—too little, too late. The key to success had always been its rapid seizure and, failing this, its by-passing and isolation.[163]

D'Este goes on to ask whether such an overwhelming bombardment was really used by Montgomery as the ultimate tactic, and one forced on him to reduce the pressure that had been building up for him to break his stalemate and whether Caen was not sacrificed in order to maintain Montgomery's image. And in posing these questions he does not take into account the military casualties and equipment losses—5,000 killed and over 300 tanks lost—most of which could have been avoided if a frontal assault had also been avoided. Although Montgomery had such an embarrassment of riches that he had replacement tanks piling up on the beaches, the needless loss of life was a sad epitaph. Again, here was a situation where Montgomery knew he had plenty of tanks waiting to be used, a luxury the Germans just did not have. The annals of the 11th Armoured Division, *The Black Bull,* recount that if a Sherman tank was even slightly damaged, the crew could afford to abandon it in the knowledge that just a few miles back was a field with several hundred new Sherman tanks just waiting to be picked up.[164] And yet he hesitated: undecided? Worried? Uncertain? Unable to change the plan?

In further comment about this delay at Caen, Carlo D'Este also quotes from Patton's *War as I Knew It,* where Patton has said:

> One does not plan and then try to make circumstances fit those plans. One tries to make plans fit the circumstances. I think the difference between success and failure depends on the ability, or lack of it, to do just that.[165]

The countryside around Caen is fairly open compared with the close network of sunken lanes and hedgerows of what is known as the bocage area in the west of Normandy. So why was it not simply encircled as it so obviously could have been? The surrounded defenders could then have been dealt with at leisure. This is a question that does not appear to have been asked of Montgomery, who was riding the crest of a British popularity wave, although Eisenhower was fuming that it had taken 7,000 tons of bombs for a gain of 7 miles and that they could not go on paying the price of 1,000 tons of bombs per mile. To add to the scenario of Montgomery's unimaginative but overwhelming bludgeoning force, the aerial bombardment of Caen had been carried out by 2,100 bombers from three air fleets, one British and two American—almost twice as many bombers as were used in the subsequent and similarly unnecessary annihilation of Dresden some 7 months later. The battle for Caen was, in a phrase used by German military historian Paul Carell, 'the tactics of attrition—the rich man's war.' But then Montgomery had always been able to fight as a wealthy man.

It would seem that the fundamental reason for this bulldozing show of force was simply that capturing Caen was one of the objectives in Montgomery's original plan, and irrespective of changed circumstances he was not going to alter his ideas; this had been part of his set plan and it must stay. It speaks of an obsessive mindset similar to that of Stalin and Hitler over Stalingrad. Yet again in the Caen episode there is the suggestion that Montgomery felt any amendment to his plan might be seen as a fault in the original design, which he had claimed was his and therefore he could not be seen to have made a mistake. No battle ever goes completely to plan and a genuinely strong, more confident commander would have quickly recognised the need to adapt to the circumstances, for to quote von Clausewitz once more, 'It is even better to act quickly and err than to hesitate until the time of action is past'. What was required, and what seems to have been beyond the grasp of the hidebound Montgomery, was what Britain's leading military strategist, Basil Liddell Hart, called 'the strategy of the indirect approach'. In his 1946 book of the same name he lays out his maxims of war, the leading precepts being:

1. Adjust your end to your means;
2. Chose the line (or course) of least expectation;
3. Exploit the line of least resistance.[166]

George Patton died as a result of a freak motoring accident in December 1945 but those might well have been his words.

With his customary rationale, Montgomery later attempted to deflect criticism by claiming that there had been no unexpected delay at all as it had always been his plan to draw German armour towards him so as to allow the Americans more leeway in the west. But if this was the case, then is he also saying it had always been his plan for there to be a final demolishing barrage that virtually obliterated the city? Would he be prepared to admit that? He cannot have it both ways. Anthony Beevor puts this nicely in his book *D-Day: The Battle for Normandy* when he writes:

> Monty liked to keep his objectives vague, often with Delphic cricketing metaphors, so that if there was a break-out he could claim credit for it and if the operation ran into the sand he could say that they had simply been tying down German forces to help the Americans.[167]

Help the Americans? Montgomery was aware that Patton was to arrive in France on 7 July 1944 and was scheduled to immediately take over in the west. Was he attempting to convince everyone to accept that his real strategy all along had been deliberately designed to make things easier for, of all people, George Patton? Whatever his true motives and although it had been a hugely costly exercise, and had taken him 5 weeks instead of 2 days, Montgomery would claim that he had won yet another battle and of course it had all gone according to plan.

That might be exaggeration enough at the time, but in a statement that borders on farce he says in his 1958 *Memoirs* that the battle for Caen would be 'a victory acclaimed as the greatest achievement in military history.'[168] Megalomania? Was a psychiatrist needed?

CHAPTER 10

MOUNTBATTEN'S MALAYAN MADNESS— OPERATION *ZIPPER*

*Every effort was made to hush it up and the story was
censored . . . If the Japs had been in their fox-holes—
as they would have been but for the surrender—
our troops would have been mown down as they
floundered in the quicksands. It would have been the
most grisly story of the war, the most ghastly failure.*
— FRANK ROSTRON,
    Daily Express war correspondent

Excluding the Pacific, which was the sole American bailiwick of General MacArthur and Admiral Chester Nimitz, it was decided at the 1943 Quebec Conference that the Allied Asian HQ would be based in New Delhi. The experienced General Auchinleck at the age of 59 would seem to have been an obvious choice to command this new operation but he was rejected by Churchill, who frequently interpreted measured professional judgement as indicating a negative attitude. In any event, Churchill had sacked him a year earlier and was not about to allow any resurrection, however vaguely implied, because it might also be seen as a criticism of himself. The next proposal came from Churchill, the 50-year-old Air Chief Marshal Sir Sholto Douglas, but he was rejected by Roosevelt who then suggested either Admiral Andrew Cunningham (aged 60) or Air Chief Marshal Arthur Tedder (aged 53).

They in turn were declined by Churchill, Cunningham probably because he had refused Churchill's hare-brained plan to sink two warships to block the port of Tripoli, and although it is not known why Churchill would not accept Tedder, it seems likely this was because it had been Churchill's plan all along to contrive that the job should go to Mountbatten. At 43 years and relatively inexperienced, Mountbatten was handed the overall command which would be called South-East Asia Command, or SEAC for short. Since Churchill had brought Mountbatten with him to the conference, his choice was perhaps not surprising, but due to Mountbatten's age he could only be promoted to the rank of acting rather than full admiral, a rank which would normally have gone with the command. Even this 'acting' rank provoked such resentment that Admiral Sir James Somerville, the 61-year-old commander of the Far Eastern Fleet thereafter refused Mountbatten permission to board any of his ships.

SEAC was however not to be a solely British command but would operate under the auspices of a combined US/British chiefs of staff with Mountbatten's deputy being the American General Joseph Stilwell. Although ostensibly a command covering the existing British campaign in Burma under Lieutenant-General Slim and Anglo-American support for Chiang Kai-shek under Stilwell, it soon became apparent to the Americans that Churchill's underlying priority was not primarily military but one of British political prestige in Asia and the recapture of Britain's imperial possessions there. 'A grievous and shameful blow to British prestige must be avenged in battle',[169] Churchill had told the Americans, and it was not long before they cynically, but with some justification, referred to the acronym SEAC as really meaning 'Save England's Asian Colonies'. Perhaps they realised that Churchill was seeking some personal redemption for his own culpability over the fall of Singapore in 1942. As we have seen with the unnecessary battle at El Alamein, fought for the benefit of Churchill's reputation, he was now seeking another 'battle' to rescue his standing. The fact that such a confrontation would unavoidably involve loss of British lives was a factor that did not even enter his head, for as Clive Ponting has written, Churchill was remarkably indifferent to British casualties.[170]

Although anxious to have a hand in the ultimate defeat of Japan, Britain could in fact offer very little by way of any meaningful contribution to the American effort in their theatre of operations. The massive American naval presence in the Pacific totally dwarfed anything that Britain might be able to scrape together and consequently however much Britain wanted to get in on the act, Japan was, logically and quite rightly, to be an American operation. Churchill, ever on the lookout for a political opportunity and always conscious of Britain's standing as the pre-eminent colonial power, could see an opening for the retaking of Malaya and Singapore by force of arms as victory was assured in Europe and the war in Burma was drawing to a successful conclusion. Plans were made early in 1945 for what was to be called Operation *Zipper*; it required a force of some seven divisions to be assembled in India and Ceylon with invasion landings to be made in the Strait of Malacca on the west coast of the Malayan peninsula between Port Swettenham and Port Dickson, sometime between late August and early November 1945. Little is known of this undertaking, and as will be seen, for very good reasons.

Churchill was a great monarchist and Mountbatten, being closely connected to the British monarchy, made him one of Churchill's blue-eyed boys, although, as already detailed, prior to his SEAC appointment his performance in the war had been distinctly chequered. Mountbatten had an amount of the superficial panache that sometimes goes with the confidence of inherited social privilege but he had shown no great signs of intellect nor demonstrated any particular flair for strategy. In his book *Engage the Enemy More Closely,* Corelli Barnett describes Mountbatten as 'a man rivalling Nelson in his hunger for admiration and surpassing him in appetite for personal aggrandisement who chose to run South-east Asia Command on authoritarian lines'[171]—so authoritarian that, according to Stephen Harper, one of Mountbatten's first SEAC decisions was to remove his HQ from the heat of New Delhi to Ceylon in the spring of 1945 where he 'assembled in the cool hills near Kandy a staff of around 7,000. His glittering court included scores of pretty women in uniform'.[172] Gordon Corrigan goes further, describing the scene as 'swollen to over 7,000 bodies, many of whom seemed to have been selected on grounds of breeding and ability to make small talk at cocktail parties rather than for any military qualities.'[173] And as if to demonstrate that he was still 'untouchable', Mountbatten even went so far as to import his own personal barber from Trumper's of Mayfair, bringing him in with the theoretical rank of RAF sergeant.

Stephen Harper was on board the destroyer HMS *Petard* taking part in

*Ebullient and self-centered, Churchill had little time or space for other people
and their opinions—Biographer John Charmley.*

—FDR Library and Museum

Auchinleck & Wavell. Two of Britain's finest generals, sacked by Churchill to deflect attention from his own flawed dictates.—*Imperial War Museum* (JAR783)

Major-General Eric Dorman-Smith. Auchinleck's right-hand man, he was an inventive and original planner of the 1st Battle of Alamein. Dismissed without reason, probably due to jealousy in an orthodox and snobbish British Army; a talent that would not have been wasted by the Americans or Germans. detail.—*Imperial War Museum* (E15298)

Destroyer HMS *Kelly*. Mountbatten's first WW2 command, a ship in which many of his crews died because of his irresponsible antics.—*Imperial War Museum* (A2287)

HMS *Kelly*. Under tow after being severely damaged by a German E Boat *(see Chapter 5)*. —*Imperial War Museum* (A1960)

Montgomery. Shortly after being given command of the 8th Army, wearing his multi-badged hat to make him stand out.—*Imperial War Museum* (E19699)

Montgomery. Posing in front of one of his new Grant tanks after his victory at the Battle of El-Alamein. —*Imperial War Museum* (18982)

Churchill's strategy, Algiers 1943. A classic depiction of the manner in which Churchill attempted to control all military decisions. Seated around him are British Foreign Secretary Eden, General Brooke, Air Marshall Tedder, Admiral Cunningham, General Alexander, General Marshall, General Eisenhower and General Montgomery.
—*Imperial War Museum* (NA3286)

Churchill's political survival. Generals Alexander and Montgomery, with Churchill, August 1942. With the overwhelming advantages in men, materials and intelligence, Churchill knew the coming battle would ensure his political survival.
—*Imperial War Museum* (E15905)

General Erwin Rommel. Gifted, legendary commander who's defeat became an obsession with Churchill. He said Wavell was the only British general who showed a sign of genius and described Patton as outstanding.

Post El-Alamein. Montgomery watches the German retreat from his tank; the problem was that he just watched, and didn't pursue.—*Imperial War Museum* (E18980)

Mountbatten's disaster. Tanks and landing craft burning on the beach at Dieppe. Of the 24 landing craft which took part, 10 managed to land a total of 24 tanks, all of which were lost.—*Imperial War Museum* (HU1904)

Dieppe.
An exhausted
Lord Lovat
after the
debacle.
According to
Lovat, 'It was
a bad plan and
had no chance
of success'.
IWM H22583.
—*Imperial
War Museum*

Arnhem. A beleaguered General Roy Urquhart, British 1st Airborne CO, shortly before his desperate plea for evacuation.—*Imperial War Museum* (BU1136)

Arnhem. British paratroops being marched away to captivity. Some 6,400 of the 10,000 who had landed were taken prisoner; a further 1,000 had been killed.—*Imperial War Museum* (HU2129)

Generals Sosabowski & Browning, Arnhem. A photograph that seems to encapsulate Sosabowski's suspicions about Browning.

Casablanca Conference, January 1943, Churchill and Mountbatten. There was no rational reason for Mountbatten to be there other than the fact that Churchill had already decided his blue-eyed boy would be in charge of South-East Asia, a decision he formally announced eight months later at Quebec.—*Imperial War Museum* (A14107)

The Ardennes. A tank of Patton's 3rd Army advances through thick snow in his rapid northward thrust.—*Imperial War Museum* (EA68715)

The Ardennes. Generals Patton, Eisenhower and Bradley meet at Bastogne after having halted the German offensive.—*Imperial War Museum* (EA52043)

The Ardennes. General Anthony McAuliffe, the US 101st Airborne commander who said 'nuts' to the Germans.

General George S. Patton. Sometimes controversial, but very highly regarded by the Germans who described him as 'the most aggressive Panzer general of the Allies, a man of incredible initiative and lightning-like action'.
—*CMGworldwide*

South-East Asia. Lord Louis Mountbatten (right) conferring with American General Stilwell CO US Forces in China. Mountbatten's official attire compares with Stilwell's functional dress. Stilwell could be caustic in his criticism, hence his name 'Vinegar Joe', but unlike the British, the Americans valued competence over courtesy.—*Imperial War Museum* (20073)

South-East Asia. Mountbatten (left) with General Douglas MacArthur. Again note the formality of Mountbatten's uniform as compared with the practicality of MacArthur.—*Imperial War Museum* (SE8488)

Field Marshall Sir Claude Auchinleck. Outstanding leader, without whom Slim said he could not have succeeded in Burma, and Rommel's No 2, Fritz Bayerlein described as 'the best Allied general in North Africa.' —*Imperial War Museum* (IB2095)

South-East Asia. General Sir William Slim—'Uncle Bill' to his troops. The Burmese campaign was almost a forgotten theatre, but according to military historian Correlli Barnett, Slim was the finest British general of the war. —*Imperial War Museum* (SE3310)

General Dwight Eisenhower. A typically informal photograph of the Allied
Supreme Commander. A man of remarkable patience and forbearance.

Louis & Edwina Mountbatten 1923. A marriage of great convenience. She wanted his Royalty and he needed her money.—*Library of Congress*

Lord Louis Mountbatten. Adored wearing uniform and medals. Irresponsible and impatient in his rushing of Indian Independence because he was more interested in getting back to the navy.

Field Marshall Sir John Dill, equestrian statue at Arlington National Cemetery. Removed by Churchill who could not stand wise advice that went against his own ideas, but admired by the Americans who recognised the experience and wisdom that was beyond Churchill's grasp.—*Arlington National Cemetery*

Winston Churchill. Britain's war leader and self-appointed expert whose dictatorial style was a consistent impediment throughout the war. —*Imperial War Museum* (MH26392)

Operation *Zipper* and his book appears to have been the only account, anywhere, of what actually happened when the operation was launched. With such high-handed priorities and with the spectre of Dieppe still lurking as a 'skeleton in the closet', the question must be asked whether Mountbatten was really the right man to be in command.

A spanner was thrown into the planning of the operation when, with political opportunism that belied their apparent support for the coalition government in the UK over the previous 5 years, the British Labour Party called for a general election almost as soon as Nazi Germany surrendered. That the bipartisan arrangement would finish with the end of the war was never in doubt, but although the Labour leaders themselves apparently favoured postponing this until the final victory had been obtained against Japan, the party conference at Blackpool at the end of May 1945 voted overwhelmingly against continuing the coalition. Political opportunism was now the card played by the Conservative Party when, to attract popular support, the Conservative secretary for war, Sir James Grigg, announced almost immediately a speed-up in demobilisation with the qualifying period of service for repatriation being reduced to 3 years and 4 months. This change affected about one-third of the men in South-East Asia who had been earmarked for Operation *Zipper* where the majority had served for 4 years or more without any of the home leave that had been available for many of those fighting on fronts closer to home. Although protesting vehemently at the weakening of their forces that these early demobilisations would involve, the planning for *Zipper* went ahead but with the reduced number of six divisions.

A substantial force of men, together with thousands of vehicles and tons of supplies and fuel, had to be assembled and transported to rendezvous at the top of the Strait of Malacca. It was an exercise that would be fraught with uncertainty and dangers and due to the very size of the fleet and the distance it had to travel from its starting point in Ceylon and the east coast of India, it would be almost impossible to maintain total secrecy. The longest voyage, that undertaken by the landing crafts, would take 13 days whilst even the relatively fast troopships would take 7 days to reach the invasion location. By comparison Plymouth was probably the furthest away from the Normandy beaches and then that was only 250km

The navy reported that the tides in the Morib area, which was approximately halfway between Port Swettenham and Port Dickson on the western coast of Malaya, would be suitable on just two dates within the projected timeframe—27 August or 9 September; the latter date was agreed upon due to last-minute rearrangements necessary within the army because of the early demobilisation enforced on them by politics in London. If they were to arrive at Morib as planned on 9 September, the landing craft had to depart by 27 August. However, whilst the final touches were being put on these plans at Mountbatten's headquarters in Ceylon, two events that were to be marked down in history occurred some 6,400km away to the east: an atomic bomb was dropped on Hiroshima on 6 August 1945 and a second bomb was dropped three days later on Nagasaki.

Six days later on 15 August 1945, and after a period of complete turmoil within the top military and civilian echelons in Tokyo, Emperor Hirohito of Japan publicly accepted the Allies' surrender terms. When Mountbatten visited Churchill in Potsdam in July, he was warned by Churchill in strict confidence that he might have to change his plans due to the proposed use of the new weapon. With the dropping of these bombs and the Japanese accepting the demanded surrender terms it looked as though Mountbatten was to be robbed of his moment of glory.

Although there were Japanese commanders who initially either refused to believe or accept that their government had surrendered, by the time the troops of Operation *Zipper* were due to storm ashore on 9 September, it was nearly 4 weeks since the surrender and it was known through contact with Japanese senior officers that no resistance would be encountered at the landings. In fact from recently declassified war records it is now known that General Seishiro Itagaki, the Japanese area commander for Singapore and Malaya, had signalled Mountbatten on 20 August that he would abide by his emperor's decision to surrender. The glory of the 'avenging battle' that Churchill had so looked forward to was to be denied him and, as Stephen Harper writes, when Mountbatten visited General Macarthur in Manila in early July, 'Mountbatten was feeling buoyant at the prospect of commanding the next great Allied campaign, confident that the Malayan invasion would put his name in the pantheon of great British military commanders'.[174] Now it seemed even the remaining victory chalice of 'invasion' was to be snatched from his hands at the eleventh hour. This would have been something of a setback for any commander but for a man of the ego and ambition of Mountbatten as described by Correlli Barnett, it must have been a crushing blow. On top of this bitter disappointment came another shock, when on 19 August, just 4 days after the surrender, General MacArthur, the Supreme Commander in the Pacific, decreed that no landings were to be made on enemy-held territory until the formal surrender had taken place. The Combined Chiefs of Staff had handed complete control of the Japanese surrender to MacArthur and a formal surrender ceremony was planned for 2 September on board the United States battleship *Missouri* in Tokyo Bay.

There may, in principle, have been some degree of humiliation that the British could not reoccupy their erstwhile colonies until this American-staged surrender had been completed, but from MacArthur's point of view it made great sense. He was genuinely and understandably concerned that some Japanese armies might continue to fight unless the formal surrender was publicly and clearly signed in the name of the emperor. This order was therefore aimed at avoiding any further unnecessary casualties; enough blood had already been shed in this conflict without needlessly risking any more.

There was a period of 3 weeks between the dates of MacArthur's edict on 19 August and the landings planned on Malayan soil for 9 September. Because of the known desperate plight of prisoners of war in Japanese hands, it was decided to turn a blind eye to what was technically a 'landing' in order to provide urgently needed food, medical supplies and clothing, and these were flown in and dropped by parachute along with relief teams. As far as the assembled invasion fleet was concerned, Mountbatten claimed in his report to the British chiefs of staff in 1956 that his ships, landing craft and forces were already at sea when MacArthur's directive came through and could not be turned back, particularly as this would have meant heading into the south-western monsoon. It is almost impossible to accept how this could have been the case since even the slowest landing crafts would not have taken more than 13 days to reach the area and, as mentioned earlier, none of these vessels would have been likely to have commenced their voyage before, say, 26/27 August. There must therefore have been a gap of at least a week between the date Mountbatten received MacArthur's order, 19 August, and the earliest planned date of departure of the first ships, 26 August. Was this another example of Mountbatten's 'rewriting of history' as described by biographer Philip Ziegler?

Why it took 11 years for his report on the landings to appear is not clear but it should be noted that by then Mountbatten had risen to First Sea Lord; so perhaps the chiefs of staff were reluctant at that late stage to question the detail. Was this therefore the Churchill 'show' that had to go ahead, or was Mountbatten personally determined that he was not going to be denied the opportunity to demonstrate his grand scheme? In his book *Defeat into Victory,* which came out at about the same time as Mountbatten's report, Field Marshal Sir William Slim makes only brief mention of Operation *Zipper* and merely says that the landings on the west coast of Malaya went in on 9 September as what he nebulously and perhaps diplomatically described as 'a tactical operation'. He went on to state: 'There was no resistance and even if there had been I think the operation would have been a success for the Japanese plans as we afterwards discovered, were based on our landing elsewhere.'[175]

Mountbatten's Dieppe fiasco, mentioned earlier, seems to have been due to an ego that demanded he alone make decisions, irrespective of contrary advice or changed circumstances. This character trait was to reveal itself again several years later when, picked by Attlee as the last Viceroy of India, Mountbatten rushed through the complex question of Indian Independence in a matter of 14 weeks rather than the 14 month period suggested by the Attlee government, which in itself was widely regarded as extremely optimistic. Then, as in earlier cases, and going against experienced advice and warnings from just about every quarter, Mountbatten insisted on pushing through the partition of India. This involved the rapid drawing of arbitrary boundary lines, particularly through Punjab and Bengal and resulted in the deaths of millions, the tragic legacy of which continues today in Pakistan, Bangladesh and Kashmir. The underlying reason for such irresponsible haste was Mountbatten's ambitions within the Royal Navy, to which service he was anxious to return as quickly as possible. Was Operation *Zipper* 'pushed through irrespective' in a similar manner?

As Mountbatten was well aware prior to the Normandy landings in June 1944, the beaches and coastlines had been fully surveyed not only by way of photographic evidence from the air but also by extensive core samples taken of sand and the underlying strata. Indeed, in attempting to rationalise his Dieppe fiasco he had said that one of the lessons learned had been about beach material. The D-Day beach samples were obtained by teams landed from submarines at night and the information was then used to judge the suitability or otherwise of the beaches for the landing of various weights of tracked or wheeled vehicles. Compared with Malaya such operations were of course much easier to accomplish due to the relative proximity of English home ports, Portsmouth to the Normandy beaches, for instance, being only about 160km and a round trip that could be undertaken under cover of darkness. In addition, a considerable amount of information was obtained from French holiday photographs and from those who were familiar with the coastline concerned.

On the other hand very little information of a similar nature was available for the beaches selected for the *Zipper* landings. The Malayan west coast could not be reached in anything like the same manner since the closest British bases in India or Ceylon were about 2,400km away; any reconnaissance would have required a voyage of several days and nights through Japanese-controlled seas, and considerable care would need to be taken to avoid discovery. Several investigation teams were dispatched but what little information was obtained did not look promising. Port Dickson was believed to have beaches of firm sand and was thought to be an obvious location for the landings but it was well defended by the Japanese, and so Morib, a small Malay fishing village some 50km to the north, was chosen for the main thrust of the invasion. However, it was found that deep mud lay only 8 inches below the surface there and what should have been an ominous finding was given scant attention by the navy personnel responsible for assessing the intelligence. The fact that the Morib beaches were unsuitable seems to have added to the theory that they would not be well defended. Even if a landing could be achieved, Morib hardly featured on a map in 1945 and compared with Port Dickson further down the coast had very little in the way of recognised roads inland for access to the interior.

In such circumstances it seems remarkable that little reference appears to have been made to existing Admiralty information at the time. *The Malacca Strait Pilot* was first published by the Admiralty in 1904. It is a guide to navigation and comprises detailed information for shipping in the Malacca Strait and its northern approaches, the Singapore Strait and the west coast of Sumatra; a second edition of the *Pilot* was published in 1934. Whilst the fresh editions contained changes in harbour developments and aids to navigation such as buoys, beacons, lights and so on, the fundamental information regarding flora, fauna, seabed composition, shorelines and the like remained the same. For the landing locations selected and the stretch of coast some distance either side, the third edition, published in 1946, makes consistent reference to aspects such as 'soft mud', 'mud-banks', 'shallow mud-banks', 'bottom is soft', and for the area of Port Swettenham itself there are more warnings of 'extensive mud-banks', 'islands formed of black mud', 'shallow mud-banks' and areas to be avoided. To the south of Port Swettenham there are warnings of mudflats that extend about 8 cables (roughly 1,400m) from the coast with consistent and unreliable combinations of mud and sand.

All this information was available, and taken together with the Admiralty chart shoreline notations which clearly show an intertidal area of marsh, swamp, sand and mud for the whole length of the coastal area from Port Swettenham to Port Dickson, warning bells should have sounded loud and clear. The charts also indicated a shoreline fringed almost entirely by mangroves, which would present serious obstacles. Despite all these hazards and warning signs Mountbatten decided that the operation had to go ahead irrespective of the unfavourable geographical and maritime information. This 'unfavourable intelligence' would only risk jeopardising the lives of the servicemen involved in the operation and would not imperil those making the decisions; the circumstances had about them the eerie omen of Dieppe.

What actually occurred when some of the landings in Malaya were eventually made is described below, but the question that has to be asked is why was the operation not changed into a simple reoccupation force? We know there was time, and that ships could have been docked alongside wharves where it would be possible for the organised disembarking and offloading of cargoes of men and materials. This is what was done at Penang at the northern end of the Malacca Strait and similar procedures could have been followed at harbours such as Port Weld, Telok Anson, Port Swettenham, Port Dickson, Malacca and river estuary ports further down the coast. Some of the carrying vessels were landing craft but that would have presented little problem because the Malacca Strait, particularly between Port Swettenham and Singapore, is approximately 45km wide, and nearly always calm due to it being sheltered from the effects of the south-west monsoon by the highlands of Sumatra, which rise to a height of over 4,000m.

Any of the carrying vessels could therefore have safely awaited their turn to disembark their cargoes in an orderly and perfectly safe manner at any of the above mentioned ports. It was known beforehand that there would be no resistance, that the Japanese commanders had, albeit with some reluctance, accepted their emperor's decree of surrender and this had been communicated to Mountbatten; so why even the pretence of an invading force taking the country by storm? Although never admitted, quite clearly the underlying reason was the need to at least stage some semblance of a forceful return. At Singapore, British troops were put ashore in orderly fashion following the signing of the surrender document by General Itagaki on board HMS *Sussex* in Singapore harbour and there was no reason why a similar procedure could not have been followed in Malaya.

The landings at Morib went ahead without the aerial cover and naval bombardments originally planned because they were not needed due to the Japanese surrender. It was just as well they were not required, for the Morib landings were, for the most part, an unmitigated disaster due to the sand/mud beaches and poor intelligence. In his book *Miracle of Deliverance* Stephen Harper recounts talking to a number of personnel who took part in the landings. A Royal Engineers lieutenant recalled:

> vehicles were breaking through the thin crust of sand and sinking into the underlying mud all along the beach, often as soon as they came off the ramp, and that meant they blocked the exit for all the following vehicles. Immediately we started disembarking we had several of our vehicles bogged . . . the REME [Royal Electrical and Mechanical Engineers] Beach Recovery Unit had already lost all its tractors and a Naval Unit's armoured bulldozer was hopelessly stuck deep in the mud.

Another officer, a Royal Artillery Captain said: 'Ultimately we got some vehicles ashore, but the scene on the beach was pathetic. It was common to hear remarks like "My God, one sniper would have done for the lot of us."'[176] A similar comment came from a Royal Artillery lieutenant-colonel, who remembered: 'In the next few days we saw an awful lot of Japs, and I've always had the impression it would have been a bloodbath if they had still been fighting. It was a shambles that, luckily, we didn't have to pay for.' The Royal Engineers lieutenant quoted earlier sent recovery vehicles back to the landing areas some weeks later, his drivers reporting that: 'some 800 vehicles were written off as well as several smaller landing craft which could not be towed back as they had settled in the mud', and even without any opposition it is not as though this unnecessary show of force did not suffer casualties. To quote Stephen Harper once more, he recounts the experience of an able seaman, a veteran of similar landings in Italy, Normandy and Rangoon, who said Morib was a near disaster and described being stranded on the roof of a lorry along with its driver and a crowd of very frightened Indian soldiers, none of whom could swim. 'It was heartbreaking, he said, to see bodies floating among the crates and crates of stores that covered the surface of the sea.'

This was merely a reoccupation force, an operation that could and should have involved no loss of life at all, but one where the original plan was quite unnecessarily pursued with reckless abandon and for no other apparent purpose than to stage some dramatic gesture to satisfy the ego of Mountbatten. Perhaps the final description of this scenario of determined incompetence should come from an RAF armourer, a veteran of the Burma campaign, who commented to Stephen Harper: 'But for the atomic bombs I don't think we would have stood a cat in hell's chance. We would have been murdered in the biggest massacre of the war. They would have annihilated the lot of us.'

The official version said everything had gone according to plan. The force's newspaper, *SEAC*, published its own account of the landings about a week later, announcing with some pride:

A few days ago we landed our troops in Malaya. It was a magnificent sight. Scores of ships, every kind of warship present, and hundreds of landing craft lying squatly in the water as they wallowed inshore laden with troops and equipment. This was no invasion over a small distance like the English Channel, but the biggest Combined Op we ever carried out. A vast invasion force had to be conveyed hundreds of miles from numerous bases and put ashore, maintained there by the Navy. I was able to get ashore a couple of hours after the first troops touched down. A splendid scene, with every kind of supply and equipment pouring ashore.[177]

Who wrote that glamorised rubbish? Was it Mountbatten? To repeat what has been said before—the first casualty of war is the truth. The Official War History rationalises what took place by saying that: 'Despite the chaos on the beaches there is little doubt that, had it been necessary to take Malaya by force of arms, Operation *Zipper* would eventually have achieved its object'.[178] Whether it would have achieved its object is very much a moot point. Contacted by Stephen Harper in 1984, the commander of the operation's land forces, General Sir Ouvry Roberts, noted: 'I was indeed happy from every point of view that we were not involved in fighting. Had the Japanese defended Malaya it is more than probable that our operation would have been a failure . . . and I don't suppose I should have been here today.'[179] Stephen Harper's book quotes numerous other eyewitness accounts, all of which describe similar scenes of chaos and many making the same sort of comment as that of General Roberts—'Had the beaches been defended, I wouldn't be writing this.'

However, a final question remains: it was known there would be no resistance and it was also known that what intelligence had been obtained showed that the beaches were unreliable to say the least, so why was it decided to persist with the original plan, known to be very chancy, when there was a much safer and orderly alternative? Chances, calculated risks, sometimes have to be taken in wartime, but when hostilities have ceased, the taking of such risks is unnecessary, unless perhaps there is a point to prove, 'recapturing' having a far greater dramatic ring to it than mere 'reoccupying'. As has been seen the Second Battle of El Alamein was unnecessary and was launched a few days before the Americans landed in North Africa in order that Churchill could proclaim a great 'British victory'. All the signs point to Mountbatten, for similar reasons, having pursued a parallel course; this was after all, exactly what he had done when running Special Operations. Although invited, Mountbatten declined to attend the official Japanese surrender on board the battleship USS *Missouri* in Tokyo Bay on 2 September 1945, saying that 'he could not have stood the sight of them' i.e. the Japanese. Had he been there, he would of course have had to play second fiddle to MacArthur, and as we have seen Mountbatten always preferred to be orchestra leader. So instead of being 'upstaged' as it were by the ceremony in Tokyo Bay, he presided over his very own ceremony in Singapore 10 days later, where he accepted the surrender of all Japanese forces in South-East

Asia, by which time, presumably, the 'sight of them' had become less un-bearable.

What was ultimately achieved tells its own story. It took 2 weeks to fi-nally clear the shambles at the Morib beaches, by which time 44,500 per-sonnel had been put ashore, and after a similar period 19,300 were landed at Port Dickson: a total of 63,800. In that period the two beaches had also managed to land 26,000 tons of stores and 7,300 vehicles. These figures, achieved without any opposition whatsoever, should be compared with the original targets set for Operation *Zipper* under combat conditions of fierce resistance, which were that 97,500 troops, 82,000 tons of stores and 9,200 vehicles would be landed. As they should have done from the outset, all ships in the following convoys discharged their cargoes using only port facilities.

Frank Rostron, who after the war became a well-known and respected sports writer with the *Daily Express*, had accompanied the force as a war correspondent for that paper, but instead of stopping at Morib his ship sailed straight to Singapore. Stephen Harper recounts a conversation he had with Rostron who told him that the correspondents only heard of the Morib chaos later, and as quoted earlier, he said:

> Every effort was made to hush it up, and the story was censored. We had plenty of things to write about, and it was weeks before we heard what a disaster *Zipper* would have been. If the Japs had been in their fox-holes—as they would have been but for the surren-der—our troops would have been mown down as they foundered in the quicksands. It would have been the most grisly story of the war, the most ghastly failure.[180]

Although a brief summary is available, the full official report is still, apparently, among classified Cabinet papers and has never been released. Even now it looks as though Mountbatten is still being protected.

Just how many did lose their lives so unnecessarily? There must have been hundreds, maybe thousands, but no figures have ever been published which detail the number of those who perished in this 'tactical operation' and even now casualty figures are merely shown as 'Not Available'—mean-ing unpublishable. The questions remain: why was a censorship blackout imposed on what was, ostensibly, only a peacetime reoccupation, and who imposed it? Someone at the top at SEAC? For those who were involved in Operation *Zipper* and the chaos of their attempted landings it was indeed a 'miracle of deliverance' that Japan had surrendered, but that is not the point: it is more likely that this Mountbatten 'operation' had been pushed through in its original form for no reason other than to polish his own prestige.

As a postscript to this saga of imperial postures, Mountbatten visited Morib beach in 1972 'and expressed amazement at the apparent firmness of the sand, commenting that he could hardly blame his intelligence for their misleading reports.'[181] 'Apparent' is the crucial word here, for one would have expected experienced intelligence to require more than just what seemed apparent on the surface. One might ask whether the information obtained in 1945 was known to be inadequate for such landings to proceed, but they went ahead anyway.

In 1965 the author drove his Vauxhall Victor onto dry sand at Port Dickson at low tide. Port Dickson was described by the commanders of Operation *Zipper* as having the best beaches on the whole of the west coast of Malaya. This medium-sized saloon weighed only about 2,000 pounds but within a few yards of the grassy bank the wheels went straight through the apparently secure hard sandy surface leaving the car completely bogged in the soft mud immediately beneath the thin crust. This embarrassing situation was resolved when the car was rescued by a group of Malay fisherman who helpfully ganged together to pull it out. But if even a light passenger car could suffer that fate, and on what was supposed to have been the best beach, what chance was there for the heavier military vehicles such as 3- to 5-ton trucks or 20-ton tractors at Morib? Is it any wonder there was such chaos?

It should be added that Mountbatten had contributed little to the actual victory in Burma, which had been achieved by the Fourteenth Army under the avuncular but brilliant leadership of General Slim—'Uncle Bill' as he was known to his troops—who in turn had been given huge support by General Auchinleck from India. The accolades for the successful Burma campaign therefore went quite rightly to Slim. However, when Mountbatten was created an earl in October 1947, he made sure that it was his name that was associated with that war, for he chose 'Burma' as the locale for the title. If the name of that theatre was to be awarded to anyone it should rightly have gone to Slim, but when he was created a viscount in 1959, the title 'Burma' had already been pocketed by Mountbatten and so Slim quite happily chose Yarralumla in Canberra, (where he had been a most popular Governor-General of Australia) and Bishopston; but then compared with Mountbatten the modest Slim was a rather different character.

CHAPTER 11

MONTGOMERY'S *MARKET GARDEN*—ARNHEM

And then Montgomery did something that was totally out of character: normally cautious, meticulous, painstaking, ponderous, he proposed a lightning thrust.
—GORDON CORRIGAN,
  The Second World War

Whereas the D-Day landings in Normandy were the result of months of planning that culminated in the best possible plan the Allies could devise, Market Garden was a military disaster thanks largely to the blunders of its architects who ignored obvious danger signals, violated established principles of offensive warfare, and failed to take note of the valuable (and sometimes costly) lessons gained from earlier operations.
—CARLO D'ESTE, Foreword to
  A Magnificent Disaster

After the charade of El Alamein, and although always having huge numerical advantages, Montgomery did eventually achieve his objectives, whether they were in Tunisia, Sicily, Italy, or in North-West Europe. Every single action was marked by careful preparation and caution, which of course is in no way a criticism, but far too often there were lengthy hesitations and indecision when original plans encountered obstacles for which there had been no provision. It is here that Montgomery tends to come undone, for if in such circumstances, which can happen to any general, he had said, 'I hadn't expected this—I'll have to re-think', then even a delay taking some time would not have been criticised or even questioned. But it was largely in his consistent refusal to concede any error or the necessity for a change in plan plus his non-stop self-pro-motion that he often shot himself in the foot and so created his own cred-ibility gap.

By 4 September 1944 the British Army had reached Brussels, and the next day Antwerp was taken intact. Eisenhower urged Montgomery to im-mediately clear the Scheldt Estuary so that the valuable port could be used to ease the acute problems with the Allies' supply chain, which still relied mainly on Cherbourg, some 600km away. Antwerp was one of the largest ports in Europe and the only one capable of handling the supplies for an Allied army of 2 million men, and had Montgomery been a 'team' player, he would have cleared the estuary because the overall benefits to the Allies' cause was obvious. Capturing the port intact was quite valueless unless the estuary could be cleared for its use. But Montgomery, as usual, had his own schedule and had other ideas which took little account of 'team' needs. This was his territory, and he was not going to have anyone else telling him what to do, however reasonable or obvious the suggestion.

In his *History of the Second World War,* Basil Liddell Hart describes this case of contradicting priorities as an extraordinary oversight.[182] Having swept into Antwerp on 5 September and captured the docks intact, Mont-gomery made no effort to take the seemingly obvious further step of im-mediately securing the bridges over the Albert Canal in the suburbs, and no orders were given to that effect. This major canal stretches 130km south-east from Antwerp to the city of Liège and has a minimum width of 25m; seizing the bridges over such a waterway would appear to have been a logical objective. Such a move should have been clear, since having captured the port in undamaged condition it was obvious the Germans had left in a hurry. Two days later the 11th Armoured Division did attempt a crossing, but by then the delay had given the retreating Germans plenty of time to blow the bridges; faced with this obstacle, Montgomery then switched the division eastwards.

The Albert Canal was only the first of the considerable physical obsta-cles of the rivers and canals of Holland and these would have to be conquered before Germany could be reached. This is where there suddenly appeared an escapade that would go down in history as Montgomery's biggest and most infamous—or famous—disaster, and yet again one where he later claimed success. Announced on 10 September the plan was named Operation *Market Garden*, an ambitious venture, particularly by Montgomery's cautious standards, to capture the main bridge over the Rhine at Arnhem in Holland through the combined use of British and American airborne troops and ground forces. Given the advantages of men and materials that the Allies had at their disposal plus virtual control of the skies, the problems of these canals and rivers would, one by one, have been overcome by conventional methods—but this would have taken time, and for once Montgomery was in a hurry. Virtually nothing was heard of this debacle until Cornelius Ryan's book *A Bridge Too Far* appeared in 1974, and for good reason, for it was a completely avoidable disaster. It was to be yet another nail in Montgomery's quietly crumbling coffin.

The overall concept was so outrageously risky and daring, and so un-Montgomery, that it caused total astonishment amongst the top Allied command. American General Omar Bradley, writing in his memoirs, said he never reconciled himself to the venture: 'Had the pious, tee-totalling Montgomery wobbled in with a hangover I could not have been more astonished than I was by the daring adventure he proposed.'[183]

What was even more amazing was the plan that his grand idea should take off in just 7 days, on 17 September. Montgomery rationalised his proposal to Eisenhower on the grounds that it would enable his British Army to race on to Berlin and end the war in 3 months. His projected operation, which at the very best was optimistic, involved airborne troops seizing and holding the bridges over each of four waterways before they could be demolished by the Germans, in order to reach the objective—the final bridge over the Rhine at Arnhem. They would hold the bridge for 3 days before being relieved by ground troops, who would arrive to make the capture of the bridge permanent. It was a high-risk venture that depended entirely upon the combined success of a number of vital factors: effective communications, clear skies, accurate intelligence, no unexpected obstacles that would affect crucial timing and coordination and, as always in an operation such as this, the existence of a 'Plan B'. If any one of the factors failed, the whole scheme would be in jeopardy.

Eisenhower had grave doubts but allowed the operation at least as far as Arnhem to proceed because of the likely political reaction if he, as American overall commander, was seen to be holding back what would have been described as an imaginative British initiative. Had Montgomery's plan not been approved, he would probably have gone to the British Chief of the Imperial General Staff, General Brooke, saying that here he was producing an ingenious and original concept for his British Army, only to have it knocked on the head by the Americans. Ever since D-Day such considerations had become a frequent headache for the long-suffering Eisenhower.

And there was another possible factor. On 1 September 1944 Montgomery was elevated to field marshal and therefore he probably felt he was now senior in rank, if not in authority, to any American except Eisenhower. As a mere general Montgomery had been a problem, but as a field marshal? This promotion itself was little more than a compensatory gesture from London for having been relieved of his command of all the Allied ground forces and given the smaller job of being in charge of just the 21st Army Group. Such a demotion would have been painful for anyone, but for an individual of Montgomery's ego it would have been excruciating.

There was, however, one serious threat to the plan. The port of Antwerp, although having been captured, lay some 70km up the Scheldt Estuary and on the southern bank at the mouth of the estuary were 60,000 men of the German Fifteenth Army who had been encircled by Montgomery's Canadian 1st Army. Montgomery was aware of this and the probability that unless the Fifteenth Army was eliminated or intercepted it would escape across the estuary and up into Holland, thus reinforcing the German defences in the very location at which Montgomery was aiming. However, he refused to change his plan, insisting that his troops were required for his own operation and could not be spared for clearing out the Fifteenth Army position further down the estuary.

What Montgomery had refused to accept was immediately recognised by Field Marshal Gerd von Rundstedt, the German Commander-in-Chief West. He quickly ordered the almost trapped Fifteenth Army out of the area, leaving just enough units to defend the estuary ports and by doing so strengthened his forces by giving himself another 60,000 men. The tragedy is that the Fifteenth Army's only possible getaway route could have been severed by a simple 20km thrust north from Antwerp, which was already in Montgomery's hands. As it was the Germans were able to escape, an omission that would prove to be a major factor in the failure of *Market Garden*. This stubborn and irrational decision by Montgomery was so blatantly at odds to the logical steps that should have been taken that it became the specific subject of a book by military historian Reginald W. Thompson, *The 85 Days*,[184] which detailed what should have taken place.

Shortly before Operation *Market Garden* was to be launched, intelligence from the Dutch Resistance reported to the Supreme Headquarters Allied Expeditionary Force (SHAEF) in London, that two SS panzer divisions, the 9th and 10th, whose whereabouts had been a mystery for some time, had reappeared right where the main airborne assault on Arnhem was planned to land. This was further confirmed by intelligence received in England through unscrambling of the German Ultra intelligence signals. The 1st Airborne Corps' intelligence officer concerned, Major Brian Urquhart, was so worried that he arranged for the information to be checked and confirmed again by British aerial photographs. These clearly showed numerous tanks in the area, and all this new and alarming information he relayed to Eisenhower and Montgomery. Eisenhower was so concerned that he sent his deputy, General Bedell Smith, to confer with Montgomery. Knowing his propensity for extreme caution it might have been thought that Montgomery would have taken care to assess the implications of this intelligence; but not a bit of it—he dismissed it as ridiculous.

Here, tragically, was yet another situation where Montgomery would not, or could not, contemplate altering his plan to take account of changed circumstances or fresh information, and as a consequence this vital but unpalatable evidence was ignored as if it were some sort of peripheral inconvenience. In some quarters there has been an attempt to rationalise this on the basis that Dutch intelligence could be unreliable. That was quite true, but when such a warning is substantiated through independent photographic evidence, the excuse does not stand up. But there was worse to come. In order to completely discredit the intelligence he had obtained, Major Urquhart received an unexpected visit from a medical officer, Colonel Arthur 'Austin' Eagger, who had been told by senior members of Montgomery's staff that Urquhart had become 'hysterical'. Obviously working under instructions from on high, and despite Urquhart telling Eagger that he was convinced the proposed operation was 'madness', Urquhart was diagnosed by Eagger as suffering from 'exhaustion' and was sent on leave. Montgomery had thus removed from the immediate scene an uncomfortable witness to the existence of unpalatable intelligence. Urquhart later felt he should have tried harder to convince the high command of the dangerous accuracy of his intelligence, although it is difficult to see just what more he could have achieved when confronted with an official blank wall that directed such intransigence. Urquhart was not the only source of unwelcome intelligence. A distinguished air intelligence officer, Wing Commander Asher Lee, investigated more deeply into the sources of the Ultra information and personally conveyed his conclusive evidence of substantial German armour at Arnhem to Montgomery's headquarters in Brussels. Nobody but several junior staff officers were prepared to see him, and his corroborating information was again ignored.[185] Even at much higher levels considerable misgivings were being felt. On 9 September Lieutenant-General Miles Dempsey, commander of the British Second Army, wrote in his diary:

> It is clear that the enemy is bringing up all the reinforcements that he can get his hands on for the defence of the Albert Canal, and that he appreciates the importance of the area Arnhem-Nijmegan. It looks as though he is going to do all that he can to hold it. This being the case, any question of a rapid advance to the north-east seems unlikely—Are we right to direct Second Army to Arnhem?[186]

If Dempsey was to be so wary, it would seem highly unlikely that he was the only senior commander for whom fresh intelligence indicated that great caution should be exercised. Whether Dempsey relayed his fears to Montgomery is apparently not known, but one must ask an obvious question: would a responsible, experienced military commander deliberately remove or ignore such evidence unless the plan was one of such personal fixation that it bordered on an obsession? The only logical explanation for such a dismissive rejection of clearly documented evidence of serious new information that could obviously have a considerable bearing on the outcome of the whole operation is that it did not 'fit in' with Montgomery's personal ambitions vis-à-vis Berlin; this was a classic case of reluctance to accept information that is unpalatable—cognitive dissonance.

Behind his plausible aim there was a hidden personal agenda—that of attempting to compete with the Americans in the east, Patton's Third Army in particular, which had raced across France and was now only 50km from the German border. Montgomery was desperate to be the first to reach Berlin and feared being left in Patton's shadow. As has been explained, from the very beginning the fundamental concepts of *Market Garden* were tenuous, finely balanced and full of 'ifs' and 'buts' with a whole range of influences and factors being interdependent for the accuracy and successful accomplishment of what was planned. In other words, it would require only one spanner to be thrown into the works for the whole scenario to collapse, and yet when presented with documented proof of a serious and existing problem, such was Montgomery's preoccupation with the race to Berlin he brushed it aside. A commander not taking council of his fears is one thing, wilful dismissal of documented fact is quite another—and so the show went ahead with the first airborne landings taking place on 17 September.

Montgomery's plan proposed that once the airborne had successfully seized the bridges, an armoured thrust would then force its way in 3 days over 100km through territory that was held by the Germans. The success of the plan rested on assumptions in a chain of planned events; if one of the links were broken or not taken, then the whole operation would either grind to a halt or would be driven back by the German defenders. At the outset there occurred the first of these fears; although airborne forces did capture three of the bridges, the southernmost bridge at Zon, and therefore the first that would have to be crossed, had already been blown up by the Germans. A replacement Bailey bridge was constructed by the Royal Engineers, but this caused severe delays right at the start of a so-called thrust that depended desperately on accurate timing and speed of execution. At Arnhem itself airborne troops landed too far from their objective and then encountered fierce resistance from the very German armour that Montgomery had said did not exist. Narrow elevated dyke roads with marshy ground either side meant that armour was very exposed to fire from anti-tank guns, and once the leading tank was hit, or for that matter had to stop for any reason, the whole tank column behind it would come to a halt. Assuming enemy anti-tank fire allowed this, the tank could be manoeuvred aside but this would take time and time was of the very essence. Again, the

Dutch Resistance had also warned about this risk but once more Montgomery decided to ignore it. Even so it should not have required any military intelligence for the problem to have been perceived at the outset: raised narrow roads are a very limiting factor, it should not have needed anyone to point this out. All these issues severely delayed the ground forces resulting in the airborne troops being isolated.

The entire plan was based on nothing going wrong, and yet was so finely balanced that it was absurdly unreal to have gone ahead without there being built-in provision for alternatives. Radio sets, which would be vital in bad weather, were notoriously unreliable, had a maximum range of 8km in daylight and less at night and were not robust enough to withstand the shock of air dropping. All of this was known before the operation commenced and as a result, and almost inevitably, vital communications broke down nearly immediately. The skies were not clear and there was early morning fog causing the airborne starting from England to be delayed by many hours, but again this was known to be a distinct risk in the fen country of East Anglia in September. Intelligence was not what it should have been, and even then was ignored if it was unwelcome, and there was no 'plan B' if the unexpected should happen. The total Allied strength was roughly 41,000 airborne and 45,000 ground troops, which it may be noted is only a little more than the 60,000 men of the German Fifteenth Army that had been allowed to escape from the mouth of the estuary.

Nothing, however, should be taken away from the courage and tenacity of the Allied troops involved. They fought magnificently but were prevented from achieving their assigned objectives by the hopelessly unreal optimism of a basic plan that left no room for unexpected circumstances. SS Obersturmbannführer (Lieutenant-Colonel) Walter Harzer commanded the 9th Waffen SS Panzer Division 'Hohenstaufen' at Arnhem. This division played a key role in preventing a bridgehead being obtained across the Rhine, and Harzer later paid tribute to his opponents, saying: 'The British 1st Airborne Division that landed in Arnhem was an elite unit. Its performance, especially at the road bridge was, in the last analysis, acknowledged as really heroic'.[187] The problem did not anywhere lie with the performance of the various individual units on the ground, who grappled as best they could with a collection of factors that were foreseen but had been ignored. When the inevitable chickens came home to roost, they were the ones who paid the price, whilst the grand director himself stood aloof and claimed that his brilliant plan had been a total success.

Some 70 years later there came to light a radio message from the British 1st Airborne Division to Montgomery's headquarters dated 24 September 1944, which revealed just how desperate was the position they faced:

> URQUHART[188] TO BROWNING. Must warn you that unless physical contact is made with us early 25 Sep consider it unlikely we can hold out long enough. All ranks now exhausted. Lack of rations, water, ammunition and weapons with high officer casualty rate. Even slight enemy offensive action may cause complete dis-integration. If this happens all will be ordered to break towards bridgehead if anything rather than surrender. Any movement at present in face of enemy NOT possible. Have attempted our best and will do so as long as possible. (NOT for general distribution).

Of the 9,000 British Airborne troops, who had only been intended to hold Arnhem Bridge from the Germans for 3 days before being reinforced, 1,174 were killed and 6,000 captured. The remaining 1,900 were success-fully evacuated 24 hours later under the cover of darkness. Instead of the projected 3 days they had been forced to hold out for 9 days.

In summarising Operation *Market Garden* in his 1976 book *On the Psy-chology of Military Incompetence,* Dr Norman F. Dixon wrote:

> Far from being demoralised, the enemy fought like tigers to defend the gateway to their homeland. And far from sweeping across Hol-land to aid the hard-pressed paratroopers the tanks were reduced to a crawl by the combination of unsuitable terrain and determined opposition. Defeat was absolute and terrible. Total Allied losses— in killed, wounded and missing—exceeded 17,000 some 5,000 more than those who became casualties on D-Day.[189]

With an 80 per cent casualty rate the 1st Airborne Division was never reconstituted. Dutch civilian casualties have been estimated at between 500 and 10,000, a wide range of figures but including disruption and displace-ment it gives some idea of the overall impact on the civilian population then and ensuing starvation enforced by the Germans as a reprisal in the bitter winter that followed. The starvation was made worse by the port of Antwerp not being available until much later than it should have been.

And yet once more Montgomery was quite unrepentant, claiming that *Market Garden* had been a 90 per cent success; such an opinion makes one shudder to think what he might have considered a failure—after all, just where was the success? There had been huge casualties and the loss of 88 tanks and 144 transport aircraft, and finally an ignominious rescue and retreat of the survivors all the way back to square one. So, asking the question once more, just what had been achieved that Montgomery could even faintly lay claim to any success? It was patently and obviously absurd, and it was a statement that almost inevitably provoked the caustic comment from Prince Bernhard of the Netherlands: 'My country can never again afford the luxury of a Montgomery success.'[190]

Even if it had not been a complete failure, it was unrealistic to assume that the German commanders for the Arnhem area—battle-hardened veterans like Field Marshal Walter Model or his immediate superior, Field Marshal Gerd von Rundstedt, Hitler's leading general—would not have recognised the inherent weakness of the narrow corridor to Arnhem; it was just 25km in width and 100km in length. In his 1989 appraisal of Walter Model, Carlo D'Este describes his ability to adapt rapidly to constantly changing conditions on the field of battle. He could easily and most probably would have cut through the corridor, thus isolating those in Arnhem; and once that was done, how would the war have been shortened by Montgomery's 3 months?

Eventually, but only after peremptory orders from an exasperated Eisenhower, Montgomery did turn his attention to making the long-awaited port of Antwerp available for Allied shipping. Clearing the Scheldt Estuary had become more difficult due to the delay he had created. This had allowed the Germans time to reinforce their forts at the mouth of the estuary and as a result the port was not ultimately cleared for supply convoys until 28 November. This was 85 days since Antwerp was taken on 5 September and hence the title of Reginald W. Thompson's 1957 book; over 12 weeks had been wasted, in men, materials and time. It was only common sense that this should have had priority over any other 'plan' Montgomery might have had in mind, indeed with Antwerp cleared for use it should have made

Market Garden easier to accomplish. This was particularly so since the deep-water port had been captured intact, the Germans having amazingly not destroyed any of the port installations or facilities. It could therefore have been used immediately and of all the Allied forces in Europe at that time it would have been Montgomery who would have been the main beneficiary. Obviously that is except for one factor: if immediate clearance of the Scheldt Estuary had been undertaken and the German Fifteenth Army removed or captured after the occupation of Antwerp, this would have taken time and Montgomery was impatient to launch his operation before the Americans could advance even further. Time was of the essence in his desperate bid to be the first to Berlin. On 28 November the first convoy of eighteen ships made its way cautiously up the Scheldt Estuary and the first 10,000 tons of badly needed cargo was unloaded.

Bewildered by such priorities, General Omar Bradley later stated: 'Of all the might-have-beens in the European campaign, none was more agonizing then the failure of Montgomery to open Antwerp.' And as he observed in his book *A General's Life,* he went on to comment: 'Because of this blunder, Antwerp, captured on September 4 as a matter of highest strategic priority, would not become available to us until nearly three months later— November 28'.[191]

With the Allies steadily and inexorably forcing the German defences back across a wide front there was never any need (ignoring Montgomery's personal ambitions) to mount such a chancy undertaking; it was quite unnecessary. As Gordon Corrigan stated in his book *The Second World War: A Military History*, without the use of the port of Antwerp it is difficult to see what *Market Garden* might have achieved even if it had been successful, but because *Market Garden* was so much the focus of Montgomery's plans the port would not be cleared for a number of weeks. *Market Garden* was never essential to the Allies advance anymore than the Second Battle of El Alamein was necessary for victory in North Africa. Both had been launched because of the ambitions of individual men. El Alamein had successfully saved Churchill's political position at home. *Market Garden* was a gamble in the hope, remote though it might have been, that it could provide a launch pad for Montgomery giving him a quicker path to his own personal goal. Both cases involved the tragic and quite avoidable loss of thousands of lives. Moreover, since the chaos of *Market Garden* was due to fundamental mistakes in planning, it was perhaps clear evidence of precisely why Montgomery had always been so rigid and cautious. He hadn't a clue how to mount such a daring operation, but having made the commitment he could not bring himself to make any changes, even when presented with menacing but incontrovertible intelligence. For a man renowned for meticulous planning and caution, to have deliberately ignored highly unfavourable information and overlooked the detail of the exposed dyke roads seems to point to a motive that was unrelated to considerations of military strategy but simply an overriding personal obsession with his own glory.

As usual Montgomery made sure that any critical odour was deflected and quite unfairly laid what blame he could, which was not much, on Lieutenant-General Sir Richard O'Connor, who had been in command of one of the flanking corps and on Polish Major-General Stanislaw Sosabowski. This was the same O'Connor who had achieved the spectacular victory over the Italians at Beda Fomm in February 1941, had been captured by the Afrika Korps, spent some time in captivity in Italy but had escaped. Several weeks after *Market Garden* he resigned in disgust because of Montgomery's command style and was reassigned to India, where he was welcomed with open arms by Auchinleck.

The Polish 1st Independent Parachute Brigade had fought very bravely, suffered a high casualty rate and had performed as well as could have been expected in the inevitably confused circumstances. Their role had been made particularly difficult due to the brigade being divided into several parts over a period of 3 days due to a totally foreseeable shortage of transport aircraft and then being dropped in the wrong places. Several days after the operation had been brought to a halt Sosabowski received a letter from Montgomery, commending the bravery of the Polish troops and offering ten medals. Then, 9 days after that Montgomery wrote to the British high command adding Sosabowski to his list of scapegoats, and accused Sosabowski of criticising him. As a result, and pressured by Britain to do so, the Polish general staff was obliged to remove him as the commanding officer of his brigade.

Sasobowski's crime was to have been brutally honest in his opinions regarding various aspects of the proposed operation, practically all of which were proved to be right. However, as was often the case with the British Army, it was more important to be polite than to be right, and like the American General 'Vinegar Joe' Stilwell, Sasobowski could be very caustic about anything he felt made no sense or which had been a shambles. Such bluntness was just too much for the British to stomach, especially when his views were later proved to have been correct. His main arguments had been with British Lieutenant-General, and Old Etonian, Frederick 'Boy' Browning who just could not stand anyone proving him wrong. Posthumously, and despite intense diplomatic pressure from Britain to prevent this, Sosabowski received the recognition that was his due when in 2006 the Dutch government awarded his brigade the Military Order of William and he himself was awarded the Bronze Lion. It had taken some 64 years, but justice had eventually been done.

As a postscript, let us consider a peripheral thought, a factor that Montgomery may have had at the back of his self-promoting mind. He had arrived in Normandy on 7 June and in the 90 days to the capture of Antwerp on 5 September he had covered about 400km, by an odd coincidence his usual rate of just over 4km per day. Of this 90-day period, Montgomery had spent 35 days dithering over Caen before bludgeoning his way through with a massive onslaught of artillery and aerial bombardment; this had taken 35 days or 5 weeks, because he was incapable of changing his original plan which had forecast taking the city in just 2 days. Patton had arrived in Normandy a month later, 7 July, and in the 60 days to the same date, 5 September, he had advanced about 650km, or nearly 11km per day; and had it not been for a lack of petrol, his advance would have been much greater. In strict military terms the analogy is not entirely meaningful, but press headlines did not concern themselves with such niceties when comparing the dazzling speed of Patton's advance and the general public would have cared even less. In any event the speed and success of Patton's army certainly had not been lost on the Germans, for in speaking of the advanced tactical handling of the American by their generals none other than Rommel described the Patton army in France as 'one of the most astonishing achievement in mobile warfare'.[192] Although as usual making no comment about the successes of others, was this obvious comparison praying on Montgomery's mind?

This seems to be confirmed by Cornelius Ryan in his book *A Bridge Too Far,* where he recounts that when requesting the necessary supplies for his operation, Montgomery was promised that Patton's drive to the Saar would be checked; Ryan states that Montgomery's response to this news was one of elation.[193] So, was Montgomery 'elated' simply because the supplies he had asked for would be forthcoming, or in reality was it because he had also been told that his requested supplies would have to be diverted from material designated for Patton and would thus bring Patton to a halt? And let it be noted that the only thing that seemed likely to halt the Patton momentum was going to be the problem of supplies and the logistics of keeping pace with his forces. That all of this may have been due to nothing more than personal ambition and perceived rivalry might seem an unpleasant suggestion, but is there any other rational explanation?

Montgomery, the operationally demoted but newly elevated field marshal, was determined to find some way to push ahead of everyone else—his ego demanded this. In his *Memoirs,* Napoleon stated: 'There is a gift of being able to see at a glance the possibilities offered by the terrain . . . and it is inborn in great generals'.[194] The corollary to that of course is that a great general would also immediately have recognised the almost prohibitive obstacles presented by such difficult ground. Thus almost in desperation, he had hatched a plan that would never have even been considered except in extremely dire circumstances. At that stage in the European conflict the Allies had no need at all for anything other than measured planning and coordination, and certainly no necessity for sudden unconventional and highly risky theatrics—unless, that is, one of their senior commanders had a personality who would go to any lengths and take almost any chance (with the lives of others) to maintain his image and destiny.

As mentioned earlier the port of Antwerp was not opened until 28 November. Montgomery's totally inexplicable attitude caused such anger with the Americans that when the first draft of the official United States military history of the war in Europe came out, it was so critical in reference to this campaign that it had to be revised on the personal intervention of Eisenhower before a toned-down version could be published.

And well might there have been such anger in the United States. Churchill had been away in Canada at the time of the debacle but he was to write in his sixth volume of *The Second World War* entitled *Triumph and Tragedy*: 'Had we been more fortunate in the weather, which turned against us it is probable that we should have succeeded'.[195] And speaking of Arnhem, he then went on to state that whilst he was away 'glorious reports had flowed in'. But he went even further and stated that he had sent a cable to Field Marshal Jan Smuts saying: 'As regards Arnhem, the battle was a decided victory. I have not been afflicted with any feeling of disappointment over this and am glad our commanders are capable of running this kind of risk'.[196] Smuts was aware of exactly what had happened and must have been mystified by the cable, but Churchill does not recount his reply.

Let us read those Churchillian words again: 'Glorious reports had flowed in', 'The battle was a decided victory'—was this wishful thinking, senility or just normal politics? It was completely out of touch with the reality of what had actually happened and totally untrue, but if Churchill, as British Prime Minister, accepted so willingly what he was being fed at that time and believed he could get away with repeating such distorted statements and moreover proceeded to repeat them again in his book, then it does perhaps explain why Montgomery managed to hold on to his job.

Some 14 years later, when he came to write his *Memoirs*, Montgomery had become a little more contrite. He conceded that although he had made a few mistakes, the real reasons for what he called 'not gaining complete success' were completely outside of his control and involved the weather, lack of support from Eisenhower and unexpected German armoured strength; no mention is made of *any* intelligence.

But such has been the notoriety of this 'success' that the United States Army War College felt it was worthy of detailed analysis, and in 2009 they published *Operation Market Garden: Case Study for Analyzing Senior Leader Responsibilities*. This 46-page report concludes:

> Most of the responsibility for the failure must fall on Montgomery. In addition to be being the plan's architect, he repeatedly ignored key intelligence and information, including weather and terrain, which should have altered the plan, if not causing its cancellation. He disregarded warnings from senior advisors and commanders.[197]

And of course this was purely an operational assessment—it did not, and could not, venture into the murky realm of underlying personal motives.

The intelligence officer who was removed because his accurate warnings were inconvenient, Major Brian Urquhart, was an experienced intelligence officer whose ability was such that soon after *Market Garden* he was recruited to join T-Force, an elite intelligence-gathering unit established by SHAEF soon after D-Day. After the war he went on to become Under-Secretary-General at the United Nations, where in 1961 his integrity and acute intellect for the truth led him to say that he felt United Nations Secretary-General Dag Hammarskjold had been murdered when his plane crashed in Africa. Urquhart was knighted when he retired in 1986. During an interview on *Market Garden* in New York in May 2003 he made the following comments:

> My first reaction to Market Garden was that it was unbelievably risky, a plan for which there were grossly insufficient resources. As an operation to get across the Rhine, it was in the wrong place, requiring the capture of three major bridges, not one. Strategically, the operation made no sense. It would have been far better to have supported Patton's drive, which was proceeding against light opposition and which had a much better chance of getting across the Rhine. My own explanation, which I arrived at only much later, was that the operation was to feed Montgomery's ego and secure his reputation by a dashing manoeuvre to end the war. I put the responsibility for the operation squarely on the shoulders of Montgomery, who launched it, then refused to listen to anyone who wished to modify a bad plan.
>
> Finally, he made the incredible statement that the operation was ninety per cent successful.[198]

Given all of the above, Britain could be extremely thankful for such forbearance on the part of the Americans. And what is the first casualty of war?

CHAPTER 12

MONTGOMERY'S BULGE— THE ARDENNES

Montgomery would be a psychiatrist's delight were he alive today; an extraordinary mixture of insecurity and bombast, of meticulous preparation and cautious execution, his reputation as Britain's greatest general was largely manufactured by himself.
—GORDON CORRIGAN

Wars may be fought with weapons, but they are won by men. It is the spirit of the men who follow and of the man who leads that gains the victory.
—GENERAL GEORGE S. PATTON

Corrigan's assessment might, at first sight, appear to be just an attack motivated by the advantage of hindsight, were it not for the fact that an investigation of the facts demonstrates a huge gap in so many areas between what Montgomery claimed to have achieved through his own trumpet blowing and what actually happened. This aspect of his personality—the consistent claims that were clearly nowhere near the truth—emerged once more during the German Ardennes offensive in December 1944, what became known as the Battle of the Bulge. This chapter has deliberately been headed *Montgomery's Bulge* for the simple reason that he contributed very little to defeating the German attack. The latter was almost entirely due to the Americans, and in particular to Patton, and yet Montgomery later held a press conference in which he gave the distinct impression that he had saved the Americans. Outwardly admitting nothing, but inwardly smarting following his humiliation in September, Montgomery was, as ever, on the lookout for any opportunity for his usual grandstanding. Whatever he might claim was one thing, but he was aware that the Americans, knowing the truth, regarded him with even less trust than they had before—and that was saying something. Montgomery was therefore keener than ever to grasp any opportunity to recover his prestige.

Having been given a breather by the failure of Montgomery's plan at Arnhem, by the end of October 1944 Hitler was assessing what remaining options he might have. In Italy, Rome had fallen some 3 months earlier and his forces under Field Marshal Albert Kesselring had been pushed back to Bologna in the north. In the Pacific his erstwhile ally Japan was fairing no better. The Japanese forces were gradually being rolled up by the American behemoth under General MacArthur and Admiral Nimitz and the Americans had just landed in the Philippines. On his eastern front matters were even worse; the Russians had maintained their advances and were now close to Warsaw and had entered Belgrade. Hitler desperately needed some final spark of inspiration, that streak of genius that he was convinced he had, and remembering the success of the 1940 blitzkrieg through the Ardennes he felt he could use the same lightning tactics. He would thrust through the same area, cutting off and destroying the Allied forces to the north and reaching Antwerp. Thus, the master strategist predicted, the Allies would be forced to sue for peace. It was to be his last desperate gamble, but deluded as ever in the twilight of his career, Hitler was sure he could yet hold the destiny of Germany in his hands and Field Marshal von Rundstedt was instructed accordingly. In his grasp at the historical precedent, Hitler had overlooked the massive change in the Allied dispositions since 1940. Then he was only up against a static French army that lacked mobility and spirit; 1944 would be different. Experienced commanders were selected by von Rundstedt: General Josef 'Sepp' Dietrich for the Sixth Panzer Army, General Hasso von Manteuffel for the Fifth Panzer Army and a largely infantry Seventh Army under the command of General Erich Brandenberger, all of them battle-hardened veterans. In the coldest winter for 38 years, in deep snow and under cover of fog and overcast skies, these armies, involving over 250,000 men, attacked at 5.30 a.m. on 16 December.

The initial onslaught came along a 60-mile front from just south of

Aachen in the north to Trier in the south, the centre of which the Americans had only lightly defended giving the Germans a five to two numerical advantage; it caught most of the Allies completely by surprise. The central German thrust rapidly penetrated westwards into ground the Americans had felt was secure; it was this central push that became known as the 'bulge'. Low cloud cover had hampered Allied air reconnaissance but not everyone on the Allies' side had been caught totally unawares. Forty miles to the south of the main attack, Patton, whose Third Army was heading eastwards just south of Luxembourg, was blessed with an exceptional G2 (or intelligence officer) Colonel Oscar Koch, an officer whom Patton had known for many years and with whom he conferred every morning. The Patton–Koch relationship was to have a decisive influence on the outcome of the German offensive and the shrewd Koch's almost intuitive perspicacity is described by the following extract from Carlo D'Este's *A Genius for War: A Life of General George S. Patton*:

> In the Third Army it became apparent at Oscar Koch's 7.00 AM intelligence briefing that something unusual was afoot. For some time Koch had not only been keeping a close eye on German dispositions but reporting a build-up of panzer and infantry divisions and ammunition and gasoline dumps west of the Rhine in the Saar, and in the areas opposite the First Army from Aachen to the southernmost extremity of the Ardennes forest. Massive rail movements, of increasing frequency and size, were noted, most north of the Moselle in the First Army sector. As the build-up continued the possible ramifications became a matter of serious concern for Patton. On December 16 Koch reported the Germans were in a state of radio silence, and when Patton asked him what it meant, the G2 replied that when American units went under radio silence it invariably signalled an impending attack. 'I believe the Germans are going to launch an attack, probably at Luxembourg' he predicted.[199]

Working on what his instincts told him this intelligence meant Patton immediately ordered his chiefs of staff to change the direction of the whole of Third Army 90 degrees and instead of facing east it was to prepare to attack north. Since his sector was some 70 miles to the north from where the

German breakthrough occurred, Montgomery's forces were too safely distant for him to have been caught on the hop as had been the Americans and he had plenty of time in which to prepare his response. What was required of him, in effect, was not the rapidly formed defence that had been hurriedly forced on the Americans, but to counter the German attack. However, before doing anything he sent a misleading cable to London reading:

> The situation in the American area is not repeat not good—great confusion and all signs of full scale withdrawal. There is definite lack of grip and control and no one has a clear picture as to situation. There is an atmosphere of great pessimism due to the fact that everyone knows something has gone wrong and no one knows what or why. I myself have had no orders or requests of any sort.[200]

Nothing would be served by quoting here the full text of the long, distorted and offensive message which, as usual for the opportunistic Montgomery, was designed and intended to disparage his colleagues and enhance his own prospects. By far the largest contribution to the Allies' cause came from the Americans who had four times as many divisions in Europe than the British; most of the tanks and other equipment were American and had it not been for the Americans, Montgomery would never have left North Africa. Loudly blowing his own trumpet at every conceivable opportunity was his unfortunate style, but in this case intentionally causing anger and offence to those who he depended on was, even for Montgomery, a new low. In fact, he was so out of touch with the realities of the situation that when he learned of the German breakout, he sent a message to his own troops reading: 'The enemy is at present fighting a defensive campaign on all fronts; his situation is such that he cannot stage major offensive operations. Furthermore at all costs he has to prevent the war from entering the mobile phase'.[201]

On 19 December Eisenhower called a top-line conference at Verdun to discuss the new situation. Present were all Eisenhower's top commanders, except Montgomery, who decided such a meeting did not warrant his attendance, sending his number two instead; if a further slight was intended, this was it. The general consensus at the meeting was first to concentrate on blunting the German offensive and once they had been contained then as soon as possible to go on the offensive. Prior to leaving that morning for the meeting, Patton had ensured his Third Army was poised to move north immediately if required and when asked by Eisenhower how long it would take for him to be ready to counter-attack, Patton told the astonished gathering that 48 hours would be sufficient. At the end of the conference Patton telephoned his commanders and gave them the orders they had been expecting and the Third Army began its momentous sprint northwards. They were aided by blue skies that arrived on 23 December, which enabled Allied airpower to attack the German forces.

It might have been thought that there was now overall agreement on how the Allies were to react to the German offensive, but Montgomery was intent on stirring things whenever he could, again telling London on 25 December: 'The American armies in the north are in a complete muddle'.[202] The truth was that, as usual, Montgomery had decided to 'tidy up' the defences on his front and was making sure that his enemy had safely exhausted itself before contemplating any counter-offensive. This caused an unnecessary pause of some days before the forces under his command would make any impression on the Germans. However, and as he had intended, the British press had an absolute field day with his distorted comments and the *Daily Mail* carried the following headlines:

MONTGOMERY FORESAW ATTACK
HIS TROOPS WERE ALL READY TO MARCH
ACTED 'ON OWN' TO SAVE DAY[203]

No one could blame the paper for what they had printed because the impression they gained was precisely what Montgomery had intended. The problem was how to undo the damage he had deliberately caused because no newspaper was likely to print a retraction of what Britain's leading field marshal had said.

Even before he had made his eventual move to attack the Germans, Montgomery had caused such annoyance with his continuous criticisms of the way Eisenhower was handling the Ardennes offensive that matters came to a head in late December. The final straw was a letter from Montgomery to Eisenhower in which he virtually informed Eisenhower what he should be doing and how to do it, and did so in a fashion of such provocation and insolence that, being written by a subordinate, even the patient and mild-mannered Eisenhower had had enough. Coming on top of his distortions for the British press, this was just too much and resulted in a telegram from General George Marshall in the United States, making it totally clear to Eisenhower that no concessions to Montgomery's ideas should even be contemplated.

Totally reinforced in his position, Eisenhower wrote to Montgomery telling him to keep quiet in future, or if he didn't like it, to take issues up with the Combined Chiefs of Staff. This ultimatum should have got through even Montgomery's thick skin, but the fundamental seriousness of the situation that he faced still did not sink in until it was driven home to him in no uncertain terms by his chief of staff, the now Major-General de Guingand, who, unlike Montgomery, had sensibly maintained friendly relations with Eisenhower's HQ and was only too aware of the serious implications behind the unusually threatening tone of Marshall's telegram. The reality of his delicate position did sink in this time and on 31 December Montgomery was forced to write an almost grovelling letter of apology to Eisenhower, reading:

> Dear Ike, I have seen Freddie [de Guingand] and understand you are greatly worried by many considerations in these very difficult days. I have given you my frank views because I have felt you like this. I am sure there are many factors which have a bearing quite beyond anything I realise. Very distressed that my letter may have upset you and I would ask you to tear it up. Your very devoted subordinate, Monty.[204]

And thus, as Alun Chalfont says, did Montgomery, a recently appointed field marshal, 'narrowly escape having his head cut off.'[205] It is not generally realised just how close Marshall and Eisenhower came to demanding that Montgomery be removed and replaced by someone else, and had he not written that 'very devoted subordinate' letter, it seems almost certain that he would have been. But the Allies cause had always been as much political as purely military and although there were bound to be instances of differing opinions, Montgomery's attitude and behaviour towards his superiors had been nothing less than discourteous, disobedient and rebellious. Montgomery was not a habitual gambler, but he seems to have tested his luck in the knowledge that he had Brooke as his mentor behind him and in the belief that, politically, the Americans would probably not have wanted to embarrass their British allies by making such a demand. Not that it would have caused much in the way of operational difficulties to replace Montgomery because at that stage in the European campaign and with the inevitable result being only a matter of time, there were plenty of senior commanders who could easily have taken over.

Fortunately for Montgomery Eisenhower was not a vindictive person but a patient man of quiet demeanour, and his letter was not released. Given the degree to which Montgomery had consistently acted as if he and not Eisenhower were in charge, publication of that letter might have been fully justified if only to finally put a stop to his insubordinate antics. Had it been released, it would have caused huge humiliation for him, a man who had only recently been elevated to the most senior rank in the British Army and now was being forced into an abject kowtow to an American general. The papers of the day, especially in the United States, would have run riot with their headlines and for once Montgomery might have found he was the prey and not the hero of the press. It is not clear whether Churchill was aware of the letter—probably not—but he too would have been highly embarrassed that a man he had judged to be fit for top promotion had been obliged to write such a letter. Field marshal rank carries with it obligations that go beyond the merely military—innate instincts for tact and diplomacy are expected—and yet here was his most recent appointment behaving as though he was some recalcitrant corporal.

However, a personal letter written to Eisenhower was not going to put any stop to Montgomery's self-serving and twisted press announcements, and just one week later he set about things once more, holding a news conference where he said:

> Von Rundstedt attacked on December 16th. He obtained tactical surprise. He drove a deep wedge into the centre of First US Army and split the American forces in two. As soon as I saw what was happening I took certain steps myself to ensure that IF the Germans got to the Meuse they would certainly not get over the river i.e. I was thinking ahead. I employed the whole available power of the

British Group of Armies. Finally it was put into battle with a bang and today British divisions are fighting hard on the right flank of First US Army. You thus have the picture of British troops fighting on both sides of American forces who have suffered a hard blow.[206]

According to his biographer Alun Chalfont, Montgomery's version of the way the Germans were halted caused even more offence. Chalfont wrote: 'He said he had put his men "into battle with a bang." But he did not begin offensive operations until 3 January—twelve days after Patton, from the south, had counter-attacked, and effectively sealed the fate of the Germans'.[207] The facts were distinctly different. Rather than taking steps as soon as he saw what had happened, Montgomery had in fact virtually sat on his hands for a couple of weeks and had made no real move against the Germans until 3 January. For the first week the Americans had handled every aspect of the German breakthrough and had then counter-attacked. Before making any move, Montgomery had waited until the skies had cleared and he could have the support of the formidable Allied airpower that could be unleashed against von Rundstedt's forces. A case of the heroic British going to the aid of the beleaguered Americans, it most certainly was not.

Quite naturally, this grotesque misrepresentation provoked fury amongst the Americans and confusion within the United States media, who naturally wanted to know exactly what was going on. Shaking his head in sad resignation, General Bradley described Montgomery's actions as pouring gasoline on a fire. Eisenhower telephoned Churchill to explain their annoyance and asked that the British press should take steps to clarify the false impression that had been created. Churchill could not do much about the papers and nothing appeared in the press, but the political repercussions resulting from what were not mere indiscretions but deliberate insults from a British commander of Montgomery's standing did require some public clarification to put the Ardennes matter straight.

The widening rift between the two allies caused by Montgomery's lies and distortions was such that on 18 January Churchill felt obliged to correct the matter by making the following detailed statement of the true position in the House of Commons:

I have seen it suggested that the terrific battle which has been proceeding since December 21 on the American Front is an Anglo-American battle. In fact, however, the United States troops have done almost all the fighting and suffered almost all the losses. The Americans have engaged 30 or 40 men to every one we have engaged and they have lost 60 to 80 men for every one of us. That is a point I wish to make. Care must be taken in telling our proud tale not to claim for the British army an undue share of what is undoubtedly the greatest American battle of the War and will, I believe, be regarded as an ever famous American victory. Let no one lend themselves to the shouting of mischief making when issues of this momentous consequence are being successfully decided by the sword.[208]

When writing his memoirs in 1953, however, Churchill included only a much-sanitised version of this statement, carefully omitting the full facts he had been obliged to state publicly; Montgomery's reputation was still being protected.[209]

The German offensive was not finally defeated until 23 January 1945. Exact casualty details are not available but in rough figures the Americans suffered some 89,000 killed, wounded, captured or missing as against Montgomery's losses which totalled some 1,400. Figures can sometimes be misleading, but in this case they do provide an accurate comparison of the relative contributions made by the two allies to defeat Hitler's gamble: 98.5 per cent of the load had been carried by the Americans and despite his posturing, Montgomery's share had actually been no more than about 1.5 per cent. The American's ultimate success had of course not been solely due to Patton and his speedy reaction, but by his quickly changing the direction of an army of 250,000 together with 130,000 tanks and trucks in thick fog and over icebound roads. It meant that the German's encountered firm resistance and were strongly counter-attacked far sooner than they had thought would be possible.

It had been a situation that required speed and flexibility of response, neither of which were exactly Montgomery's best-known characteristics, the essence of which was encapsulated by Eisenhower in his 1948 book *Crusade in Europe*, where he states:

Our flexibility was nowhere better illustrated than during the German counter-offensive in the Ardennes when Patton's army ceased its preparations for an eastwards attack, changed front, and undertook a movement extending over sixty to seventy miles at right angles to its former direction of advance. In less than seventy-two hours from the time Patton's staff had its orders an entire corps of his army had initiated a new attack.[210]

In his *Memoirs* written some 14 years later, Montgomery makes only fleeting mention of the Ardennes offensive, stating: 'I think the less one says about this battle the better, for I fancy that whatever I say will be resented'.[211] For once, given the facts of the matter, Montgomery was unusually right to keep his thoughts to himself. However, although he does indeed say little, his book includes a misleading map of the 'Bulge' showing only what he terms the 'Allied Counter-Offensive Launched 3 Jan 1945'. This shows the Allies, British and American, attacking from the north, west and south— there is no mention of the attack made by the Americans from the *south* some 12 days earlier, nor the fact that Patton had started moving several days before that. Even when actually saying little, through deliberate omission Montgomery still contrived to distort facts to his own advantage. In his brief narrative he goes even further and describes the German action as having caused the American command to be 'crestfallen'—it was just as well for Montgomery that George Patton had died as a result of a freak road accident some years before he made that scurrilous allegation; but Patton—crestfallen?

It was because of distortions such as these that Correlli Barnett felt compelled to write *The Desert Generals*. That it had indeed been Patton's swift reaction that caused the German offensive to lose early momentum is confirmed by General Heinz Guderian in his book *Panzer Leader*.[212] He says there that disruption was caused by Manteuffel having to move parts of his Fifth Panzer Army armour south to strengthen the left flank of the Seventh Army and from that point on a breakthrough in the grand manner was no longer possible. He goes on to say that by 22 December it was plain that a less ambitious objective should have been chosen and by 24 December it was clear to any perceptive soldier that the offensive had finally broken down. All of this was some 10 days before Montgomery himself admitted that he made any move.

That it had indeed mainly been Patton's almost lightning response that had caused the German breakout to stall at the very beginning is mentioned thus by General Omar Bradley:

> True to his boast at Verdun, Patton, having turned his Third Army ninety degrees, attacked on December 22. His generalship during this difficult manoeuvre was magnificent, one of the most brilliant performances by any commander on either side in World War II. It was absolutely his cup of tea—rapid, open warfare combined with noble purpose and difficult goals. Patton's objective was to inflict maximum damage on the German salient. Equally important was to relieve our forces at Bastogne.[213]

Patton's almost instinctive reaction was essentially what is described as *coup d'oeil*, a confident commander's strategic intuition, and that intuition itself being based on experienced insight, inquisitiveness, comprehension and determination. It is what has been termed a high level of situational awareness that the mind would ordinarily miss or would perceive only after long study and refection.[214] *Coup d'oeil* is also the swift reaction to a situation that is perceived as demanding an immediate response. This may involve acting upon the instant recognition of an opportunity to be exploited, or, as in the case of the German Ardennes offensive, the speedy appreciation of a danger requiring rapid reaction. In either case it is the quickness of response that either takes advantage of an opportunity or enables a dire situation to be contained or averted; above all perhaps, acting upon a *coup d'oeil* requires confidence and courage. As Basil Liddell Hart put it in his 1944 book *Thoughts on War*: 'A vital faculty of generalship is the power of grasping *instantly* the picture on the ground and the situation, of relating one to the other, and the local to the general'.[215] Instinctive and rapid reaction was a characteristic hallmark of Patton but it was one that was virtually non-existent in Montgomery.

It was during the initial German thrust that the US 101st Airborne Division was besieged at Bastogne. Their commanding officer, General Maxwell Taylor, was away and in his absence General Anthony McAuliffe was in command and became famous when he replied 'nuts' to a German demand that he surrender. When he heard of this retort, Patton commented: 'Any General of mine who is capable of such eloquence deserves to be rescued'.

Despite all his posturing, lies, distortions and exaggerations, Montgomery's contribution to stemming the German Ardennes offensive had been minimal, probably of the order of the above mentioned figure of 1.5 per cent. As usual, while it seems he just could not stand the thought that someone else might gain any kudos, the fact that 'someone' was Patton perhaps explains the quite extraordinary lengths to which Montgomery went to claim a disproportionate contribution for himself and play down all others. It seems remarkable that Montgomery had been allowed to get away with spreading so much fiction, insulting so many people, in so many places and caused so many problems for so long, but by this time—early in 1945—it seems possible that if they could avoid it, neither Churchill nor Brooke could see much point in changing their top horse in Europe so close to what must be nearing the end of the race.

Reference has been elsewhere made to Eisenhower's extraordinary patience in his handling of Montgomery and having to put up with his consistently offensive behaviour and insolence. His calm demeanour is all the more remarkable when one considers that at the time of the Ardennes offensive Eisenhower had under his command some seventy-three divisions, of which twelve were British as against forty-nine American (the balance being made up of eight French, three Canadian and one Polish). In other words the Americans made up some 68 per cent of the Allied effort as against Britain's contribution of around 16 per cent and yet despite this massive disparity in forces Montgomery was behaving as if he was at least an equal partner if not in overall charge. It says a lot about the Americans' generosity of spirit and patience that they tolerated this and that neither Roosevelt nor Marshal demanded Montgomery be replaced, which given the Allies overwhelming superiority in numbers would not have been difficult.

But, in the end, were all these bizarre transgressions really just symptoms of the underlying psychiatric condition from which it now seems certain that Montgomery suffered? As already quoted, military historians Anthony Beevor and Nigel Hamilton have both pointed to evidence of a deep-seated insecurity and lack of confidence, Hamilton going so far as to describe Montgomery as an 'emotional cripple'. Therefore, it seems entirely possible, perhaps even probable, that his insecurity coupled with an inferiority complex and yet craving the public eye, there was an uncontrollable compulsion to continually proclaim his greatness, as much as to quell his own self-doubts as to further his career. His consistent refusal to concede that anything had not gone completely according to his plan would be consistent with the self-delusion without which he could not perform. Admittedly, this is speculation, but it all fits and provides a very plausible explanation to what is otherwise an enigma.

CHAPTER 13

MOUNTBATTEN'S CATASTROPHE— INDIAN INDEPENDENCE

Attlee appointed Admiral 'Dickie' Mountbatten,
the favourite cousin of King George, to serve as
Britain's last viceroy. But Mountbatten was
neither wise enough nor patient enough to accomplish
what many older and more experienced British
predecessors had failed to do.
—STANLEY WOLPERT, *Shameful Flight*

Winston Churchill may well have been the ruthless and meddling politician who caused more problems than he solved during World War II but he did have a sense of history and national obligation. Independence for India had been set by the government of Clement Attlee for 30 June 1948 and during the parliamentary debate over Indian independence in March 1947, Churchill asked:

Was this to be Operation *Scuttle*? The Government by their 14 months time limit have put an end to all prospects of Indian unity. How can one suppose that the thousand year gulf which yawns between Moslem and Hindu will be bridged in 14 months? It is astounding.[216]

Churchill called the proposed time limit a kind of guillotine designed to cut all the long-united services, and that it would not merely partition, but would bring about the fragmentation of India. He went on to say:

> How can we walk out of India and leave behind a war between 90 million Muslims and 200 million caste Hindus? Will it not be a terrible disgrace to our name if we allow one fifth of the population of the globe to fall into chaos and carnage? Would it not be a world crime that would stain our name forever? We must do our best in all circumstances but, at least, let us not add by shameful flight, by a premature hurried scuttle to the pangs of sorrow so many of us feel, the tint and smear of shame.[217]

It is not at all clear just why British Prime Minister Clement Attlee decided that Mountbatten was the right man or even the best person Britain could find for a complex, difficult and sensitive task that clearly required wisdom, patience and a willingness to listen and learn, for he had not one of these characteristics. In 1946 British India (excluding Burma) covered a vast area of some 4,200,000km² with a population of 340 million and over 20 different languages; 60 per cent of this area consisted of British provinces, and the remaining 40 per cent was made up of 562 princely states, one of which was Hyderabad, which was only slightly smaller than present-day Germany. It was an undertaking that would require diplomacy, tact and moreover a deep understanding and appreciation of the diverse histories, cultures, religions and politics of a land that had been held together as an entity only through the firm and sometimes brutal hand of an independent third party—the British Crown.

Mountbatten was headstrong, convinced that he was always right and unless they could be useful to him, he was not interested in other people or their views; he was above all else interested in promoting himself. In many reckless actions throughout the war he had demonstrated a complete indifference to the consequences of a succession of rash decisions, and bolstered by support from Churchill had been concerned only with enhancing his own reputation. In an ironic twist, Mountbatten, who had seemed untouchable in his irresponsible wartime escapades, was to adjudicate a culture where to be 'Untouchable' (to use the contemporary term) was quite the opposite of the privileged and protected standing in his own society.

From 1943 to 1945 Mountbatten had been in charge of South-East Asia Command (SEAC), in which role his actual contribution to victory in Burma had amounted to little more than top-level window dressing since all strategic decisions were taken by his subordinates. It is possible that this geographical experience may have influenced the British government, after all, superficially at least, 'he'd been there, hadn't he?' However, he would have had little if any meaningful contact with the local populace since his role was essentially to assist in winning the war against the Japanese, and in any event soon after assuming his command Mountbatten moved his head-quarters from New Delhi to a much more comfortable and cooler setting in the hills of Ceylon. During this earlier time, moreover, both Gandhi and Nehru were in prison, having been banished there by the British Raj for their roles in the 1942 'Quit India' campaign.

Before departing on his mission Mountbatten would have done him-self, the British government and India no harm by keeping in mind the words of a man who had spent some time in India, Rudyard Kipling:

> Now it is not good for the Christian's health
> To hustle the Aryan brown
> For the Christian riles and the Aryan smiles
> And he weareth the Christian down;
> And the end of the fight is a tombstone white
> With the name of the late deceased
> And an epitaph drear 'A fool lies here
> Who tried to hustle the East.'

Words of wisdom indeed, but they would have fallen on the stony ground of Mountbatten's persona. Moreover, as anyone who has held dis-cussions in Asia will tell, and this is as true today as it was then, one must first get to know the person with whom one would like to negotiate; one does not just charge in and immediately start talking business. As Kipling wrote, 'the Christian riles and the Aryan smiles'. Commenting on this, American historian Stanley Wolpert wrote in his 2006 book *Shameful Flight*: 'Mountbatten did not have the humility or good sense to listen to India's two wisest political leaders, Mahatma Gandhi and Mohammed Ali Jinna, both of whom tried their frail best to warn him to stop the runaway jug-

gernaut to Partition before it was too late'.[218] Humility was another trait
that was singularly absent from the Mountbatten persona and any suggestion that he was in any way humble would have been greeted with hilarity.
In fact such was his vanity and obsession with his image that when originally advised to arrive in India wearing an informal lounge suit, he had
protested. Thus provoked, when he did arrive on 22 March 1947, it resulted
in him appearing at the door of his aircraft on landing, wearing a glittering
white dress-uniform together with medals all across his chest. Thus dramatically attired he and Edwina were driven to the viceroy's residence in
an open landau with cavalry escort. Style without substance perhaps, but
this was Mountbatten.

Beset with a myriad of financial problems at home and, through its
own political dogma, anxious to be rid of India as soon as possible, the
British Labour government decided in February 1947 that independence
should be completed by 30 June 1948. The date was demanded by Mountbatten if he was to take the position because he feared that being away from
the navy for too long would jeopardise his ambitions at the Admiralty; he
also made it clear to Attlee that his absence from the navy was to be regarded as only temporary. In true British fashion, the government intended
this to be presented to the world as a triumph of British wisdom, states-
manship, benevolence and a long-intended culmination; the truth was that
Britain was bankrupt at the end of the war and had little alternative but to
bow out with as little overt humiliation as possible. The target date allowed
only a fairly short horizon, an assignment that would have been daunting
for even the steady and most experienced of hands, but under the self-as-
sured yet amateurish stewardship of someone like Mountbatten it was
rather like putting him on a bobsleigh on the Cresta Run and at the same
time telling him to go slowly.

There does not appear to be any evidence that he took any pains to study
his coming responsibilities in any depth as might have been expected for
anyone asked to venture upon such a complex task, merely asking Attlee for
a deadline. That his onerous mandate was to find a mechanism for the orderly transfer of over 300 years of British rule in a matter of some 15 months
did not seem to faze him in the slightest.

Surprisingly, considering his aristocratic connections, he was known
to be left-wing in his political views and this, plus the fact that he had spent

a couple of years in that part of the world, may also have supported his suit-ability. An unfortunate indication of his shallow priorities came at the very beginning of his tenure. In his 1994 book *Eminent Churchillians,* Andrew Roberts recounts Mountbatten's childish glee when describing the pomp and ceremony of his installation as viceroy:

> What a ceremony! Everyone who mattered was there. All the Princes. All the leaders. All the diplomats. I put on everything. My white full dress uniform. Orders, decorations, medals, the lot . . . Obviously I wore the Order of the Garter. I then wore the Star of India, I was the Grand Master of the Order. I wore the Star of the Indian Empire and then I wore the Royal Victorian Order and that made four; that's all you're allowed to wear. And I wore the aigu-illettes as personal aide-de-camp to the King-Emperor.[219]

It all sounds rather like having put Dracula in charge of the blood bank.

Limited by his own narrow appreciation of people, Mountbatten was liable to form naive opinions far too quickly. To quote Andrew Roberts once more: 'He saw Nehru as an aristocratic radical leader in his own mould. "When Nehru began to call Edwina and me 'dear friends'," Mount-batten was later to gush, "I began to get the feeling that we were half-way home."' He had no experience at all in diplomacy and this impressionable view was to prove only a half-truth. His biased estimation was in complete contrast with his opinion of the elegant and shrewd Muslim leader Muham-mad Ali Jinnah whom he said he found negative and evasive, and this prej-udice was made all the more dangerous by the fact that Nehru and Edwina Mountbatten quickly established what was widely seen in New Delhi as a 'relationship'. As had been the case in the past, Mountbatten seems to have regarded such a 'friendship' perhaps as an asset, which in the public eye it certainly was not, or alternatively to have turned his own blind eye to it. Either way it meant that very early on he had allowed himself to be com-promised—both in the marital sense and as an impediment to the achieve-ment of the British government's objective of impartial consensus.

In the 47 years from the turn of the 20th century to the time of his ar-rival, there had been eight previous viceroys, none of them serving for a period of less than 5 years and one or two somewhat longer. His immediate predecessor, Field Marshal Sir Archibald Wavell, had spent much of his childhood in India and had over 2 years' experience of the country as Commander-in-Chief, India before becoming viceroy in 1943. All of the others had either significant diplomatic and/or political experience to draw on and several had been governors in the Dominions before assuming the position.

The distances were vast: New Delhi to Madras was 1,800km, and across the country Karachi to Calcutta was even further, some 2,200km. In addition to the cultural, racial and religious mix, there were huge differences in topography and climate. For such a complex job Mountbatten had none of these experiences and yet, instead of taking time to settle in, travel the country and familiarise himself with as many aspects as possible, he charged in at breakneck speed. Viewed in retrospect it seems fairly clear that from the very outset he had decided that he was going to get even the most complex issues decided as soon as possible and that the various completion dates had been in his mind from the beginning.

Mountbatten began meetings with his staff immediately and at the fourth of such meetings within just a week of his arrival, he was already stressing the importance of speed. This in itself seems strange, for if he was intending to work within the framework of the 15-month period agreed with the British government, there should have been no need to move with such urgency right from the very beginning. The wisest course would surely have been for him to gradually find his feet in what was a totally new environment and situation. That he did not do so points to the fact that he never had any intention of considering 30 June 1948 as his goalpost but had firmly at the back of his mind returning to the Admiralty in time to achieve his long-standing ambition of becoming First Sea Lord, the role his father had held before being sidelined for political convenience by Churchill in 1914.

When he did eventually meet Mahatma Gandhi for the first time, he found him tedious; a more experienced negotiator might have recognised the need for an indulgent and forbearing attitude in order to elicit and weigh up the depths and meanings behind Gandhi's words. It was well known that Gandhi could be abstruse, thus requiring all the more subtlety and perception. Mountbatten decided that although he could not ignore Gandhi because he was an iconic figure, he had said nothing of any value. From then on his relationship with the devout and honest Gandhi was nothing like as trusting or appreciative as would probably have been the case had Mountbatten been a man of greater diplomatic experience. He could and should have realised that, above all, Gandhi wanted to avoid a break-up of India and that Gandhi was in neither the Muslim League nor the Indian Congress camps, but blinded by his haste, Mountbatten had no time for the niceties of patient discussion and negotiation with someone he had never understood and could not be bothered to even attempt to.

Both Mountbatten and his wife, in their somewhat differing ways, spent far too much private time with Nehru. The reason, for Mountbatten at least, was that he did find Nehru congenial company, but in so doing he seemed to be totally indifferent to the unavoidable subliminal influence of the relationship. Jinnah could sometimes be rather oblique, but here again what was required was an ability to see through the overt and immediate façade. Had he spent as much time with Jinnah as he did with Nehru then India might have been spared the traumas consequent on Mountbatten's own ill-inspired ideas.

Within a few short weeks Mountbatten felt he knew enough to produce his first plan, known now as 'Mountbatten's May Plan', which he announced on 3 May 1947. Although it was a mere 6 weeks since he had arrived, Mountbatten still felt that even in such a short time he had produced a solution that had eluded more experienced and wiser men before him. In just 42 days he had come up with an answer that others, even after months and years of consideration, had found impossible. This plan was rejected by his friend Nehru on the basis that the divisions proposed would involve too much of what Nehru called the 'Balkanisation' of the country. Completely undeterred and convinced of his own infallibility and determined to quickly force something through, Mountbatten went back to his personal drawing board, and just 4 weeks later unveiled his 'June Plan', which proposed the partition of the country between India and what was to be called Pakistan. Believing that the areas allotted for Muslim majorities could never survive economically and would return to the fold, Nehru and his party agreed; Gandhi was non-committal and the despairing Jinnah was pressured by Mountbatten to accept what was in effect a fait accompli.

In so pressuring the various parties, Mountbatten had shown little or no concern for the monumental demographic/religious problems that his proposals would present to those areas where there were mixed Hindu/

Muslim communities. Shortly after the shelving of his May Plan he told the British government that communal trouble would not be tolerated and would if necessary be dealt with through the use of bombing and machine gunning from the air. The likely problems were especially acute in the north-west province, the Punjab and in Bengal in the south-east and there were other areas of minority religions such as Sikhs, Buddhists and Christians. These difficulties might have been resolved, or certainly far better handled, had a reasonable time frame of some months been provided, which could possibly have been achieved given the original deadline of 30 June 1948; but with his frenetic pace ever accelerating, any such concerns were given short shrift. Such was Mountbatten's impatience that it prompted the Secretary of Bengal, Sir John Dawson Tyson, to write with some prescience from Calcutta on 5 July:

> Mountbatten is a hustler: ever since he came out he has pursued shock tactics. He made his plan and soon after that the blitz began. And since the time when he launched his blitz he has given no-one any rest—the Indian leaders least of all. He has kept them so busy— so much on the run—that they have not had time to draw breath and criticize. There will be very unsettled conditions in India for some time to come but the trouble will be primarily between Hindus and Muslims—not anti-European. The India after 15th August will not be the kind of country I should want to live in.[220]

Dawson Tyson had held various positions in the Indian Civil Service since 1920 and during that time had travelled widely throughout the country. Like most who had served India for so long, he was genuinely concerned for the wellbeing of its peoples, he was aware that even in the best of settled times large swathes of the population faced a fragile and precarious existence, and human beings could not be coldly moved around like so many pawns on a political chessboard. Under Mountbatten's direction, a Boundary Commission was quickly established to resolve these problems, its instructions being to 'demarcate the boundaries on the basis of ascertaining the contiguous majority areas of Muslims and non Muslims. In doing so, it will also take into account other factors.' As an ominous precursor, the 'other factors' were left undefined.

Appointed as chairman of the Boundary Commission was Sir Cyril Radcliffe, a 48-year-old English lawyer who although having achieved some legal prominence after World War I and having served as director general of the Ministry of Information from 1941, had no experience at all in the well-established procedures and information needed to draw a boundary. Radcliffe was in charge of two commissions, one for the Punjab and another for Bengal. Radcliffe had never previously set one foot on Indian soil, and although this was, naively, accepted by the Indian parties concerned as an indication of impartiality, it did not of course prevent him from looking after the interests of the party who had engaged him, Britain. Radcliffe was also given considerable leeway by the words *'other factors'* in his terms of reference.

So frantic was Mountbatten's programme for early independence that when Radcliffe did eventually arrive in India on 8 July 1947, he was immediately instructed that he had to complete his redrawing of boundaries within 5 weeks. This absurd time frame was total madness, for as Radcliffe himself said later, it was so complex an assignment that he might have been able to make a reasonable job of it had he been given 18 months instead of 35 days; but having accepted the engagement he got on with the job. Working with equal commission numbers of Muslim League and Indian Congress representatives, who could never agree, Radcliffe found himself as the only person prepared to make a decision, but never having visited India and knowing no one there, his position was almost impossible. Nonetheless he persisted, and in total secrecy he gradually carried out his instructions with complete indifference to the local consequences of boundaries drawn though thickly populated areas, or in some cases a boundary that even ran right through the middle of a house. Certainly this was, on the face of it impartial, but it was also the recipe for massive communal violence on a scale the world had never seen.

In all this Radcliffe was in frequent touch with Mountbatten, but having completed his appointed task, he carefully destroyed all his papers and made sure he had left India before his boundaries were published. He later said that he was so shocked to learn of the loss of life caused by his new boundaries that he returned his fee of 40,000 rupees, or about £21,000. Whether as quietly promised or as an official reward is not clear, and of course it might have been quite coincidental, but shortly after returning to England

Radcliffe was made a privy councillor and a lord of appeal (although he had never been a judge), and was also created a life peer as Baron Radcliffe of Werneth in the County of Lancaster. The whole affair had about it the nasty miasma of underhand dealings, of tacit deals between 'chaps who understood each other', for if not, then why the need to destroy papers that might have justified and explained decisions that were ostensibly made on a basis that was totally impartial? Adding to that, when questioned about this, Mountbatten expressly denied he'd had any special knowledge and nor had he influenced anything.

It smelled then and it stinks today, and what adds even more unsavoury odour to the whole affair was the fact that although Mountbatten had scheduled Independence Day for midnight 14/15 August 1947, the Congress and Muslim parties were given no more than 2 hours to study the boundaries late in the afternoon of the day before. To take the stench of this foul-smelling manipulation even further, if that were possible, Mountbatten then delayed publication of the new boundaries until 2 days after the actual ceremony of independence. This resulted in innocent but suspicious communities all over what had been British India being bewildered, not to say outraged, to discover that they were living in a country different from that which they had, logically, believed themselves to be in. The new boundaries were controversial, provocative and divisive but politically convenient, and Mountbatten knew there would be massive violence. By delaying the publication of the new boundaries he had ducked any responsibility for public order and dropped the problem into the laps of the fledgling governments of the new India and Pakistan, neither of whom were either prepared for or had the resources to handle the disturbances. It would thus no longer be Britain's problem. Almost 2,000 years previously Herod had washed his hands; in 1947 Mountbatten was now doing the same. The expression 'Perfidious Albion' is believed to have originated in France but it could just as easily have been coined in India.

One of the most ill-considered steps taken by Mountbatten was to award the north-western Princely State of Jammu-Kashmir to India. With an area of some 130,000km², it was second in size only to Hyderabad, with a population of 4 million of which 76 per cent were Muslim and only 22 per cent Hindu. The ruler was, however, a Hindu and although other states had, logically, been awarded either to India or Pakistan according to the religious majority of the population (irrespective of the wishes of their rulers), in the case of the strategically important Jammu-Kashmir Mountbatten made an exception and allowed the ruler to make his own decision.

This was flagrantly pro-Nehru, whose home state was Kashmir, and was seen as such. The ruler initially wanted to stay independent of either of the new states but Kashmir had an 800km border with the new state of Pakistan and following publication of the new boundary there were incursions by indignant Muslim irregulars from Pakistan. Upon this the ruler requested military help from India and Nehru was prepared to provide assistance. For reasons that have never been properly explained Nehru's arm was twisted by Mountbatten advising him to do nothing unless the ruler first agreed that his state would join India.

Prior to this, however, and in another 'exception', large portions of the Punjab which were predominantly Muslim and therefore should clearly have become part of Pakistan were nonetheless awarded to India rather than Pakistan to allow India access to the state of Jammu-Kashmir. The first boundaries drawn by Radcliffe in line with this rule of thumb were altered at Mountbatten's behest, despite months of dire warnings from the governor of the Punjab, Sir Evan Jenkins, who had been in India for over 45 years. Without such 'access' India would have had no claim to Kashmir, and even ignoring the strategic value of that area, it was the homeland of Nehru and as we have seen Mountbatten felt that Nehru was his 'sort of chap'. To go further and suggest that Edwina Mountbatten might have had some sort of influence is of course speculation, but the possibility is worth bearing in mind. The whole arrangement was transparently duplicitous and set the stage for a tragic, avoidable but understandable conflagration that continues to this day.

To such an extent was it known that the new boundaries would provoke sectarian violence that a special Punjab Boundary Force was put together a month before Independence Day. Required to safeguard an area the size of Ireland, the force of some 15,000 that was so frantically assembled was pathetically inadequate, meaning as it did just one soldier for every 600 civilians. In the event the controversial new boundaries in the Punjab caused the displacement of over 9 million people, 5.3 million being Muslims with the balance Hindus and Sikhs, moving either east or west in what became known as the Punjab Holocaust of 1947. The total number killed in what would now be called 'ethnic cleansing', has never been accurately established, but certainly the numbers were well over 500,000 and may be as high as 800,000. In Bengal, the new boundaries also caused a huge east and west movement of humankind involving millions of people, and although the numbers were lower than in the case of the Punjab, thousands of lives were lost. But, just as in the Punjab, the new lines of demarcation were so hurriedly and arbitrarily drawn that they made little if any sense, and they still do not today. True to form, Mountbatten professed regret at what he termed the tragic loss of life and claimed he had had no idea that this was likely to occur. In truth, he was as callously indifferent to the outcome of his actions as he had been to the loss of life he caused as Captain of HMS *Kelly*, his ordering of the tragic attack on Dieppe and his disastrous 'invasion' of Malaya.

A brief summary of the way in which the transfer of power should and could so easily have been handled appears in Andrew Roberts' *Eminent Churchillians*:

> Mountbatten should have given Radcliffe at least six months to make his Award, from, say, April to October 1947. During the next six months he should have deployed a massively enlarged Punjab Boundary Force in the general area of Radcliffe's proposed frontier—and particularly in Sikh territory. The Indian army could have been split between the two Dominions in that time, and also deployed. Then in 1948 he could have announced the Award, sustained by an undertaking that Britain would provide safe conduct for any Hindu, Muslim or Sikh family which wished to migrate across the frontier. The original deadline could then have been adhered to, and the new states not born during a bloody haemorrhage.[221]

The accuracy of what this plan might have achieved is borne out by the control that the governor of the Punjab, Sir Evan Jenkins, achieved. He was able to prevent large-scale killings until he was obliged to hand over control to the newly born governments on 15 August.

Mountbatten had successfully managed to persuade the British government that relentless speed was essential for a successful withdrawal from

India. He had told them that it would only be the shock of suddenly realising that the British were going, and going immediately, that would bring the dissenting parties to their senses; there is not one jot of evidence to support his theory. The ulterior motive and the real *raison d'être* for his haste had little if anything to do with Indian politics or personalities, but concerned his lifelong ambition to seek retribution for his father's treatment at the hands of Churchill in 1914 and become the First Sea Lord. He had gone along with Attlee's 30 June 1948 deadline, so he was committed to India in one shape or form until then; to have returned to London immediately following the August 1947 independence date would have revealed his hand. As it was, following independence, he became India's first governor-general, but conveniently only until 21 June 1948. He had wanted to hold the same position in Pakistan too, but Jinnah would have none of it. When he left, he received a glowing tribute from Nehru, who said: 'You came here, Sir, with a high reputation, but many a reputation has foundered in India. You lived here through a period of great difficulty and crisis, and yet your reputation has not foundered. That is a remarkable feat.'[222] Well might Nehru have voiced those sentiments, because through Mountbatten's haste, incompetence and bias, Nehru and India had obtained by far the largest slice of the cake. The small slice that became Pakistan was divided into two parts. In the west there was only one port, Karachi, and no industry. The eastern portion should logically have included Calcutta, but without that city, the economic viability of the eastern portion was bleak.

In view of the stigma that would be attached, several of those who had served in Mountbatten's administration declined his 'independence' honours. Andrew Roberts recounts the indignation of Mountbatten's chief of staff General Hastings Ismay when he discovered that, without consultation, Mountbatten had listed him for a GCSI (Knight Grand Commander of the Order of the Star of India). Ismay already held a higher order, GCB (Knight Grand Cross of the Order of the Bath), but apart from the lack of courtesy in not having been consulted, he told Mountbatten:

> You should have asked if I was willing to be recommended to a lower order. But that is not the point. Nothing on earth would induce me to accept an honour for the most painful and distasteful episode of my career. I must ask you to delete my name at once.[223]

Also not wishing to be part of any celebration was Field Marshal Sir Claude Auchinleck, Commander in Chief, India. Auchinleck, who had spent some 40 years of his life in India, loved the country and its peoples and spoke several local languages. He said he would accept a KG (Knight of the Order of the Garter) if offered, but not if it came on the recommendation of Mountbatten. Undeterred by such peripheral trivialities, on Independence Day Mountbatten had his own viscountcy raised to that of an earldom.

Those who had given their lives to the Indian Civil Service, such as the aforementioned Sir John Dawson Tyson and Sir Evan Jenkins, or who served in the Indian Army, such as Sir Claude Auchinleck, were distressed and sickened by the style of Britain's irresponsible and undignified scuttle, and what author Stanley Wolpert rightly described as a 'shameful flight'. What had required knowledge and understanding of the kaleidoscopic shades and nuances, the subtle and not so subtle influences, the gradual historical aggregation of what had made India what it was, had been handed to a shallow, self-absorbed individual more interested in maintaining his own glamorous image than caring for the welfare of others.

The pervading feeling of nausea was well described by John Connell in his book *Auchinleck,* where he stated:

> Parliament, the Press and the public at large in Britain had no idea, then or subsequently, of the ordeal to which the last of those who had held watch and ward in India were compelled to submit. It was expedient that the careers of these men should be terminated: was it necessary that their hearts should be broken, that they should have to stand, powerless, watching the destruction—or what at the time seemed the destruction—of all that they and their forebears had striven to build?[224]

Mountbatten wasted no time in pursuing his long-time objective. Only 4 days after leaving India he reported to the Lords of the Admiralty in London to see what opportunities were going—and that was just 5 days before the 30 June 1948 deadline originally agreed with Attlee.

CHAPTER 14

WORLD WAR II WITHOUT CHURCHILL?

*If Churchill was the man who won the war, as
election posters in 1945 said he was, then he was also
the man who by his flights of fancy, his unwillingness
to trust professionals and his unshakable belief that
he knew better than anyone else was very nearly
responsible for losing it.*
—GORDON CORRIGAN,
  Blood, Sweat and Arrogance

For some decades after the war the feeling of triumph that comes with victory persisted, and all who had featured prominently in that conflict were championed as having been the architects and/or heroes responsible. Since Churchill had been Prime Minister from 1940 to 1945 and had been portrayed as emblematic by the British press, it was only natural that this should have been especially so for him. However, after the first couple of years the glow of his image had dimmed and, much to the astonishment of many, Churchill and his Conservative Party were soundly beaten in the 1945 general election. To some this was base ingratitude but to most he and his social class seem to have been identified with the very reasons Britain had become embroiled in the first place. As he was warned by General Slim when he and Churchill first met in 1944, a very large proportion of the armed services in the Far East would not be voting for him and moreover they were hardly likely to vote into power the very sort of people who had been giving them orders for

200

the past 6 years. The print media might say one thing for national morale, but those actually involved saw a different side of the coin and knew the truth.

Nonetheless, being out of office did provide Churchill with the time and opportunity to write his own version of what had happened, the six volume set entitled *The Second World War,* which prominently featured himself, his orders and his own interpretation of events. However, more recent evaluations have caused a rethink of what he actually achieved as opposed to the conventional and orthodox view of the omnipotent and all conquering statesman. What would previously have been regarded as heresy is now being considered from a more rational and dispassionate perspective as the consequences of his impetuous or stubborn decisions have come under a microscope that would earlier have been left well alone as too hot to handle.

The enormous morale boosting value of Churchill's inspiring rhetoric cannot be denied, and almost certainly could not have been performed by anyone else. His 'British Bulldog' defiance and pugnacity gave heart to the nation when just about everything in Europe had fallen to Adolf Hitler. This cannot be taken away from him but the question should be asked whether his contribution was in fact more symbolic than material or functional. In other words, apart from this defiant image of proud nationalism at the beginning just what did Churchill actually accomplish that was so unique or could not have been achieved by anyone else in the same circumstances? Although having, however superficially, sustained British self-confidence during the initial period of anxiety, was the Churchill persona subsequently not at least as much a liability as an asset? Reassuring oratory that was heartening at the beginning later became little more than flowery grandiloquence. In other words, is Churchill's World War II reputation really based on his words in 1940, just as Montgomery's standing is based entirely on El Alamein? The difference is of course that Churchill's oratory was his and his alone and cannot be taken away from him, whereas Montgomery's standing rests on a self-created myth.

When Chamberlain stood down on 10 May 1940, there were really only a few possible candidates for his job, the foreign secretary Lord Halifax and Churchill; Sir Stafford Cripps might have been added as an outsider to that list. Just about everyone in all parties favoured Halifax, except Halifax himself who clearly did not relish the position, whereas Churchill was positively straining at the leash to obtain it. This was the post that he had coveted and had been his all-consuming target for well over 20 years, but in finally obtaining it in these circumstances he really became Prime Minister only by default. There is no doubt he relished this role at a time of war. He has been called a 'warmonger', a description that is perhaps unkind to the man, but as military historian Basil Liddell Hart accurately described him, he was 'the Great Animator of War', and Churchill himself admitted that he missed it when it was all over. To him war was a drug and he was hooked on it, but in administrative style he was more of a 'bull in a china shop' than a cohesive and rational manager.

Even before he grasped the mantle for which he had been aiming for so long, in his prior role as First Lord of the Admiralty he had already been largely responsible for the disaster at the neutral Norwegian port of Narvik in April 1940. Although it is some 250km north of the Arctic Circle, Narvik remains ice-free during winter. It is connected by rail through to Sweden and thus Swedish iron ore could be imported by Germany during winter when the Gulf of Bothnia is ice-bound; the idea was to prevent this. The whole hare-brained operation had mainly been his own creation and yet when almost inevitably it collapsed, Churchill, as would be the case so often in the following years, laid the blame in all directions; these were shades of things to come. Even Narvik was his second inspiration because a little earlier he had suggested that a battle fleet be dispatched to the Baltic, until it was pointed out to him that this really was not a very bright idea since the Baltic was almost completely landlocked. The price for Narvik was paid by Neville Chamberlain, for as Clive Ponting describes the position in his book *Churchill*:

> The political and military situation at the end of April 1940 was remarkably similar to that in May 1915. In both cases, after about nine months of war a botched military operation, largely brought about by Churchill's direction, produced a political crisis that led to the collapse of the Government and the creation of a national coalition. The difference was that the first time it almost ended Churchill's career; the second time it made him Prime Minister.[225]

For Churchill, war was like a boy playing with his tin soldiers, moving them here and there as the impulse came to him, and if it did not work or the moved went wrong, he could always start all over again. His penchant for making decisions without consultation provoked an open revolt within the military circles of Whitehall, a situation unknown to the public at large, which still thought of him as the man who had warned about German rearmament.

It has been stated, for instance by Richard Overy in his book *Why the Allies Won*, that Churchill was clear sighted in his pursuit of American assistance and his support for air power.[226] Given Britain's geographical and financial position in 1940, was this not merely recognising the obvious? Would or could another leader have made a different decision, or would they have had any other option? This is a question that appears either to have been avoided or overlooked, but it suggests that the steps taken were uniquely Churchill's whereas that is not the case. This is just one example where a common sense and obvious action taken by Churchill is elevated to the individual action of a genius.

Following the celebration about Dunkirk—in reality a defeat—the one way in which an island nation like Britain could retaliate at that time in the war was through air strikes, and it did not need any genius to have seen this. Hitler, too, recognised this and hence materialised the Battle of Britain only a couple of months later in July and August 1940 as a precursor to a possible German invasion. Churchill had nothing to do with either of these but the vital contribution that could be made by the RAF was clear in circumstances where both the army and the navy, much as they may have resented it, were dependant on the protection of the RAF.

However, within just a week or so of becoming Prime Minister, a hasty and opportunistic Churchill gave his first controversial and unilateral order of the war: the sinking of the French fleet which was lying peacefully at anchor at Mers-el-Kébir in French Algeria to prevent it falling into German hands. A 6-hour ultimatum was given by Churchill and even though just a little more time had been requested by the French navy for them to consider this deadline to allow British control, the British naval and aircraft bombardment went ahead.

Although this order was strongly opposed by both vice admirals Somerville and Cunningham, who at one point even considered resigning and refusing an order they considered would cause a totally unnecessary and shameful tragedy, it was rationalised by Churchill on the specious grounds that it was carried out to impress the Americans. Just how you create a positive image for someone you hope will help you by killing 1,300 of another friend's sailors is something of a mystery. Perhaps it was staged to show everyone just who was in charge; if so it would fit in with the ruthless and determined persona. But, once more, there are those who rationalise a decision that was made in haste whereas it has been demonstrated that a few more hours would probably have engendered a rethink on the part of the French, and a few hours in which the French could not have handed their ships to the Germans anyway. Unfortunately this episode was just a precursor to the ham-fisted but single-minded and impatient manner in which so many issues would be handled in the future.

In any event, although neutrality was America's official policy at that time, it did not need any brutal theatrics from Churchill for Roosevelt to clearly recognise that it was not in his country's interests for there to be a European continent completely dominated and controlled by a totalitarian state like Nazi Germany. Therefore, and despite Roosevelt's continued domestic statements reaffirming non-alignment, help, even though disguised, would be forthcoming. In various ways United States support gradually increased up to the Lend-Lease Act of 1941. The point should be made here that although British Prime Minster Churchill was credited with having achieved this, it had in fact been Roosevelt's initiative and there is no evidence that it would not have occurred had the Prime Minister of Britain been anyone else. Britain was desperate for American help and Washington DC was the obvious, indeed the only place, to go to seek operational and material assistance. For reasons of national prestige it was portrayed, without the full details being made public, as the outcome of the singular talents of Winston Churchill.

Numerous books have either been written on or have portrayed the relationship between Roosevelt and Churchill as being 'special', as a partnership that could only have occurred between those two individuals. Of course the idea makes good reading but the reality is that personally they had virtually nothing in common other than their shared purpose to defeat Germany and Japan; and despite there being areas where the interests of their respective nations did not coincide, it made strategic and political sense to find agreement where possible. Lord Moran, Churchill's physician, travelled with him constantly and wrote of his relationship with Roosevelt:

> Apart from some passing tribute to Roosevelt, he seldom seems to
> allude to him in his conversation. He never tells us of Roosevelt's
> views, nor are we regaled by what he said, or by stories about him.
> The cast of Roosevelt's mind—I am thinking of his preoccupation
> with social problems and the rights of the common man—struck no
> sparks in Winston's mind. The war was all they had in common.[227]

Again, and as in other areas, there is no evidence that another British
leader could not have found the same degree of mutuality or indeed might
have improved on it. At all of their meetings throughout the war, from the
first at Placentia Bay in August 1941—disguised as a fishing trip for the
benefit of the American public and kept secret in Britain—they were each
accompanied by their respective military advisers, but although Roosevelt
deferred to the views of his military chiefs, it soon became clear that
Churchill would be wearing several hats of his own choosing; this would
be the pattern for all future such meetings.

The difference between the two attitudes was not lost on the Americans, Diane K. DeWaters of the University of Texas describing it thus:
'Churchill always demanded that political matters be left to the politicians
and military matters be left to the generals. He himself, of course, could
be an exception to that rule'.[228] Despite official statements of total agreement Roosevelt was continuously telling Churchill that his thinking was
18th-century and that he was mainly concerned with the interests of the
British Empire and maintaining that empire—and Churchill being the imperialist that he was, Roosevelt's statement was entirely justified. The one
thing that can be said about the relationship is that it worked, because it
had to be made to work, but nothing like as well as it could have done if
the views and beliefs of the British leader had been less dogmatic and not
so rigidly anchored in the past.

Had there been another personality at the helm, someone less immersed in his own heritage and destiny and more inclined to recognise and
accept alternative views and wider experience, then it is quite likely that
Singapore might not have been lost. What can be said in that context is that
the loss of HMS *Prince of Wales* and HMS *Repulse* together with 800 lives

almost certainly would not have occurred. As we have seen in the chapter *Churchill and Singapore*, the resources so badly needed for Singapore could have been made available but were withheld on the direct orders of Churchill. Would any other Prime Minister not at least have considered the dire warning from Sir John Dill? It took a strange personality, which Churchill was, to dismiss out of hand such a categorical warning.

As military historian John Keegan described him, 'he was averse to the exegetical', and he did not like recommendations in writing because he could not then deny them having been made. Add to that the bipolar condition with the massive swings in mood and who knows in what state of mind Churchill might have been at any particular point in the war.

Major-General Sir John Kennedy was Director of Operations and Plans at the War Office from 1940 to 1943 and was therefore in a unique position to observe and experience the dictating style that Churchill imposed on others. In his book of that period, *The Business of War*, he writes:

> When Churchill's projects were finally thrown aside, after the useless expenditure of much labour and energy, he obviously did not realise that he had been saved from disasters. On the contrary, he seemed to think he had been thwarted by men who lacked initiative and courage. At times such as this, we often felt that we would give almost anything for a less colourful occupant of No 10.[229]

His book was published in 1957 when Churchill was still alive so it can be safely assumed that Kennedy was being restrained in his comment, but even then he goes on to criticise Churchill's consistent interfering, stating of one cable to Wavell:

> I said this was absolutely wrong; that we should not dictate strategy and tactics from London to a commander in the field, and that, if I were in Wavell's place, I should disregard it. In the desert the game to play was to fall back, as we did originally with the Italians, and choose the moment when the enemy was extended to fall upon him.

But Churchill was incapable of understanding this, or at least he refused to accept it. If a different individual with a more measured and less emotional style had been in charge, what might have been the outcome in the Middle East and the fate of those who were there? This is of course pure speculation but it would not be too fanciful to posit that had Wavell's problems (many of which had been created by Churchill) not been denigrated and had his achievements been appreciated and supported, then with the massive build-up in materials that was underway, that theatre might well have turned out in favour of the British without the need for the eventual support of the Americans through Operation *Torch*. This was Churchill's brainchild and although he persuaded Roosevelt, it was not favoured by either his own or the American chiefs of staff. But it does not require too much perspicacity to see that what he was also seeking, and what was at the back of his mind, was some way to clear north Africa so as to make the Mediterranean safe for the benefit of his empire's sea traffic; the ideas of Sicily and then Italy had not been planned then and were tacked on a year later.

Twelve months after *Torch* it was Churchill once more who insisted on the disastrous Dodecanese campaign of late 1943. Ever convinced of his own strategic genius and vision, he was certain the islands could be used as a base to attack the Balkans and that it would persuade Turkey to join the war on the side of the Allies. The likelihood of Turkey seeing any advantage at all was extremely remote and was whistling in the wind. The Americans refused to participate as they could see no benefits but simply a diversion of resources from Italy, shrewdly saying that if Britain wanted to launch such an attack, they were on their own. General Alan Brooke tried to get him to see sense but Churchill would listen to no one. Writing in his diary Brooke recorded: 'He has worked himself into a fury of excitement about the Greek islands. He refuses to listen to any arguments or to see the dangers. The whole thing is sheer madness.'[230] It would seem that this was yet another of Churchill's 'manic' episodes, the periods of exuberant omnipotence that frequently occur between interludes of depression. Individuals with bipolar often exhibit flights of fancy or ideas that are out of touch with reality during a manic period and are likely to persist with these notions irrespective of rational argument to the contrary.

The plan, codenamed Operation *Accolade,* envisaged the capture of the main island of Rhodes, together with other smaller ones and the expected surrender of the Italian garrisons following the recent surrender of Italy.

Landings were successfully made and the Italians did surrender, but with customary efficiency the reaction from the Germans was immediate and effective. Making the most of their almost complete air superiority they quickly mobilised successful airborne and amphibious attacks in response and one by one the British forces were driven from all the islands. In short, and as warned by his chiefs, the plan was ill-conceived and underprovided. The total cost was the loss of 6 destroyers, 113 aircraft, 10 minesweepers and coastal defence ships and 2 submarines; 8 cruisers were badly damaged and 4,800 men were killed wounded or captured. The German losses were minimal. When he came to power Churchill had also made himself Minister of Defence. The problem was that there was a minister but no real ministry and as has been mentioned elsewhere, Churchill was indifferent to casualties.

Twelve months further on and it was Churchill who pushed through Operation *Shingle,* the disastrous British–American landings at Anzio in January 1944. He had attempted to obtain agreement to this idea some time earlier but had been rebuffed by the Americans; stubborn as ever, Churchill again pressed for it at the Tunis Conference of December 1943 and this time the Americans reluctantly went along with it. Anzio was not a disaster on the same scale as Churchill's previous inspirations at Gallipoli in 1915 and Greece in 1941, but once more it was political rather than operational in its concept. Obsessed with historical and romantic visions, Churchill wanted to be able to announce that Rome had been 'liberated by British troops' and as a consequence of his urgings and with barely 3 weeks planning, the landings went ahead. Rushed preparations, inadequate resources and poor intelligence resulted in Rome eventually being reached but only after a slog of another 6 months and the loss of 7,000 dead plus 36,000 wounded or missing.

Although he would not have appreciated the analogy, his detailed meddling and consistent demands for attack that were made of Wavell and Auchinleck in North Africa were a mirror image of the problems created for von Rundstedt and Rommel by Adolph Hitler in 1944, who demanded that there should be no retreat anywhere following D-Day. Hitler's refusal to sanction any withdrawal was regarded as grotesque and prompted the resignation of von Rundstedt. Neither Wavell nor Auchinleck were anything other than realists and one can only imagine the resigned shaking of their heads at this barrage of impatient and unrealistic extortions. Both Churchill and Hitler gave orders that were, in opposite circumstances, virtually impossible to implement, but again the two of them believed themselves to be military geniuses. In his book *D-Day: The Battle for Normandy*, Antony Beevor states: 'Hitler was out of touch with reality and, when his dreams failed to materialise, he looked for scapegoats.'[231] Exactly the same could be said of Churchill. Hitler's refusal to allow General Friedrich Paulus to surrender at Stalingrad was the same sort of rejection of unpalatable facts as Churchill's angry demands for consistent attack in North Africa or his order that Singapore should be defended to the death. For some this might be an unsavoury comparison but nonetheless the similarities are there.

It is not generally realised just how valuable the continued existence of the empire was for many in the higher echelons of British society before World War II. For a young man from a socially reputable family the most favoured and respectable career options open to him were the army, the Church or the Colonial Service, for none of which was a high IQ or university education a necessity. In her book describing the development of the Malay Peninsula, *Taming the Jungle: The Men who Made British Malaya*, Pat Barr recounts that for entry to the Malay Civil Service all that was required was 'a white face and a public-school education.'[232] The same went for most commercial posts there and this was the case throughout the British colonies. When advertising for staff, British trading companies operating in the colonies, such as the United Africa Company, British-American Tobacco or Harrisons & Crosfield in Asia, would state 'public school and/or University degree required'. It was a subtle form of social apartheid whereby it was possible that an applicant without the preferred style of education might be considered provided he also had the cultural veneer that was deemed to have been acquired by way of a university 'experience'.

Instead of the expected business priorities of intelligence, financial competence, initiative and foresight, more highly valued were predictable conformance to the social mores of a class-conscious colonial society. Like the top echelons in the British Army, competitiveness and overt efficiency were considered less important than conventional behaviour and thus it was almost unavoidable that so many British trading companies quickly folded when they were exposed to the realities of global competition after the various colonies achieved independence. Although this did not apply to the 'white' dominions of Australia, Canada, New Zealand and South Africa, for the most part India and the colonies were run by and for a fairly exclusive stratum of British society whhich comfortably fitted in with such socio-cultural priorities. It was an elitist club but one whose continued existence depended on the artificial environment provided by colonial protection.

Whether this was anything of a factor in Churchill's almost missionary vision of an everlasting British Empire ('if [it] last for a thousand years') is not known, but he would have been aware of it. For the average man in the street in Britain 'the empire' offered nothing special in the way of opportunities, its existence was of no tangible benefit and it was fairly meaningless except as a form of national flag-waving for the establishment. The fruits of Britain's mines, mills and factories that fed the empire went to a very slim sliver of society—the owners of those industrial undertakings, which although providing employment were manned by underpaid workers toiling long hours in the most appalling coolie-like conditions of dirt and grime and living in unhealthy and congested housing.

These realities at home were in stark contrast to the almost romantic idealism of empire genuinely felt by those responsible for administering Britain's overseas territories. Up to 1941 Charles Vlieland had for 20 years been a senior officer in the Malayan Civil Service, and in a letter to Correlli Barnett in the late 1960s he stated: 'Naturally we believed whole-heartedly in the greatness of Britain and the permanence of the Empire. I think we believed in our hearts that the creation of the British Empire was the best thing that ever happened to mankind'.[233] Churchill's constant emotional harping on about the empire is perhaps just one more example of how out of touch with reality were his many priorities, or perhaps with the realities of a wartime situation staring him in the face, he recognised that Britain was in fact not an industrial powerhouse and had little more than her 'empire' to hang on to.

One of the numerous biographies of Churchill, that by James C. Humes, is subtitled *Speaker of the Century,* and without doubt such a caption was unlikely to have been used to describe any other leader. Churchill's gift for words was unique and cannot be challenged, and Humes, as a former White House speech-writer who wrote for five presidents, was himself in a unique position to pass judgement. Churchill was a master of oratory, and as US President John F. Kennedy so aptly put it: 'He mobilized the English language and sent it into battle'.[234] The problem with Churchill is that if his words are taken away, there is precious little left upon which history can pass any sort of positive opinion. His actual behaviour and modus operandi as Prime Minister during World War II was often scarcely less than eccentric and his hold on the power that he loved was maintained through political ruthlessness and sheer force of personality that enabled him to domineer. There were achievements in the partnership with the United States, but for it to be suggested that this could not have occurred or even been possible without Winston Churchill is an exercise in wishful thinking—however much Churchill himself might have wished that we should think this.

An example of the recent revised opinions of Churchill is the following comment in Richard Overy's *Why the Allies Won*:

> It is difficult not to conclude that Allied strategy succeeded despite Churchill, though his pugnacity and spirit remained a valuable symbol of the Allied will to win. Both his Allies and his military staffs soon learned how to cope with their mercurial companion by diverting and ignoring his interventions. He was a poor administrator, and left much of the machinery of war, once it was established, to run itself. He grew out of touch with policy on the home front. In military affairs he met his match in Brooke who managed to blunt his excesses. His notorious habit of interfering with front-line operations, and sacking generals and admirals he did not value was curbed with the emergence of strong personalities who ensured that his bark remained worse than his bite. By 1943 his influence on the war effort was much reduced.[235]

But not reduced enough to avoid the Dodecanese debacle or Anzio. And it was just as well he could no longer meddle, for whatever the historical greatness of his oratory, and his choice of words, the evidence of history is that he caused more problems than he solved.

James C. Humes wrote of Churchill: 'Early in his life he determined that command of the English language would be his staircase to power and greatness. He would wield that mastery to advance his career.'[236] After the war Churchill himself confirmed this in a conversation with Lord Moran when he said: 'I am not an orator, an orator is spontaneous. The written word—ah, that's different. It was my ambition, all my life, to be a master of the spoken word. That was my only ambition.'[237] In reality his whole reputation rests on the brilliantly constructed heroic and pugnacious words in his 1940 speeches:

> I have nothing to offer but blood, toil, tears and sweat etc; we shall fight on the beaches, we shall fight on the landing grounds, we shall fight in the fields and in the streets, we shall fight in the hills; we shall never surrender.

> You ask, what is our aim? I can answer in one word: It is victory, victory at all cost, victory in spite of all terror, victory however long and hard the road may be.

> Let us therefore so brace ourselves to our duties, and so bear ourselves that, if the British Empire and its Commonwealth last for a thousand years, men will still say 'This was their finest hour.'

> Never in the field of human conflict was so much owed by so many to so few.

It was of course stirring language—the genius being in the peroration. In the darkness of that time few could gainsay the heart-warming effect of those inspiring words, and to go along with them he adopted a grim, ebullient and pugnacious expression, which together with a cigar clamped in his jaws, successfully heightened the effect of this defiance. Churchill's physician Lord Moran quotes veteran civil servant and diplomat Sir Oliver Franks, who spoke eloquently of Churchill: 'He gave us faith. There was in him a demonic element as in Calvin and Luther. Churchill became a prophet.'[238] But the problem was of course that wars cannot be won with words alone, not even with his eloquence. Once Churchill stopped speaking and started functioning, then the shortcomings in his character rapidly began to emerge and made themselves felt, for the pugnacious image was no mere façade, it was in fact a direct reflection of his bellicose and combative personality. unfortunately he was doggedly convinced he had inherited all the military genius of his 18th-century ancestor, Marlborough. In the self-appointed role of commander in chief he became an autocratic military, naval and air-force tactician and strategist, and it was there, in his interfering and intruding into areas that he did not understand, that he was a menace and sometimes a complete disaster.

In his aptly named book *Blood, Sweat and Arrogance: The Myths of Churchill's War,* military historian Gordon Corrigan sums up a range of problems caused by Churchill's domineering character:

> His conduct as First Lord of the Admiralty during the Norway campaign was disastrous; his demands to sink the French fleet at Mers-el-Kebir unnecessary for as Cunningham showed the French would have come to an agreement without the threat of force and thus the Syrian campaign need not have happened and the 'Torch' landings might not have been opposed. His insistence on sending troops to Greece when Britain was no longer under any legal or moral obligation to do so; his constant chivvying of successive commanders-in-chief Middle East to go on the offensive when all their military instincts told them to wait, and his insistence on an Italian campaign which then got so bogged down that it was neither a distraction from Normandy nor an enabler of a Balkan front, all dissipated what few assets Britain had and wasted lives to little avail.[239]

Wars are won by the side that makes the fewest mistakes, and there will always be mistakes, but in Churchill's case it is plain to see that the errors were of such magnitude that in many cases they defy any rational explanation, except that they were the product of a stubborn self-conviction of military genius that just was not there. This is not a view obtained with the benefit of hindsight, it was plainly seen then but without an open revolt there was nobody to stand in his way. His was a personality that felt compelled to be the source of all strategy and one that continually longed for the acclamation that would spring from being the author of victories. Churchill just could not allow others, however extensive their experience, to be or to be seen as having been responsible; he had to be the font of all action and when he did apportion some praise, he made sure that he was also seen as having had a hand in it.

Ignoring the Japanese theatre there were four key leaders during World War II: Roosevelt, Churchill, Stalin and Hitler. Two of these, Stalin and Hitler, were complete dictators of brutal totalitarian regimes—and although it could never be said that he was a 'dictator', Churchill was equally adept as those two at issuing his own strategic and tactical orders and appointing and firing top commanders as the whim took him. As military author Reginald W. Thompson wrote, he was a veritable 'Generalissimo'.[240]

In his book *Churchill: The End of Glory* John Charmley writes: 'Churchill took the view that "wars are won by superior will-power"', [241] and yet this concept of 'superior will-power' was exactly what Adolf Hitler had always proclaimed—the 'will' of the Fuhrer'; another parallel that many will probably find unpalatable, but nonetheless the similarities are there.

And here we can see why it was that Churchill did not understand or distrusted anyone, irrespective of ability, who was not an extrovert because he would have seen this as lacking in 'will-power'. Hence his support for colourful egotists, like Mountbatten and Montgomery or even Wingate, whereas he was unable to understand the real achievements of the more modest men like Wavell and Auchinleck. Fortunately for Slim he took over in Burma later in the war when Churchill's influence had waned and he had very little contact with him, but it seems likely that he too would have been suspected by Churchill of being too modest to be effective.

In the same book Charmley went on to state that by early 1941, 'Churchill had surrounded himself with "yes men" and lacked anyone to "provide ballast"; the "Rogue elephant" had broken loose from his keepers.'[242] Again this is almost an exact parallel with the way in which Hitler operated, both of them dismissing almost anyone who disagreed with them, and particularly anyone who said so face to face. In typical 'dictator' fashion, Churchill was a man obsessed with the personalities of his enemies and this was recognised by Liddell Hart and Correlli Barnett when they said that he became fixated with beating Rommel.

In a parallel manner and instead of a rational and measured approach to the war with Germany, he regarded Adolf Hitler as some sort of personal adversary against whom there was an all-consuming individual vendetta. Because of this almost monomaniacal preoccupation he would grasp at virtually any opportunity, however outlandish, to land some retributive blow, even if it was only symbolic. Hence, again, his placing the security of Singapore at the very back of his mind, Singapore having a very low priority when all of his attention was directed at beating a man he had come to regard as an individual rival. He virtually said as much himself when he stated he would deal with the devil himself if it would help him beat Hitler.

Because of the looming world crisis Roosevelt had been re-elected for an unprecedented third term in 1940 but thereafter, although closely involved as President, he mostly concerned himself with the overall and ultimate political aims, and wisely left details of armed service strategy and deployments to his service chiefs. Therefore at no point was Roosevelt in any way personally responsible for any military setbacks. In the case of Churchill, however, there were a string of disasters resulting from actions he had demanded that were either totally unnecessary or virtually impossible to comply with, or where he refused to accept strong and experienced advice—and in either case he then blamed others for the consequences. Lord Moran put the position succinctly when he wrote of Churchill:

> He felt that he was born to govern men. The trouble was that he did not seem to be designed by nature for the part. Winston was without the first attribute of a good administrator, namely that ability to pick the right man, and then to let him get on with the job.[243]

Roosevelt was a leader at the head of a wide-based and delegated pyramid; in Churchill's case he sat atop a self-constructed steeple, a pinnacle of complete and individual power.

Even after the war, Churchill continued to distort in order to attract praise for what he projected as his own, unique turn of phrase. In March 1946 he delivered a speech in Fulton, Missouri in which he made the much-quoted statement: 'From Stettin in the Baltic to Trieste in the Adriatic an iron curtain has descended across the Continent'.[244] This aphorism was taken, as he had intended it should be, as yet another great Churchillian creation and ever after has been called the 'Iron Curtain speech'. It became a catchphrase and slogan for the West and was attributed to Churchill. The truth is somewhat different. Hitler's Minister for Propaganda, Joseph Goebbels, had founded *Das Reich*, a weekly newspaper, in 1940. He was not involved in the actual running of the paper but he wrote an editorial. In the edition of 25 February 1945, Goebbels wrote:

> If the German people lay down their weapons, the Soviets, according to the agreement between Roosevelt, Churchill and Stalin, would occupy all of East and Southeast Europe along with a greater part of the Reich. An iron curtain would fall over this enormous territory controlled by the Soviet Union, behind which nations would be slaughtered.

Not only was Churchill's much-vaunted expression not his own, but it had in fact been lifted from a publication that only 13 months earlier had come out of the very regime that he condemned and treated with contempt. Not only was this plagiarism but hypocrisy as well.

CHAPTER 15

UNSUNG HEROES—
WAVELL AND AUCHINLECK

No other British soldier of the day had the strategic grasp, the sagacity, the cool nerves and the immense powers of leadership.
—CORRELLI BARNETT, on Wavell

If Auchinleck had not been the man he was—and by that I mean the best Allied general in North Africa during the war—Rommel would have finished the Eighth Army off.
—GENERAL FRITZ BAYERLEIN,
    Rommel's chief of staff

Because such characteristics were not encouraged, men with imagination and initiative were somewhat rare in the British high command in World War II, and therefore it was all the more important that those who did stand out should have been used to best advantage. It is thus worth looking briefly at the effect of Churchill's political interference on the careers of two such men in North Africa who became victims of his brainstorms in order to enhance his own position. These might be called the *'unsung* heroes'—Wavell and Auchinleck.

Sir Archibald Wavell did come from a most conventional educational and military background but his promotion and success was not due to social class; in his case it was due to intellect and innate ability. His father was a major-general in the Indian Army and Wavell spent much of his childhood in that country. He was wounded in the Second Battle of Ypres in 1915, losing his left eye. His career between the wars was conventional and saw gradual promotions until he achieved the rank of full general in 1939. Early in World War II, Wavell was unfortunate in being ordered to undertake a succession of difficult if not almost impossible tasks in East Africa, North Africa, the Middle East, Malaya, Singapore and Burma. In each of these theatres the resources at his disposal were either woefully inadequate or he was asked to rescue a situation that was already lost. He was regarded by Rommel as a most gifted general,[245] and military historian Correlli Barnett rates him as outstanding, and yet in his incessant demands Churchill was oblivious of the fact that from his Cairo HQ, and with barely 64,000 men, Wavell was required to look after over 9,000,000km^2 and nine countries where three continents converged.

Rommel was so impressed by Wavell that he obtained a copy of Wavell's 1939 lectures at Trinity College Cambridge entitled 'Generals and Generalship'.[246] Rommel had them bound in leather and carried them with him throughout the war. Once more, and as in the case of the German assessments of Montgomery, here was an example of the views of an experienced enemy commander being quite different than that of a self-opinionated politician at home. After Wavell's death in 1950, Frau Rommel took Wavell's book with her to England where she presented it to Lady Wavell.

In July 1939 Wavell was given command of the Middle East and in February 1940 his responsibilities were expanded to include East Africa, Greece and the Balkans. In the early months of the war it was a peaceful command but this was the lull before the storm, which broke when Italy declared war against Britain in June 1940. Although vastly outnumbered by the Italian forces, Wavell skilfully directed tactical withdrawals in Egypt and East Africa before mounting offensives in those areas from December 1940 to February 1941. The Italians were completely routed in East Africa, Wavell's forces capturing 230,000 prisoners and using the ingenious planning mind of the then Brigadier Eric Dorman-Smith, of whom more will be written later, and with a small force, Wavell and his army commander O'Connor successfully routed the Italians in Egypt at the Battle of Beda Fomm.

In February 1941 his forces had rapidly advanced some 500km further west and were about to take Syrte and then move on to Tripoli. He was on the point of driving the Italians from North Africa and would probably have done so but for Churchill's insistence that he divert and lose about 20 per cent of his already depleted force for a disastrous foray into Greece. Had he been allowed to continue and take Tripoli and maintain the momentum he had achieved, it is quite arguable that Rommel would never have been able to gain a foothold in North Africa. It has been alleged that Wavell concurred with the Greece plan; this is not true, for he was aware that Churchill would brook no opposition to his idea of aid to Greece. Serious misgivings about the Greek venture had been discussed at the War Office, the then General Dill telling Major-General Kennedy of his attempts to get Churchill to recognise the realities of the situation:

> I gave it my view that all the troops in the Middle-East are fully employed and that none are available for Greece. The Prime Minister lost his temper with me, I could see the blood coming up his great neck and his eyes began to flash. He said 'What you need out there is a Court Martial and a firing squad. Wavell has 300,000 men, etc, etc.' I should have said, 'Whom do you want to shoot exactly?' But I did not think of it till afterwards.[247]

When measured and experienced advice provoked a reaction of such intemperate fury, it is little wonder that so many British military leaders just gave up or carried on regardless. Dill must have been relieved when he was later posted to Washington where he could work in relative peace amongst other military commanders who were not subjected to such mindless and emotional bullying.

In the meantime Wavell had also been ordered by Churchill to seize Syria and Lebanon from where air attacks on the Suez Canal had been threatened by the Vichy French. Added to Syria and Lebanon, and several weeks earlier, Wavell was instructed to put down a pro-Nazi coup in Iraq. Both of these missions were successfully accomplished but yet again they caused further diversions and depletions of scarce resources, problems that Churchill ignored.

As Brigadier Cyril N. Barclay perceptively points out in his book *On Their Shoulders: British Generalship in the Lean Years 1939–1942*:

> From Italy's entry into the war in June 1940 until he left the Mid-

dle-East in July 1941 was a period of thirteen months of almost continuous crisis. As the official historian records, Wavell felt that his war was not 'one damned thing after another: it was everything in all directions at once.'[248]

Churchill claimed that Britain had never had a victory before the Second Battle of El Alamein in November 1942. That statement was untrue, and was made solely for his personal political purposes, for not only did it ignore the First Battle of Alamein in July 1942 but it also conveniently ignored all of Wavell's achievements during the previous year.

With the means at his disposal reduced by the losses in the Greece debacle, it is difficult to see just what more Wavell could have accomplished but the irrational, stubborn Churchill always thought he knew better. In June 1941 Wavell's forces failed in an attack, named *Battleaxe*, demanded by Churchill but which Wavell had advised was premature. Refusing to accept that he had been wrong, Churchill sacked Wavell and replaced him with Auchinleck, and Wavell took over Auchinleck's role in charge of the Indian Army. When Auchinleck was interviewed by David Dimbleby some years later, he was asked about the true circumstances of *Battleaxe*:

> DD: Some people say that Wavell fought the 'Battleaxe' campaign earlier than he thought right and that as a result 'Battleaxe' was a failure. Dill told you that it was his opinion didn't he?
> CA: Yes, that's right. That's quite true. That was an indication to me of what was likely to happen.
> DD: But if that's true it would mean that Churchill caused the failure of 'Battleaxe'.
> CA: Yes, he did undoubtedly I think.[249]

As an aside it might be noted that having been made Churchill's scapegoat and having spent several years on non-stop duty in the Middle East, Wavell asked if he could spend just a few days leave in England before moving on to India. However, even this simple issue was refused by a mean-minded Churchill who did not want to be seen to agreeing to such a request in case it was perceived as excusing Wavell for his own—i.e. Churchill's—mistake.

It is worth quoting directly from Correlli Barnett's *The Desert Generals* at this point:

> There was no valid case for relieving Wavell. In his two years in the Middle-East he had built a base and a command structure from nothing. He had conquered the whole of Italian East Africa, had captured two hundred thousand prisoners, including the Duke of Aosta, Viceroy of Ethiopia. Under his strategic aegis, O'Connor had taken Cyrenaica and another two hundred thousand prisoners. Between February and June 1941 he had conducted six major campaigns, never less than three at a time, and in May, five at a time. No other British soldier of the day had the strategic grasp, the sagacity, the cool nerves and the immense powers of leadership to do all these things and steer a course free of total disaster.[250]

Another, experienced, authority of the same opinion and one who had first-hand knowledge was Erwin Rommel; in his papers he described Wavell as 'the only one who showed a touch of genius'.[251] As Barnett has also observed, Churchill's interference reversed what had been achieved and lengthened the war in North Africa by 2 years; Wavell's removal was unjust, illogical and was in no way a criticism. In the long term, however, Wavell's career did not suffer unduly.

In January 1942, and 4 weeks after the Japanese attack, Wavell was moved from his position in India and ordered to take charge of ABDACOM (American, British, Dutch and Australian Command) forces which had been hastily cobbled together in an effort to stem the Japanese tide that was sweeping relentlessly through South-East Asia. Once more, and too late in the day, he had been given an impossible task and as a functional entity ABDACOM soon collapsed. He did what he could, which in the circumstances and limited time at his disposal could never have amounted to much. When Wavell arrived in South-East Asia, the Japanese Army had already taken Manila and most of the Philippines and was halfway down the Malay Peninsula; several weeks later, and inevitably, Singapore fell. Soon after this and with their home country under Nazi occupation, Dutch resistance against the Japanese in their East Indian colony collapsed. As a result and through no fault of his, ABDACOM became redundant and on

25 February 1942 he returned to resume charge of the Indian Army.

However, it was in that capacity that he made the shrewd selection of the virtually unknown Lieutenant-General William Slim to command the campaign where he was to make his name, in Burma. Just one year after Wavell's dismissal in August 1942, Auchinleck was also summarily sacked by Churchill and returned once more to India. One can only begin to imagine the resigned conversations of disbelief these two old warriors must have had on his return there. The next year Auchinleck took over his old post as Commander-in-Chief, India and Wavell was elevated to the rank of Field Marshal and became Viceroy of India. This was a post of the utmost difficulty and sensitivity at that time but one that he performed with distinction until August 1947, when he retired after Indian independence was rushed through by Mountbatten.

In England Wavell was appointed or invited to hold a number of prestigious honorary or corporate positions but he died at the age of 67 in May 1950 following a relapse after abdominal surgery. His body lay in state at the Tower of London where he had been constable, and a military funeral was held at Westminster Abbey. Such was Wavell's reputation and military standing that the funeral procession travelled along the Thames from the Tower to Westminster Pier, the first military funeral by river since that of Horatio Nelson in 1806. Despite the attendance of a multitude of dignitaries and old colleagues, including the then Prime Minister Clement Attlee, the one person notable by his absence was Winston Churchill. Even years after refusing Wavell leave before moving to India, Churchill could remain remarkably petty and uncharitable and feared that attending the funeral of someone he had dismissed might be seen to be something of an apology. Sometimes the mind of an egocentric works in strange ways; even this small gracious gesture was beyond him. Wavell is buried at Winchester College, his tombstone reading, simply, 'Wavell'.

Perhaps the finest assessment of Wavell as a military commander is that provided by General Sir Frank Messervy, who served under him in North Africa:

> Above all he impressed you by his strength of character, his calm resolution and his brilliant ability. However desperate the situation he gave you confidence that all would be well in the end. You knew

that he would never let you down and everyone loved him and served him to the best of their ability. He was undoubtedly a very great man.[252]

Sir Claude Auchinleck, the 'Auk', one of the finest British field commanders of World War II, was allowed even less time by a politically desperate Churchill and within just 14 months of taking over from Wavell he too became another of the Prime Minister's political whipping boys. As previously noted, on assuming command Auchinleck had stated that he was very impressed with the foundations and dispositions that Wavell had established, and could appreciate what he had achieved in the face of a myriad of problems. Realising what Wavell had had to endure at the hands of Churchill, Auchinleck told Churchill that he would not be rushed.

Like Wavell, Auchinleck shared an understanding of the imaginative and inventive Dorman-Smith whom they had both known for many years. It was this relationship that resulted in a remarkable partnership of military planning, one that for the first time stopped Rommel dead in his tracks at the First Battle of Alamein in June and July of 1942. Although Churchill refused to accept its significance, this battle was a strategic victory and the turning point in the desert campaign. Thereafter Rommel was not the same menace and from an important psychological angle he was never again thought to be. As will be shown later, Rommel was surprised at the reorganisation achieved by the British and felt he had been outmanoeuvred at Alamein by a general he admired. As is observed elsewhere in this book, an opponent is often a more reliable source of the truth than the subjective views of brother officers.

Churchill and General Brooke arrived in Egypt in August 1942, Churchill fighting for his political life after narrowly surviving a censure motion in Parliament. Tobruk had fallen in June. It was of no strategic importance, but it had emotional significance to the fortress-minded Churchill. It was of value only if it was behind the British lines and could be used as a port, but if this caused Churchill some embarrassment, he only had himself to blame for having made such a public song and dance about forever maintaining its defence. Several months earlier Auchinleck had told London that he had no intention of permanently holding Tobruk and this information had been relayed to Churchill. Churchill had lost Malaya and Singapore in February 1942, by mid-March Rangoon had gone and by June the Japanese Army was advancing rapidly through Burma towards India. Although it made no strategic sense to those on the spot, Churchill had ordered Tobruk to be held. In this it was the same level of thinking as his demands that Singapore and Crete be defended unto death. If Churchill's political position was precarious, it was his own fault because he had assumed total military command of the war effort and was eager to gather the accolades, but as a corollary he was therefore seen to be solely accountable when things went wrong.

In an effort to secure his political position and even though Auchinleck had inflicted on Rommel the first defeat of the North African campaign, Churchill had decided beforehand to sack him. As mentioned earlier, at the Washington conference that had been held just a few weeks before in June Churchill had persuaded Roosevelt to agree to a joint American–British invasion of Morocco and Algeria later in 1942, to be called Operation *Torch*. This plan was of course confidential but Churchill knew that once the *Torch* landings occurred, and with the huge build-up in supplies and material that had arrived, victory against Rommel was assured. Desperate to demonstrate his successful powers of leadership and strategic vision he accordingly also knew that he could without risk display his military acumen by removing a general who had just won a great battle. The battle itself would be ignored or played down, which it was, because he did not want to be seen to be dismissing a general who had recently been victorious over Rommel. The inevitable and ensuing shift in fortunes he could claim to have been entirely due to the changes that he himself had engineered.

Churchill rationalised his actions by claiming that he had lost confidence in Auchinleck but there is not one shred of evidence with which to justify such an excuse. Auchinleck had just directed and engineered the first ever supremacy gained by the British over Rommel and was in the process of regrouping after such a gruelling duel and gathering his resources for a further action; nothing more could logically have been expected of him. But logic and understanding were not the most outstanding characteristics of an emotional man like Churchill. Auchinleck's removal had nothing whatsoever to do with his army's performance, but was a political stratagem devised by Churchill for Churchill's benefit. To such lengths did he go to justify the purge he was inflicting on a very successful fighting unit that he claimed to be amazed at how quickly Montgomery had grasped the situation. This move was publically engineered by Churchill staging a tantrum in Egypt when told, quite logically, that for an army needing to re-group after the First Battle of El Alamein, an immediate attack was just not possible or sensible. Churchill was well aware of this, but being told it was not going to happen was sufficient pretext for him to rationalise the action he had already decided. Thus, when the Second Battle of El Alamein was, almost inevitably, successful in November, Churchill could bask in the glory of a victory that he could claim he had devised; his political position had been secured.

As a sop, Auchinleck was offered a newly invented Persia and Iraq Command, but it was a pig in a poke for it would have come under the overall command of India, a position that Auchinleck had vacated just over a year before. He could see it was quite meaningless and would achieve virtually nothing and he discussed it with Dorman-Smith, saying if he accepted the post he would take Dorman-Smith with him as his number two. For Dorman-Smith this would have involved promotion to lieutenant-general and a knighthood, but with a selflessness conspicuously lacking in many others around him, Dorman-Smith advised him against it knowing this might leave himself out in the wilderness. Auchinleck declined the suggested Persia and Iraq role and returned to India, and Dorman-Smith went into limbo.

Shortly after his dismissal, Auchinleck received a letter from another who knew the truth, Leo Amery, Secretary of State for India and Burma:

> I know how you must be feeling just now. You always have the sat-isfaction of knowing that the victory of today was only made pos-sible—and indeed the whole Middle Eastern situation saved—by your getting back to Alamein and holding the position there by your personal intervention. There would have been no champagne today if you hadn't put the cork in the bottle in July. So possess your soul in patience.[253]

After spending some months in enforced idleness, and although this was in the middle of the war, Churchill could not be seen reappointing a man he had just sacked, and so Auchinleck assumed his old post as Commander-in-Chief, India in 1943. In this appointment he immediately and skilfully mobilised resources enabling India to send invaluable men and materials to Slim in Burma for whose Fourteenth Army he provided the help and support it had long been lacking. In his book *Defeat into Victory* Slim paid tribute to Auchinleck's contribution, writing:

> Whatever the causes, it was clear the supply situation was critical, and equally obvious that something vigorous would have to be done to avoid disaster. Luckily, General Auchinleck was the man to do it. There was a considerable and prompt injection of ginger into the Indian administrative machine, military and civil. It was a good day for us when he took command of India, our main base, recruiting area, and training ground. Without him and what he and the army in India did for us we could not have existed, let alone conquered.[254]

And yet this was the man in whom Churchill had said he had lost confidence? Churchill had no reason at all for any lack of belief in Auchinleck, and he knew it, but he continued to maintain this façade in order to justify having sacked him. As we have seen in the chapter *Mountbatten's Malayan Madness—Operation Zipper*, when the question of command of the new South-East Asia Command came up at the Quebec Conference in August 1943, Auchinleck was the obvious choice; a man of his seniority and experience would probably have been very acceptable to the Americans who also had a senior general on that scene in General Stillwell. Auchinleck was rejected out of hand by Churchill, not for any military reasons (there weren't any), but simply, and once again, because he did not want to be seen to be appointing someone who only a year earlier he had removed from Egypt.

Auchinleck was promoted to field marshal on 1 June 1946 and although strongly disapproving of Mountbatten's manner and methods, he nonetheless oversaw the successful but painful division of the Indian Army at independence. Through his wise intervention he was instrumental in preventing outright war in Kashmir in October 1947, a totally avoidable situation that had been brought about by Mountbatten's ham-fisted decisions. He was sounded out about becoming a Knight of the Order of the Garter but with his customary integrity Auchinleck let it be known that, whilst he would be delighted to accept such an honour, he would only do so if it was not made on the recommendation of Mountbatten.

Having done what he could for India he retired from the army, lived in England for a few years and then, missing the sun, he retired to Morocco where the climate and topography reminded him of India's North-West Frontier. As Roger Parkinson describes it, he began there a quiet life of painting, reading and walking alone in the mountains.[255] Although living alone, he was well looked after by a faithful Moroccan valet who was an excellent cook and he had regular visitors who made the pilgrimage to see him. The 'Auk' lived on to 1981 when he died peacefully in his sleep in his Marrakech home at the age of 96. Arrangements for the small funeral had previously been made for him by the British Embassy at Rabat and he was buried in the Ben M'Sik European Cemetery in Casablanca, where his headstone carries the words of Geoffrey Chaucer who thus described his knight in *The Canterbury Tales*: 'He nevere yet no vileynyene sayde. He was a verray parfit gentil knyght'. Just who chose those words is not known, but they are completely appropriate. As quoted to the joint session of Congress by Douglas MacArthur when he retired in 1951, 'Old soldiers never die, they just fade away'—and thus did Claude Auchinleck quietly fade from the scene.

Whatever might have been Auchinleck's administrative value in India, Churchill's personal political agenda had robbed Britain of the active services of one of her finest generals and field commanders. Had it not been for Churchill's interference it would have been Auchinleck who would have removed Rommel from Africa and thence it is not being too fanciful to speculate what a successful partnership he and Eisenhower would have made in Europe. They were both courteous men and of similar temperaments, and with Auchinleck heading the British forces instead of the tactless and arrogant Montgomery the relationships between the two Allies would have been far smoother, more cohesive and more effective than they were. Added to which the poor citizens of Caen would have been unlikely to have suffered as they did. After the war Auchinleck stated that he had understood his removal from North Africa was for reasons that were political rather than strategic, and he accepted it as such and not as a military dismissal. As he said later: 'A change of commander by a politician is a very different thing to a change of commander by a higher commander.'[256] Also, had it not been for Churchill, with the wise and measured Auchinleck in charge of SEAC it seems almost certain that the unnecessary and dramatically disastrous landings ordered on the coast of Malaya by Mountbatten would never have taken place.

As mentioned on several occasions earlier, opinions from erstwhile opponents are frequently more down to earth than those from the same side, for they are unbiased and are untinged by envy or politics. General Fritz Bayerlein was Rommel's chief of staff for the Afrika Korps. After the war he became a noted German military historian and he put Auchinleck's true contribution into clear perspective when he said: 'If Auchinleck had not been the man he was—and by that I mean the best Allied general in North Africa during the war—Rommel would have finished the 8th army off.'[257] As a barrister might say—*Res Ipsa Loquitur*—the thing speaks for itself.

Both of these outstanding commanders, Wavell and Auchinleck, were sacrificed and Britain's war effort stymied by Churchill for the sole reasons of concealing or rationalising the mistakes caused by his interference and thereby protecting his own political position. They were 'unsung' in another way: they both stand out because they did not, unlike so many others, 'sing' about themselves. Biographies of the two were written independently by other authors but each of them felt it would have been unseemly, unchivalrous perhaps, to have profited by putting their own pens to paper and writing about their personal parts in the deaths of others, for that is what wartime autobiographies are all about. Wavell did publish several books but rather than personal trumpet blowing they were about other people, such as Field Marshal Edmund Allenby.

Wavell and Auchinleck were outstanding but modest and self-effacing leaders, personality characteristics in stark contrast to the swagger of a number of military commanders, and that in itself makes them different, a difference that is only rarely appreciated. Unfortunately, and as mentioned earlier, Churchill's constant fear of his 'black dog', and his consequent need to avoid and distrust personalities who did not exude colour and panache meant that Britain was robbed of the services of two of her most outstanding generals, and this right at a time when they were most needed.

CHAPTER 16

THE HIDDEN HERO— MAJOR-GENERAL ERIC DORMAN-SMITH

Major-General Dorman-Smith with his contributions decisively influenced not only the outcome of the first Battle of El Alamein, but the whole of the Desert War.
—PÉTER KLEMENSITS

I owe him more than I could ever repay. He was tragically mistreated and betrayed in the end. Envy and malice pursued him but he never gave in.
—FIELD MARSHAL SIR CLAUDE
    AUCHINLECK, 1969

Major-General 'Chink' Dorman-Smith, the brilliant architect of Auchinleck's first victory of El Alamein, and one of the very few original thinkers in the contemporary British Army, had his military career totally ruined by Churchill and Brooke. Without any reason or explanation ever being provided, he was removed by Churchill at the same time that Auchinleck was axed, and was exiled by the military establishment for being too clever for them. An unusual military talent that the Americans and the Germans would have been unlikely to have wasted, Dorman-Smith is worthy of separate examination.

Eric Edward Dorman-Smith—nicknamed 'Chink'—was born in 1895 in the 18th-century Palladian house on the 1,000-acre Bellamont Forest estate of County Cavan, just south of what is now Ulster in Ireland. There was nothing unconventional about his education or social background for an officer in the British Army at that time: of landed gentry origin, Uppingham public school and then Sandhurst Military Academy. His nickname 'Chink' came from another young officer saying that he looked like the regimental mascot, a Chinkara antelope. He was commissioned in the Northumberland Fusiliers and saw action in World War I where he was awarded the Military Cross and 1914–15 Star.

In 1924 he became an instructor at Sandhurst. In 1927 he sat the Staff College examination and was awarded 1,000 marks out of a possible 1,000 in the Strategy paper by a forward-looking examiner, Major-General John F.C. Fuller. His top-scoring caused resentment and he was thereafter regarded with suspicion. It seems to have been from about that time that his flow of ideas and a readiness to question the orthodox provoked indignation in the slow, plodding but rigidly conventional minds of his peers.

The analogy between British Army leaders and cricket was examined in the chapter *Class and the British Army*. Dorman-Smith fitted in exactly with all the other characteristics and social precepts described by Correlli Barnett in his book *The Desert Generals* with one notable exception: he was highly intelligent, innovative and imaginative.[258] The examiner at Sandhurst who had awarded him 100 per cent, Major-General Fuller, was himself regarded as something of a crank because of his promotion of a fluid, fully mechanised army, a dangerous and revolutionary concept in the eyes of the cavalry establishment. It should be added here that the scope of Fuller's intellect was such that he had invented the searchlight.

Between the two wars Dorman-Smith became a close friend of famed military theorist and writer Basil Liddell Hart; they met and corresponded frequently, exchanging their respective thoughts on the ways and methods in which they felt the British Army required changing. Their mutual ideas also ranged over the likely patterns of any future war; they were both deep military thinkers. Dorman-Smith openly supported Fuller's mechanisation concepts and this provoked the resentment of Brooke, later to become Army chief of staff, because Brooke himself was from the Royal Horse Artillery, an elite amongst the elites. This hostility to change was widespread in an entity that prided itself, almost above anything else, on tradition and so the priority and influence of established convention itself made change virtually impossible. Ironically, one man who noticed and adopted Liddell Hart's ideas was German General Heinz Guderian, who incorporated them into his new plans for the German Army in what became known as blitzkrieg. In his 1952 book *Panzer Leader* Guderian states quiet explicitly that he had regarded the new ideas being promoted by both Fuller and Liddell Hart in the 1930s as far-sighted and that he owed much of the German Army's development in the use of armoured forces to the ideas of Liddell Hart. Guderian went on to state:

> It was Liddell Hart who emphasized the use of armoured forces for long range strokes, operations against the opposing army's communications, and also proposed a type of armoured division combining panzer and panzer-infantry units. Deeply impressed by these ideas I tried to develop them in a sense practicable for our own army. So I owe many suggestions of our further development to Captain Liddell Hart.[259]

Like his friend, Dorman-Smith could also see where the future lay but it was a vision rejected as heresy by the British. For the first edition of Liddell Hart's now world-renowned book *Strategy: The Indirect Approach* Dorman-Smith was asked to write a foreword.[260] Predictably perhaps, the book was virtually ignored by the British military establishment and it is significant that the forward-thinking concepts it espoused were dismissed by the British but appreciated by others such as Guderian and Patton, and also Rommel, who went as far as to say: 'The British would have been able to prevent the greatest part of their defeats if they had paid attention to the modern theories expounded by Liddell Hart before the war.' To paraphrase Correlli Barnett, already quoted, 'the spurs of a gentleman were preferred to the sprockets of an engineer', and it was the speed of Guderian's tracks that decimated the French and British hooves in 1940.

Through various postings, Dorman-Smith became known to both Wavell and Auchinleck, who recognised his original ideas and keen military thinking, and he worked closely with Auchinleck in successfully reforming the Indian Army. Such was his performance that in a matter of 10 peacetime years he was promoted from captain to brigadier and seemed set for the highest positions in the army. Even then, however, there was gossip amongst his contemporaries to the effect that he was not conforming and there was discomfort within the senior ranks at his modern ideas, whilst his peers did not like having their established and conventional styles of command changed to accommodate improvements. As Barrie Pitt described him in his 1980 book *The Crucible of War*, Dorman-Smith had 'an impatience with orthodox doctrine unleavened by imagination and administered by authority.'[261] In all, he was developing a reputation for being 'different' and not really 'playing the game', unforgivable solecisms in a slow and small-minded world of conformist precedents. The word used to describe him was 'unsound', conventional military jargon for unorthodox, for new ideas were regarded with innate suspicion.

Appointed commandant of the newly opened Middle East Staff College in 1940, he once again came into close contact with Wavell who was commander-in-chief for the area. Having a very high opinion of Dorman-Smith's military knowledge and imaginative mind, Wavell immediately used him to assist in the campaign against the Italians and it was essentially his unorthodox planning that was responsible for Wavell's great victory in Cyrenaica at the end of 1940 and early 1941. Dorman-Smith's ingenious tactic there was to infiltrate through the Italian lines at night, confuse them with an artillery barrage from the east and then attack from the west. It was so successful that 130,000 prisoners were taken—over four times the size of the British force. It would have broken every one of the orthodox rules taught at Sandhurst or Camberley, and that in itself may be why it received little acknowledgement from the War Office. Thereafter he stayed at Wavell's side, assisting his inadequate resources to handle both the newly arrived Afrika Korps under Erwin Rommel and the diversion and depletion caused by Churchill's Greek disaster. Wavell was dismissed by Churchill in August 1941 but his replacement, Claude Auchinleck, also understood the value of Dorman-Smith's imaginative intellect and retained him as a senior member of his staff, writing of him: 'I took Dorman-Smith because I knew he had a most fertile, active and a very good brain. I wanted him because I knew he was a man I could talk to—a fresh mind.'[262] Correlli Barnett goes on to comment: 'In fact, Auchinleck and Dorman-Smith constituted a formidable combination; great powers of leadership with a brilliant and original intellect. Want of either would have lost us the Middle East.' There was another link as well: they were both admirers of the theories of speed, flexibility and indirect attack propounded by Basil Liddell Hart, most of which, at that time, were regarded as heretical deviations.

In an interview with Auchinleck for his book *The Auk,* the late military historian Roger Parkinson recounts Auchinleck speaking of his first meetings with Dorman-Smith in India in 1938, saying of him:

> We discussed war and training, training mostly, and I found him very intelligent and very valuable to talk to. I got a lot out of him. Very valuable indeed. Very imaginative. Not popular because he was a little bit inclined to state his opinions very openly, and the less intelligent didn't like him very much. But I had a very great opinion of him—and he proved it afterwards.[263]

In his own analysis Parkinson describes Dorman-Smith as 'a forceful, outspoken and quick witted personality who would make his presence increasingly felt'. In the same interview and talking about Churchill's consistent meddling, Auchinleck said: 'He'd no business to interfere at all. I think he was afraid of Dorman-Smith!'

Once again, however, the old-boy net of the British Army 'club' began sniping at him, and quiet reports were filtered back to London alleging that, far from having achieved anything, Dorman-Smith was a disconcerting influence and his presence a disturbing factor that made conventional cooperative relationships difficult. Churchill confirms such 'reports' when he wrote in *The Hinge of Fate*: 'The doubts I had about the High Command in the Middle East were fed continually by the reports which I received from many quarters. Had General Auchinleck or his staff lost the confidence of the Desert Army?'[264] In other words Dorman-Smith was correcting faults and putting forward unfashionable solutions, ideas that had not been learned at Staff College, and consequently the plodders who expected a 'bad luck old chap, better luck next time' style of leadership found they were actually being criticised. It was all dreadfully upsetting.

At Auchinleck's request, Dorman-Smith remained with him when Auchinleck replaced Wavell and he was promoted to major-general as they planned and rebuilt their gradually increasing resources. It was through his skilled interpreting of intelligence gained through being able to read the German Enigma codes that the British became aware of Rommel's supply problems and began to make better use of such information. It was his planning and dispositions that resulted in the British victory at the First Battle of El Alamein in June–July of 1942. However, this largely unrecognised but considerable success was not enough a few weeks later to save either him or Auchinleck from what became known as Churchill's 'Cairo Purge'. As has been seen, Auchinleck was sacked because, for reasons of domestic politics, Churchill badly needed a victory and had conveniently ignored the significance of what had been achieved. Added to this were the biased views, personal loyalties and prejudices of the chief of staff General Brooke, who regarded Dorman-Smith's inventive ideas as a malign influence. Without any reason or explanation being provided to anyone, then or since, Dorman-Smith was dismissed.

Dorman-Smith's crime was that he did think for himself; he had ideas, unorthodox tactics and these initiatives left the uncomprehending plodders either scratching their heads or resenting the success of a plan simply because they had not thought of it. Their imbued doctrines remained shackled to the demands of a 'set-piece' battle. As a consequence, an anti-Dorman-Smith rumour mill quietly grew up amongst the unimaginative also-ran senior officers of the Eighth Army who amongst themselves, agreed that they would separately send reports to their respective London contacts, all of them blaming Dorman-Smith's 'meddling' for every setback that had occurred to the Eighth Army.

John Connell speaks of this period in his book *Auchinleck,* where he describes some officers whose:

> own weaknesses had found them out, and who had to mask this unpleasant discovery from themselves and a minority from the higher echelons whose incompetence as commanders had been nakedly exposed, who were rancorous at the exposure and desperately anxious to cover it up as quickly as possible.[265]

Unfortunately, even in the middle of a war, when it might have been thought that no talent could be wasted, personal prejudices and petty envies were allowed to prevail in the 'club' of the British Army. Unfortunately again, one of those most guilty was General Brooke himself who had made up his mind that Dorman-Smith was a harmful influence on Auchinleck.

If Brooke made any enquiries, it seems he asked only those from whom he could predict the answer he was seeking. As the senior Commonwealth statesman, South African Premier General Jan Smuts had been invited to join the War Cabinet in 1939 and had been made a field marshal in the British Army in 1941. He came to Egypt as a senior adviser whilst Churchill was there, but it appears his views were never sought; later that year he happened to meet Dorman-Smith's brother who was governor of Burma, and told him that although it was felt that morale was low and some changes should be made, 'for my part, the one man I would *not* have replaced would have been your brother. He has a brilliant military mind.'[266]

As a further pretext, Brooke blamed Dorman-Smith for (quite rightly) advising Auchinleck not to accept the Persia and Iraq Command position, knowing it was going to be a largely fictitious theatre. Here again Brooke, as a cavalry man, had been affronted by the open promotion of mechanisation during the 1930s by Dorman-Smith, Liddell Hart and Fuller. Brooke's diary says no more than 'Dorman-Smith to go', but he does not say why. In *The Hinge of Fate,* Churchill recounts sending a cable to London dated 5 August 1942 that read: 'Troops were very cheerful, and all seem confident and proud of themselves'.[267] So, one might ask, how could the troops be 'very cheerful and all seem confident', if, as Churchill had said earlier, the Desert Army had lost confidence in its leaders? It would have been with the ordinary men in the field where any lack of morale would have been most evident. The truth is that the army, as a whole, knew that for the first time they had given Rommel a hammering a few days earlier and this was the reason for their new-found confidence and optimism. However, and like Brooke, without giving any reason Churchill goes on to write: 'General Dorman-Smith to be relieved as Deputy C.G.S.' It is here that there is a complete contradiction. Smuts was saying it was felt that morale was low, but if it was, then how could Churchill have found the troops very cheerful and confident? It all seems to point to the officers described by John Connell whose 'weaknesses had been found out and incompetence exposed' that this was where morale was a problem, not with the Eighth Army as a whole.

So, was this a set-up, with Churchill having decided beforehand that Auchinleck would go, and Brooke seizing the same moment to get rid of the man his chums had been complaining about? It looks very much like it, but with this sort of small-mindedness having precedence, it is little wonder that the British Army had so much difficulty in making progress during the war before the strength of the Americans helped to obscure such cultural stupidity. Auchinleck himself later admitted that it had been the most difficult time he ever had in the war and that it was largely due to Dorman-Smith's knowledge, flair and active mind that they had been able to defend the Alamein position. And of the First El Alamein battle, Rommel was to write:

> The British command was in its element . . . showing considerable enterprise and audacity. We were forced to conclude that the Italians were no longer capable of holding their line . . . The only thing that mattered to Auchinleck was to halt our advance, and that unfortunately he had done.[268]

Major-General Sir John Strawson, was a junior officer with the 4th Hussars in Egypt at this time and he speaks from personal experience in his book *The Battle for North Africa,* where he writes:

> The ideas, which Dorman-Smith, Auchinleck's Chief of Staff, put to him for conducting the First Battle of Alamein were sound ones . . . Rommel was up against an opponent who was not going to be bluffed. Rommel's description of what happened on 2 July shows how effective the new methods of Dorman-Smith, under the resolute direction of Auchinleck were proving.[269]

Ironically, but even more tellingly and albeit some years later, there came further confirmation from, of all people, Erwin Rommel's son Manfred. As we have seen earlier, it is often the erstwhile enemy who provides the most accurate assessments of the battlefield. In her account of Dorman-Smith, *Chink: A Biography*, Lavinia Greacen recounts that in 1954 he had received greetings from an Afrika Korps reunion in Heidelberg, saying, 'In memory of hard days near Alamein during July 1942.'[270] Dorman-Smith had responded in kind, cabling, 'Hard times make strong ties', and it is worth quoting directly from her book:

In a letter of thanks, Rommel's son, Manfred, revealed it had been sent on to Kesselring, and continued: 'I have been present at many discussions during the last years. It was always pointed out that North Africa was in the moment of greatest danger saved for the British by Field Marshal Auchinleck and his assistant leaders in 1942. Even my father, who really thought a lot of FM Auchinleck, did not believe at this time that he might be able to reorganize the British Army at Alamein in the extent he really did. The German leaders—also my father—pointed out that they had been out-manoeuvred in July 1942 at Alamein.'

In August 1942, without ceremony or explanation, Dorman-Smith was dismissed, told to report back to Britain where he was reduced to the rank of brigadier and advised that there was no immediate position available for him. He was eventually given charge of an infantry brigade in England. In May 1943 Wavell, who was back in London from India for a few days, asked to see him. Speaking of the reverses his troops had recently sustained against the Japanese in Burma, Wavell said: 'If you had been there, Eric, it would have been different. My generals were too orthodox.'[271]

In the meantime, Auchinleck had repeatedly asked for Dorman-Smith to be sent out to India where he knew his inventive strategic mind would be valuable, but each of his requests were refused by the War Office without any reason being given. Then, in April 1944, Dorman-Smith was posted to command an infantry brigade in Italy where the badly planned Anzio landings were making little progress. His command there was faultless, but within a few months and shortly after the capture of Rome, the vicious sniping by the little men within the army again reached a crescendo and he was relieved of that position. Like many a journalist, BBC war correspondent Wynford Vaughan-Thomas had a nose for controversy and had noted what he called a 'poisonous' reception when Dorman-Smith arrived in Italy in April. But he had also observed the progress subsequently made in his sector and intrigued by his sudden removal, made enquiries about the reasons behind his dismissal. He quickly ran into a blank wall; nobody had any idea of why or where Dorman-Smith had gone. 'Sorry old boy, no idea' was the usual answer. In a conspiracy of self-preservation the army establishment had again closed ranks, and once more with no explanation.

Although of little consolation, the true circumstances of who had engineered the Italian intrigue began to emerge some years later. The central character and chief plotter in this conspiracy was the commander of the 1st Division at Anzio, Major-General Sir Ronald Penney, who liked to be known as 'Bunny' and was assessed by Correlli Barnett as a 'plodding mediocrity'. When Dorman-Smith arrived at Anzio, Penney's immediate words of greeting and spoken loudly enough for others to hear had been, 'I didn't want you at first and I do not want you now.' If nothing else, this public comment was hardly the action of a responsible commander. Thereafter and perhaps prompted by having to justify his own intemperate words, Penney contrived to 'frame' Dorman-Smith with fictitious complaints about his style of command.

Penny prepared a two-page report, dated July 1944, for the War Office which was headed: 'STRICTLY CONFIDENTIAL—Colonel (T/Brig) E.E. Dorman-Smith—Special report by Major-General W.R.C. Penney'.[272] The report alleged that each of Dorman-Smith's battalion commanders— lieutenant-colonels Webb-Carter, Careless and Hackett—had all spontaneously come to him to complain that they could no longer with any confidence serve under his command. The report went on to state that Lieutenant-Colonel Hackett had reiterated what the other two commanders had said. It was a pack of lies for not one of the officers named in his report had made any such complaint. In fact it was Penney who had summoned them and then attributed to each of them the comments he wanted. In her book on Dorman-Smith, Lavinia Greacen recounts that shortly before his death in 1984, Hackett had written that he was 'hopping mad' to have been asked to give an opinion of a superior officer and had refused to do so.

Possibly this first report raised a few eyebrows because Penney then sent a second, one-page report on Dorman-Smith, dated 3 August 1944 and headed 'PERSONAL AND CONFIDENTIAL'; the report was addressed to Lieutenant-General Sir Oliver Leese, GOC Eighth Army and copied to Lieutenant-General Sir John Harding, at Allied HQ Italy. This second report was nothing more than an abbreviated version of the fictions contained in the first report.

However, even then Penney was not done, for later in August he sent off a further, three-page report to the War Office headed 'The Case of Dorman-Smith and the 3rd Infantry Brigade'. This last report was a lengthened version of the first two except that this time Penney went so far as to state that the Military Secretary of the War Office (name not mentioned) was an old friend who happened to be in Rome and had suggested he write once more. It would seem his first two reports had not had the desired effect. To add a final touch to his malicious plot, Penney waited until he was about to relinquish command of the division and move to a new posting in Ceylon, and so these fictitious reports were his parting shots, made in the knowledge that if there were any repercussions he was going to be thousands of miles from the scene.

Penney was a year younger than Dorman-Smith. He was an officer in the Royal Corps of Signals, one of the non-fighting, combat support arms of the British Army, and consequently it was unusual to find a Signals man in command of a front-line division. He had previously acted as chief signals officer in Cairo for Auchinleck and in view of his proven manoeuvring against Dorman-Smith in Italy, it seems probable that he had also been one of the quiet 'snipers' reporting back to London from Egypt. The age of most officers attending Staff College was about 30–34 and it might have been expected that at that age they were fairly mature, but it seems that Penney was one of those who had been irritated by Dorman-Smith's achievement of gaining the 1927 Staff College 1,000 marks out of 1,000, something that still rankled. He had little if any sense of humour whereas Dorman-Smith's wit and repartee were renowned; these too were resented by many of his slow-thinking peers who were unable to compete. Up until World War II Penney's career had been quite ordinary, serving in China and India, and after Italy, as a signals officer, he was Director of Military Intelligence, South-East Asia. His tenure in charge of the Anzio division was only brief and his posting to a position requiring signals experience suggests that in a combat command he was out of his depth; all the more reason perhaps why he would resent the presence in a subordinate position of an older and more experienced officer than himself.

But there is another, more sinister, possibility. Was Penney, as little more than a run-of-the-mill general, given quiet directions from 'someone' in London—Brooke perhaps—to produce some reason to remove Dorman-Smith on the understanding that a position elsewhere would be found for Penney as soon as he had accomplished this? Certainly this would explain the sudden transfer of Penney and why Dorman-Smith was never able to obtain any explanation for his removal. Despite repeatedly asking why he had so suddenly been dismissed, the War Office remained silent and Dorman-Smith was left in limbo in England for some months. This is even more remarkable since Liddell Hart had told him he knew that Auchinleck, who was well aware of Dorman-Smith's value and could see what he could contribute, was doing his best to get him sent out to India. Even Auchinleck, who one would have thought carried some weight as Commander-in-Chief, India, also encountered a blank wall and his request was ignored. Dorman-Smith had to wait until the end of 1944 when the War Office clinically informed him that no further suitable employment could be found for him and he would be retired effective from 14 December 1944 with the honorary rank of brigadier; he was just 49.

In his book *The Second World War* Gordon Corrigan suggests that Dorman-Smith's crime was to have derided the mistakes of others.[273] This seems something of a red herring but if there is even a vestige of truth in it, it is a pathetic comment on the mentality and immature priorities in wartime of what purported to be a trained military team serving in the national interest. Moreover, given their ham-fisted mistakes in attempting to confront the Afrika Korps with outdated methods, surely some home truths were long overdue. What do we make of such a scenario? Possibly a high-level conversation that went something along the lines of:

'This chap might be right but he's been awfully rude to me.'

'Oh, that's very bad form, we can't have that! Well whether he's right or not is really not all that important and I can well understand why you feel so upset. What did this fellow actually say to you?'

'Well, I said we should send our tanks straight at Rommel, just like the old cavalry charge, and do you know this bounder actually laughed at me and said it was old fashioned rubbish.'

'No, we must put a stop to that sort of thing. The British Army must maintain its traditional levels of courtesy, so we'd better remove him. After all we chaps must all stick together.'

Sounds far-fetched today? Maybe, but again it is very difficult to imagine the German or American military allowing the fragile trivialities of social mores to affect the efficiency of their war machines. George Patton was notorious for his outspoken and sometimes thoughtless views but that did not prevent Eisenhower recognising his unusual leadership talents and making good use of him. A similar American example was General Stilwell, nicknamed 'Vinegar Joe' because of his highly caustic personality, but a daring tactician who was highly valued by both generals Marshall and MacArthur. Moreover, within the British Army there was Montgomery who was continuously acting like a bull in a china shop, but his excesses were strangely tolerated. Success in a war requires flexibility, new ideas and initiatives, not predictable performances according to some form of unwavering traditional ritual. Even whilst struggling to overcome Rommel the ideology of the British Army in 1942 remained hidebound by elegant protocol, regimental etiquette and social convention, all of them of far greater importance than effect and efficiency.

Another instance of the British Army's inability to imagine anything outside its rigid social codes occurred in India. In his book *Defeat into Victory*, Field Marshal Sir William Slim describes a situation in India where there were so many British troops on leave in Calcutta that the city was crowded with officers and men.[274] They had no civilian clothing so that to walk through the bustling throng on Calcutta's main streets was a tiring experience because an officer was either saluting every five steps or checking soldiers for failing to salute. To relieve this problem, Slim made the commonsense suggestion that for the duration the hot and congested city of Calcutta should be declared a non-saluting area. However, although totally practical in a wartime situation, this deviation from the norm was really too much of an innovation for the conventional thinking British top brass to stomach and accordingly his proposal was rejected.

Whether or not Brooke was party to the plot to get rid of Dorman-Smith, his decision flies completely in the face of what he wrote in his own 1942 diary note, quoted by David Fraser in his book *Alanbrooke*:

> The military performance of the army is made worse by the lack of good military commanders. Half our Corps and Division commanders are totally unfit for their appointments, and yet if I were to sack them, I could find no better! They lack character, imagination, drive, and power of leadership.[275]

Brooke was quite rightly complaining about a lack of imagination and drive and yet he was removing the one senior officer who did have those qualities and one who had contributed enormously to Wavell and Auchinleck's campaigns. Privately, Brooke was saying that he badly needed someone with Dorman-Smith's gifts but publicly he seems to have fallen in line with the conformists.

So what or who was really behind the decision to sack Dorman-Smith? If nothing else it does raise a very big question mark about Brooke's judgement and/or integrity. In his aforementioned book, David Fraser alleges that Dorman-Smith was 'widely mistrusted', but if so, by whom and why? His assistance to Wavell and Auchinleck had been both vital and beyond argument. Fraser's actual words are: 'Brooke reckoned that Auchinleck was too much under the influence of General Dorman-Smith, an imaginative officer, widely mistrusted, whose flood of ideas needed a very perceptive sifting of which he felt Auchinleck incapable.' This comment, if true, only goes to show just how warped was Brooke's judgement because it had been Dorman-Smith who had been largely responsible for Auchinleck getting the better of Rommel at First El Alamein, and Brooke knew it. The comment may also have been nothing more than prejudice on the part of Fraser himself, for although chronologically accurate his book is largely a hagiography written by an ex-Grenadier Guardsman. The book was written after Brooke's death at the specific request of the Royal Regiment of Artillery and the first page of the book states: 'This story of one of the greatest of Gunners is dedicated to the Royal Regiment of Artillery'. Such had been Fraser's commission to write the book that he would support almost any decision that Brooke made. In any event the general leaning of Fraser's judgement is also shown when he refers to Churchill as a 'genius', an opinion that many today would find either laughable or ludicrous.

Brooke's quoted attitude is all the more questionable because he was clearly aware of the values that Dorman-Smith's tactical brain had already demonstrated. That being the case, which it was, by whom was he 'widely mistrusted'? Or in reality, was the word 'mistrusted' little more than the euphemistic jargon of the military establishment, simply because the plotters could not say outright that they just did not like him because he was unorthodox? In his article on Dorman-Smith, Péter Klemensits notes that others who added their views on Dorman-Smith were Alexander and

Montgomery, who both said he was a 'menace'.[276] However, here again we can see the 'old boy' net at work, because Montgomery (who in any event would rarely miss a chance at denigrating anyone) had not seen Dorman-Smith for some 13 years and Alexander had never worked with him at all, so how could either of them, in all honesty, have been able to form any direct opinion?

It all looks like a convenient scheme to concoct some pretext to permanently remove Dorman-Smith from the scene, and one that would be beyond scrutiny and never open to explanation. Sending him to command a brigade in Italy was the subtle ploy to discredit an outstanding architect by giving him a job as a carpenter and then criticising his woodwork, but unfortunately for the plotters the artisan proved just as skilful as the strategist. There are contradictions from other authors too; Corrigan claims that Dorman-Smith's additional crime was to have ostentatiously burned Montgomery's lecture notes at the finish of Staff College. In fact it was not only Montgomery's lectures that he had burned, but all of them as he (rightly) considered the learning experience to have been worth very little.

Dorman-Smith's judgement is supported by historian John Keegan in *Churchill's Generals,* where he states that between the wars the value of the Staff College was essentially social rather than educational and that the college taught, if at all, far less well than its German counterpart.[277] The Germans were concerned not with procedural routines but inculcating intellectual powers of analysis together with rigorous mutual critique. This is precisely what Dorman-Smith had perceived to have been so badly needed and he was crucified for saying so. As opposed to the conventional and conservative officer priorities of the British described by Correlli Barnett in the chapter *Class and the British Army*, the German staff college, as described by General Heinz Guderian, was actively looking for cleverness, high intelligence and a gift for improvisation and innovation. 'Rigorous mutual critique' could never have been countenanced at Sandhurst or Camberley, for it might have shown up the mice from the men and that would have been unfair and most upsetting. Upsetting for 'morale' perhaps, as in the desert? Was it also a matter of personal prejudice or under the surface was it because Dorman-Smith was a Catholic in an army hierarchy that was almost entirely Church of England and maybe high in the arcane world of Freemasonry as well? If it was, such prejudice would have been wide of the mark, because although baptised as a Catholic, he had never shown much interest in the Catholic Church.

As a final ingredient to this odious episode, had Auchinleck been shrewd in his insight when he said he thought Churchill was afraid of Dorman-Smith? Churchill had been most upset when Arthur Bryant's *The Turn of the Tide* was first published in 1957 because he had been anxious to maintain the popular belief that he had personally directed all the principle military decisions of the war, whereas Bryant's book, based on General Brooke's diaries, reveals that this was a long way from the truth. That being the case, would Churchill have wanted to allow free reign to ingenuity and imagination beyond the grasp of his own 18th-century military mind, if in particular, the source of such original thinking became known to the press?

Lavinia Greacen recounts that after the war another trumped-up story about Dorman-Smith was being spread around the establishment grapevine of London military clubs. Once again the source was almost certainly Penney who had acquired a comfortable position as Assistant Controller at the Ministry of Supply, conveniently adjacent to club-land. The gist of his farrago was that Dorman-Smith's high-flown theories just did not work in practice and his subordinate commanders had rebelled against him. It was total nonsense but the punchline found a chuckling receptive audience in that sort of conformist milieu. However, even there Penney was not finished. Wynford Vaughan-Thomas was a passionate Welshman and the author of eleven books, all except one about Wales. The one exception was his only military book, *Anzio* (1961), at the very beginning of which he states that the book would not have been written but for the persistent urgings of Major-General Sir Ronald Penney, on whose private papers much of the book was based. Needless to say, Penney features quite prominently.

Dorman-Smith inherited his father's property in Ireland and retired there. For the next 25 years he alternately ran the estate, immersed himself in genealogy and archaeology and maintained correspondence and friendship with Auchinleck, Liddell Hart, Correlli Barnett and other military historians, having a number of them to stay as his guests. He was heartened to receive one letter from Auchinleck, who wrote:

I know what I owe you, and realise very clearly, as I have always done, that without your wise and indomitable thinking always at my side and in my head, we could never have saved Egypt . . . and all the rest. I am very glad the truth has at last been told about the decisive part you played in bringing about final victory in the Western Desert. The 'voice' certainly was yours, even if the 'hands' were mine.[278]

It did not heal the wounds but it helped to salve the hurt.

Dorman-Smith watched with indignation the warped and self-promoting depiction of events in North Africa from the likes of Churchill and Montgomery in their respective accounts of the war; he knew these denigrated Auchinleck, and through legal threats he successfully forced amendments to their texts. He had also noted with satisfaction that Montgomery ducked below his parapet and made no reply when a published letter in *The Times* from Auchinleck openly challenged as 'incorrect and absurd' Montgomery's allegation in his *Memoirs*,[279] serialised in that paper, that Auchinleck had been preparing to retreat to the Nile. Montgomery had said that he cancelled previous orders for a withdrawal. It was a typical Montgomery slander and although he kept quiet, his publishers, William Collins, felt it prudent to publish a correction in the next edition admitting that this had not been the case.

In an understandable reaction to the manner in which he had been treated by the British establishment after having given 30 years of service, Dorman-Smith changed his name to Dorman-O'Gowan (O'Gowan being the name of the local Irish clan, and the Irish equivalent of Smith), and he became increasingly supportive of Irish Nationalism.

Eric 'Chink' Dorman-O'Gowan died in May 1969 after a 2-year battle with stomach cancer; he was 74. He was buried in the small Protestant cemetery just outside Cootehill in County Cavan, Ireland. At his request— and repulsed by what he had seen of sectarianism—the funeral service was ecumenical but there was not even one representative from either the British government or the army at the service. The small minds in those institutions had still not broadened or matured. Despite repeated and justified requests for an explanation of his treatment, the War Office and its successor the Ministry of Defence remained totally silent. Perhaps this is not so surprising because if they were honest, could they have said that his removal was because he had been rude to a couple of people? If published, such an admission would have made a laughing stock of the War Office.

Lavinia Greacen recounts that when he heard the news of Dorman-O'Gowan's death, Auchinleck, who had recently moved to Marrakech and was himself then 85, was desolated:

> Two days before the cable I had said to myself that I must write to Chink. It is a long time since I had news of him. I owe him more than I could ever repay. He was tragically mistreated and betrayed in the end. Envy and malice pursued him but he never gave in. I am glad his end was peaceful but I am very sad.[280]

At least one old soldier, and one of total integrity, knew the truth.

For Corelli Barnett, author of *The Desert Generals,* the book that first revealed Montgomery in his true light, the news came as a shock because he had not realised the illness was so serious. He was then in the process of writing his historical study of British military institutions, *Britain and Her Army.* Military historians rarely dedicate their works to an individual army officer, but Barnett dedicated his, and at the beginning of the book, he says simply and quite succinctly: 'To the Memory of Eric O'Gowan (Dorman-Smith).' In that book's 530 pages, the name of Major-General Dorman-Smith appears only twice but in each case to emphasise his crucial contribution in gaining the initiative from Rommel. Barnett also finds an analogy with cricket when he writes:

> Unfortunately the cavalry and the Guards retained their traditional and disproportionate influence in the higher reaches of the army establishment, to the neglect of the tank corps, artillery and infantry officers (especially if those last were from 'unfashionable' regiments). It was the army's 'gentlemen' who lost the Gazala battle in the Western Desert in 1942; the 'players' like Auchinleck and Dorman-Smith eventually won. In Burma too, the credit for victory was due to a 'player', Slim, of the Indian Army.[281]

Barnett wrote a forward to Lavinia Greacen's biography of Dorman-Smith in which he pointed out that many of the reforms he and Auchinleck had proposed for the Eighth Army in 1942 had been adopted by NATO.

In the second edition of *The Desert Generals,* published in 1983, he included a special appendix headed 'Major-General E Dorman-Smith'. It is a withering indictment of the bigotry of the rigid protocol and holy rubric of precedent in a small-minded, slow-thinking class system that had dominated the British Army. His concluding paragraph to that appendix reads as follows:

> Most British defeats have been caused by stupidity. This continuing British military fashion, this melancholy sequence from Yorktown through the Duke of York's campaigns, through the Crimea, the Zulu and Boer wars, the two great wars to the Suez operation of 1956 is starkly illuminated by the treatment accorded to Dorman-Smith.

Dorman-Smith was a 'player', he did ask questions and he had fresh ideas, fatal characteristics in a British Army whose priorities, even in time of crisis, were such that any sacrifice was justified in order to maintain tradition and decorum. It is easy to be wise in retrospect, but in that sort of stultifying atmosphere and despite what one might have thought were the practical priorities of war, maybe he should have considered the 2,500-year-old words of the Greek philosopher, Aeschylus: 'It is a profitable thing, if one is wise, to seem foolish.'

==

CHAPTER 17

FINAL COUNTDOWN

==

*History will bear me out, particularly as I shall
write that history myself.*
—WINSTON CHURCHILL

*[Montgomery] got so damn personal to make sure the
Americans and me, in particular, had no credit, had
nothing to do with the war, that I eventually just
stopped communicating with him. I was just not
interested in keeping up communications with a
man who just can't tell the truth.*
—GENERAL EISENHOWER, in conversation
    with Cornelius Ryan

*It is a curious thing, but I have been right in
everything I have done and said in my life.*
—MOUNTBATTEN, to biographer Richard Hough

By their own words the egos of Churchill and Mountbatten reveal themselves with an almost breathtaking arrogance, and along with Montgomery none of them could countenance the possibility that they might ever have been wrong. Andrew Roberts said Mountbatten was a 'mendacious, intellectually limited hustler' and it is a description that could just as easily be applied to both Churchill and Montgomery. No one could describe Churchill as intellectually limited, although Montgomery's intellect has always been difficult to identify let alone explain. For all three of them World War II provided the stage they had always craved and they grasped the chance it provided with a ruthless and determined opportunism.

National myth has it that it was Winston Churchill alone who came to the help of Britain in her hour of need, that he alone saved Britain from Nazi invasion and it was he alone who could have persuaded the United States to help. Nothing could be further from the truth. Had it not been for World War II, he would have gone down in history as a 'nearly man', an inveterate politician who over a career of 40 years in Parliament had represented four different constituencies and had switched from one political party to another and then back again from time to time as it suited his political ambitions. He was a politician who had held Cabinet positions in various British governments with fluctuating degrees of success, one posting marked by disgrace and forced resignation. In the 10 years leading up to the war he was in a political wilderness, a period during which he continually positioned and then repositioned himself as he sought, without success, to obtain advantage for his ambitions.

In the end and although he had aimed for this position all of his political life, he really only became Prime Minister in May 1940 as a result of no one else wanting the job in a wartime situation; his election was in effect *faute de mieux*. Churchill had, moreover, been complicit in the downfall of his predecessor Neville Chamberlain, who was made the scapegoat for a disastrous expedition into Norway for which, as First Lord of the Admiralty, Churchill, had largely been responsible. His party was voted out of office in 1945, not only because his own early wartime personal popularity had diminished, but because the British public in general and particularly those who had served in the armed forces during that conflict had an understandable perception that by voting Conservative they would only be voting back the same sort of people who had been giving them orders for some 6 years.

In the far more egalitarian 21st century it is sometimes difficult to realise just how much of a 'class' society Britain was in 1945, where certain accents, social backgrounds and styles of education commanded respect and deference, almost as cultural obligations or the conditioned reflex of a structured society. Churchill's aristocratic background and his milieu were set aside in the public mind during the many periods of national anxiety when his ability to produce inspiring rhetoric made him into an icon of patriotism. But by July 1945 he was nearly 71 and he and his party was seen to be part of the past as against the more youthful Clement Attlee and his forward-looking Labour Party for the future. As in 1940, it seems that Churchill was viewed as a man to call upon in times of national emergency but not the sort of person the country would want when peace returned. His was not the image of a sound administrator but rather that of a successful war leader. Indeed, his performance from 1940 to 1945 reflected the fact that although he adored getting involved in military matters in a wartime situation, he had little or no interest in the more mundane but just as vital issues of administration.

In the 1945 election he retained his own seat in Parliament but was bitterly disappointed to find himself without power after 5 years when he had reigned supreme—for apart from a few months of political danger in mid-1942, he had been virtually unchallengeable. Like any politician, Churchill loved and even craved power, the feeling of power and the sense of omnipotence. The knowledge that having given himself two hats, Prime Minister and Minister of Defence, and that he had total control was exhilarating. Even General Brooke, Chief of the Imperial General Staff for most of the war, wrote that he was aware he could be removed by Churchill at any moment if he opposed him in the wrong way. Military author Reginald W. Thompson, who went so far as to entitle one of his books *Generalissimo Churchill,* wrote on the fly-leaf of that book: 'All attempts to persuade, or to force, Churchill to relinquish his most dangerous burdens or any part of his wide power, failed. He was indivisible. The country could take him or leave him. It took him, but it was at times a hair-line decision.'[282] Indeed, to such an extent did he insist on controlling every aspect himself that with the war in Europe ended and victory against Japan in sight, instead of elation Churchill felt an enormous sadness. Lord Moran recounted a conversation in July 1945 when Churchill confided to him: 'I feel very lonely without a war. Do you feel like that?'[283]

All of this has now been said in one way or another, both here and by other authors who have looked at Churchill without the blinkers of immediate post-war adulation, and who have seen that although undeniably a great man, he was just as much a liability as an asset. Without any doubt, he was one of the greatest orators in history (in any event he preferred to listen to himself rather than anyone else) and an author of world acclaim (Nobel Prize in Literature, 1953), but as an effective national leader and guide there are a myriad of question marks concerning his military decisions; and above all he remained an abiding politician. Had another been in his place, the United States would still have become involved in the war because there was nowhere else for Britain to go to seek support and in any event it was in the United States' interests. Once the Japanese attack on Pearl Harbor had occurred and Hitler had made the foolish mistake of declaring war on the United States, she was involved anyway and in this Churchill played no part at all. Whether another less emotional and less impulsive personality might have made a better fist of the relationship is of course complete conjecture, but it is not impossible.

Two outstanding generals, Wavell and Auchinleck, were cast aside by Churchill as he contrived to hold on to power after he had caused the loss of HMS *Prince of Wales* and HMS *Repulse* and the inevitable collapse of Singapore. These were not rational steps following advice taken by an inspired 'leader', but the reaction of a cornered politician for whom anyone's scalp would suffice in order to survive. Although denied their victories that were on the horizon, the careers of Wavell and Auchinleck were not finished for they were important and valuable men and sufficiently senior to recover and even prosper in other capacities in India. Churchill was well aware of the huge build-up in troops and supplies that was in the pipeline in 1942 and so it may be asked: why dismiss Auchinleck? Why not allow him to continue with the large material advantage that would shortly be available? The answers are political rather than military. Churchill's tenure in Westminster was so shaky at that time that he had to be seen to be doing something immediately, and knowing that the advantage over Rommel would shortly be overwhelming, then by bringing in fresh faces he could claim that it had been his own new appointments that had brought victory; it was a clever political tactic. But does political sleight of hand make a man great?

In fact if the important dismissals made by Churchill are examined, it can be seen that whenever he made a serious mistake—for example, Greece, the sinking of the *Repulse* and the *Prince of Wales,* and the loss of Singapore, all of which were entirely his responsibility—he sacked someone else to cover his tracks. Assisting Greece, which he had demanded in March 1941, was a political obligation but when this foray became the military debacle it was forecast to become, it resulted several weeks later in the dismissal of General Wavell, whose forces had been severely reduced by the loss of those he had been ordered to send to Greece. Again it had been Churchill who, against all advice, insisted that the *Repulse* and the *Prince of Wales* be sent to the Far East without accompanying aircraft-carrier protection. On Singapore, he ridiculed the consistent warnings about the threat posed by the Japanese, specifically those from the then General Sir John Dill, eventually sacking him at the end of November 1941 only for Dill to be proved right 10 days later when the Japanese landed in Malaya.

All of this culminated in such criticism and public dissatisfaction that the Conservative Party lost three by-elections early in 1942, plus the normally safe seat of Maldon in June. A motion of no confidence in the House of Commons in July was won, but as Clive Ponting described the position: 'Most felt that the Government had gained no more than a breathing space and that without military success it would not survive'.[284]

The reality was that many of the military defeats had not by any means been inevitable, nor the fault of Britain's military leaders, but had been entirely of Churchill's own making. His rhetoric had done its job in 1940, but by 1942 he was no longer an asset. It is therefore entirely arguable that it might have been better had the covernment fallen at that time and Churchill with it. By mid-1942 the tide of war had already turned in the Pacific, the Japanese having been halted at the Battle of the Coral Sea in early May, and much of their navy then decimated at the Battle of Midway in June. In North Africa Rommel had run into a brick wall at the First Battle of El Alamein and the tide there was also turning. In Russia, too, the German war machine was grinding to a halt and was about to be reversed.

However, Churchill lived on and, as has been shown, the next scapegoat to be sacrificed on his survival pyre was Auchinleck in August. It was a blessing for all concerned when, from late 1942 he could no longer behave as such a loose cannon because policy and strategy had at least to be debated with the United States. For home consumption Churchill strove to present the image of equal partners but thereafter he was more and more sidelined as the relative influences and contributions of industrial power and production of the United States became increasingly apparent. The days when he could meddle without censure were over. No more would he be able to act on a whim and dictate without fear of contradiction. From Britain's point of view the entry of the United States saved the country from more than just her military enemies—it saved her from Churchill. To quote

General Sir Alan Brooke once more, in his September 1944 wartime diary he wrote of Churchill:

> He knows no details, has got only half the picture in his mind, talks absurdities and makes my blood boil to listen to his nonsense. I find it hard to remain civil. And the wonderful thing is that ¾ of the population of the world imagine that Winston Churchill is one of the Strategists of History, a second Marlborough, and the other ¼ have no conception what a public menace he is and has been throughout the war.[285]

For Montgomery, his lack of honesty and overbearing self-promotion brought the chickens home to roost following retirement. Whereas a large number of other prominent wartime figures found leading public appointments in the Commonwealth and positions on the boards of large British companies, for Montgomery no similar invitations seem to have been forthcoming. Despite his massive reputation at the end of the war as Britain's leading general and his image in the public mind as a military hero, he was left well alone by both the commercial and diplomatic worlds.

Sir William Slim became one of the most popular governor-generals of Australia, there were board memberships of a number of UK companies, and then he became Constable and Governor of Windsor Castle. General Brooke, later Viscount Alanbrooke, was invited to join the boards of the Midland Bank, Anglo-Iranian Oil and the Belfast Bank. Similarly, Sir Harold Alexander became Governor-General of Canada, President of the Marylebone Cricket Club, a Member of the Order of Merit, Lord Lieutenant of London and was then selected to carry the sovereign's orb at the 1953 coronation. Sir John Kennedy, who had been Director of Military Operations and Plans? at the War Office, became governor of what was then Southern Rhodesia and Lieutenant-General Kenneth Anderson was appointed Governor of Gibraltar. Sir Archibald Wavell became High Steward of Colchester, Constable of the Tower of London and Lord Lieutenant of the County of London and a Director of De Beers. After he retired Marshal of the Royal Air Force, Sir Charles Portal was Chairman of British Aluminium and the British Aircraft Corporation and President of the Marylebone Cricket Club. Similarly, Sir Arthur Tedder became Chancellor of

Cambridge University and Vice Chairman of the BBC. The Royal Navy does not appear to rank very often in such appointments but Admiral of the Fleet Viscount Cunningham became Lord High Commissioner for the Church of Scotland and Admiral of the Fleet Sir James Somerville was invited to be Lord Lieutenant of Somerset. Even for Auchinleck, who had spent most of his career in India, there were appointments on the boards of various companies and for 13 years he was governor of his old school, Wellington College.

Such appointments were not only common, but in some cases expected. Later on, for instance, Field Marshal Sir Gerald Templar was invited to join the Court of Directors of the Royal Exchange Assurance and Field Marshal Sir John Harding became Chairman of Plessey. For a long established and respected company, such as the Royal Exchange Assurance founded in 1720, the personal integrity of each and all of their directors was a *sine qua non*, as also was a respected public reputation. This was not so much a question of the personality of the individual concerned, but rather whether such an appointment would without question enhance the image of the commercial entity in the public eye. Usually it was a convention that worked well, for the existence of an admired war hero on the board of a public company did add to its prestige.

So the obvious question is why was such a prominent and media hailed military figure like Field Marshal Viscount Montgomery of Alamein not invited to sit alongside other such wartime glitterati in the world of leading British companies? Surely such a figure and title would have added prestige? The truth is that although there was the 'public' image, the world of commerce has its own, quiet, information system, and it became known that although famous in the media and for self-promoted wartime success, Montgomery was quite incapable of getting on with almost anyone. It was also becoming increasingly clear that he had frequently been 'economic with the truth' and was often blatantly dishonest.

Being somewhat difficult was not unique, for Sir Gerald Templar, whom the author met on several occasions, was renowned for not suffering fools lightly and could be a somewhat explosive personality, but, and it is a big but, he was also wise enough to know when another's argument might be right. This was one of Montgomery's major failings: he was congenitally incapable of accepting any view other than his own and would therefore have contributed nothing as a board member. Although he had survived in his command to the end of the war, the fact that he had remained so was essentially because of the Anglo-American politics involved rather than for any other reason. His dishonesty could be covered up or ignored in the interests of overall wartime objectives, but once that protective rationale came to an end, there was no further way in which he could perpetuate his own myth.

Once he had left the army, nobody wanted him and he had few visitors. He spent much of his retirement as a lonely man still striving to keep his image going and in addition to his *Memoirs* wrote five books: *El Alamein to the River Sangro* (1948), *An Approach to Sanity* (1959), *The Path to Leadership* (1962), *Normandy to the Baltic* (1968) and *A Concise History of Warfare* (1972). These books largely promoted him or rationalised his actions. One of these in particular, *An Approach to Sanity*, which advocated his own views on how to handle relations with the Russians, was quite remarkable in its hypocrisy, considering his own total inability to deal with Allies let alone a Cold War foe. But nothing had changed—Montgomery was always right.

Such were Montgomery's relations with his subordinates that in November 1944 Lieutenant-General Sir Richard O'Connor—then commander of Montgomery's VIII Corps, and the victor at the Battle of Beda Fomm in February 1941—resigned in disgust and requested a reassignment because of what he felt was Montgomery's totally unreasonable treatment of American Major-General Lindsay Silvester. O'Connor was given command of the army in south-eastern India where he was welcomed with open arms by Auchinleck, who was well aware of O'Connor's qualities and capabilities. After the war O'Connor became Adjutant-General to the Forces where once again a clash caused by Montgomery's unpleasant personality made him to decide to finally retire from the army. O'Connor's biographer John Baynes describes the circumstances created by Montgomery's disposition as 'little short of deplorable'.[286]

Following the German surrender, Montgomery became commander-in-chief of the British occupation forces in Germany and was Chief of the Imperial General Staff from 1946 to 1948, an appointment that was automatic but was an almost total failure because of his innate inability to 'discuss' almost anything—he always had to be right. He had largely got away with this during times of conflict but in peacetime his personality was his

Achilles heel. He was then appointed Chairman of the Western Union Commanders-in-Chief Committee, but here also his tenure was characterised by his almost continual bickering with just about everyone whilst creating the NATO forces in Europe. All of these were military or semi-military appointments; outside those circles he was a lonely man and he was lonely because of himself. For several years he toured various countries around the world with very mixed results. Ever convinced of the power of his personal standing, he offered unsolicited and outspoken advice and opinions on almost anything and was a trenchant supporter of apartheid. Alun Chalfont, himself an ex-intelligence officer, wrote this of Montgomery in 1976:

> He was certainly not one of the great commanders—his grasp of the political and strategic context of his battlefield operations was too imperfect. As a battlefield general he made a number of serious mistakes, but he can claim to be among the outstanding trainers and leaders of men to emerge in the Second World War. To adapt one of his own comments on a contemporary, he was a very good plain cook, but he was certainly no Brillat-Savarin. There remains then the question of how this man, brave, clever and industrious, but vain, single-minded, unimaginative and often brutally inconsiderate, reached the summit of his profession and earned the affection and admiration of a whole generation. The answer almost certainly lies in the fact that the hour had come and so had the man. The situation was one which needed a Montgomery. Perhaps Britain's best hope for the future is that she will never again find herself in such a situation.[287]

As we now know the affection and admiration had very largely been a media creation, but in saying 'that she will never again find herself in such a situation', it is a moot point whether Chalfont was alluding to Britain at war as such, or having to put up with another character like Montgomery.

Let us at this point look again at the gallery of history's greatest military commanders, membership of which Montgomery claimed to be his of right, and consider whether he does in fact warrant any realistic comparison. This is admittedly largely a matter of subjective and perhaps contentious assessment because of the relative factors of the passing of time, historical perspective, differing conditions, weaponry, and the like, but a reasonable consensus might be to take the group put forward by General Wavell in 1942, himself a military historian of some note. In so doing the fundamentals of conduct, character and achievement that he laid down were:

> Those who had handled large forces in an independent command in more than one campaign: and who had shown their qualities in adversity as well as in success. Then judge them by their worth as strategists, skill as tacticians, powers to deal tactfully with Governments and Allies; ability to train troops or direct their training; and energy and driving power in planning and in battle.

As his choice he then put forward the following thirteen: Alexander, Hannibal, Scipio Africanus, Julius Caesar, Belisarius, Cromwell, Marlborough, Frederick, Wellington, Napoleon, Robert E Lee, Moltke and Ludendorf. His list was presented in chronological order and seems to have been constructed from a wide range of considerations and it is interesting that he considers what he calls 'qualities in adversity' to be as important as successes in compiling an overall assessment. In Montgomery's case this is significant because his commands commenced with the massive advantages he had inherited at El Alamein in 1942 and thereafter he never even once had to handle a situation where he faced any adversity, in fact completely the reverse—he always had the advantage. Montgomery had appeared on the stage as the tide was turning strongly for the Allies and thence forward he never once had to overcome a position of disadvantage or handle a situation where he did not have at his disposal significant superior numbers in men and materials.

Wavell's assessment was made in 1942, but if that list is broadened to include World War II, who should be taken into account? Who might stand comparison? Manstein? Guderian? Rommel? Zhukov? Konev? Slim? Perhaps MacArthur? In their own individual ways each of this group used initiative, they were planners who perceived possibility where an immediate response could provide victory. Each of them had to conduct actions of retreat, consolidation and counter-offense although for the three Germans listed offensives came before retreats. As is always the case, such a collection is highly subjective and open to debate but it is very difficult to see how Montgomery could come even close by comparison. There is a well-known and perfectly true cricket saying that it is easy to captain a strong team, but when that team has a string of successes (especially against weaker opposition) that does not make the captain concerned a great skipper; and so it was with Montgomery—competent, yes—but great? In no way.

To Wavell's selection can be added the essential attributes of an outstanding commander as considered by Basil Liddell Hart. In his foreword to General Heinz Guderian's book *Panzer Leader*, Liddell Hart listed what he called 'The qualities that distinguish the "Great Captains" of history':

> *coup d'oeil*, a blend of acute observation with swift-sure intuition; the ability to create surprise and throw the opponent off-balance; the speed of thought and action that allows the opponent no chance of recovery; the combination of strategic and tactical sense; the power to win the devotion of troops and get the most out of them and a sense of what is possible.[288]

Montgomery did win the following of his troops, but to be fair that was largely because his huge advantages gave them victories; he comes nowhere near qualifying for the other six indispensable qualities.

Reference has already been made to the post-war assessments of various German generals because they do provide professional opinions that are unbiased, free of political cant and based on experience. Very little can be found about German views on Montgomery but according to Cornelius Ryan, Field Marshal Gerd von Rundstedt did say that he regarded Montgomery as 'overly cautious, habit-ridden and systematic.'[289] As a comparison, General Günther Blumentritt, one of the Wehrmacht's chief planners, said: 'We regarded General Patton extremely highly as the most aggressive Panzer General of the Allies, a man of incredible initiative and lightning-like action. His operations impressed us enormously probably because he came closest to our own concept of the classical military commander.'[290] This view was supported by Heinz Guderian, who said of Patton: 'From the standpoint of a tank specialist I must congratulate him since he acted as I should have done had I been in his place.' Another German of the same view was military historian Paul Carell. The latter, whose real name was Paul Karl Schmidt, had served in the SS during the war reaching the rank of Obersturmbannführer (lieutenant-colonel). In his book covering the Normandy landings, *Invasion: They're Coming!*, he writes:

> The battle for France saw the emergence of another revolutionary army leader. Not on the German side, but on General Eisenhower's. George S. Patton, a tank leader commanding the U.S. Third Army, became the real victor in the West. He was a kind of Guderian and Rommel rolled into one.[291]

These opinions do not, of themselves, constitute actual criticism of Montgomery, but the apparent dearth of comment about him as opposed to views on other Allied leaders does tend to speak for itself and it may be significant that plaudits for Montgomery seem to have come only from Britain.

As has been mentioned, the truth about Montgomery began to seep out with the publication of Correlli Barnett's *The Desert Generals* in 1960. It caused something of a furore at the time, for Montgomery was still alive and the majority view continued to be that he was a hero. Barnett's assessment has gathered pace with the passing of time and a realisation that much of Montgomery's reputation was at least flawed if not fiction. A more recent assessment of him is to be found in Gordon Corrigan's *The Second World War,* and as a summation of all that has been included in this book it is worth quoting from him in full:

> Montgomery was made into a national treasure, largely because Alamein was a victory of sorts and the British badly needed a victory, but the historians of the future will not, this author suspects, be kind to him. His personality traits, his desperate desire for success and recognition, his complete inability to understand the feelings of others and his determination to do everyone else down make him a deeply unattractive figure. He won victories, but many of them were flawed and, given the vastly improved state of British industry and the substantial benefits Lend-Lease had delivered by 1942, there were any number of generals who could have achieved as much, and in some cases a lot more. Montgomery went on to

become Chief of the Imperial General Staff and was described by Field Marshal Templar as having been the worst one for fifty years, after which he became Deputy Supreme Commander of NATO where he quarrelled with everybody. He did enormous harm to Anglo-American relations, insulted Eisenhower when the latter was President, and wrote love-letters to a thirteen-year-old Swiss schoolboy, which might not have any bearing on the man's military ability, but it would certainly call his judgment into question.[292]

Corrigan's cogent line is: 'there were any number of generals who could have achieved as much, and in some cases a lot more.'

Napoleon is credited with saying: 'All generals make mistakes but, given conditions equivalent to equality, the successful ones are those who make the least'. From El Alamein onwards Montgomery never once had to worry about 'equality', he always had a massive advantage and as he so frequently claimed, he never made a mistake.

So there we have it: a competent, average general, but as the Canadians described him, 'a nasty little shit'.

And so to the third of the wartime opportunists: Mountbatten. The Attlee government naturally claimed that their 'transition' to independence for India and Pakistan had been an overwhelming success. To a large extent the true facts of the disaster were kept hidden from the British public and Mountbatten was treated as a returning hero, but not everyone was fooled that it had been so clever a thing to have completed the job in such a very short time.

Soon after Mountbatten returned from India, Anthony Eden hosted a garden party for him to which Winston Churchill was invited. Spotting Churchill amongst the other guests, Mountbatten made straight for him with arms outstretched and a broad smile of welcome. Churchill stopped him in his tracks with a pointing and arresting finger and using Mountbatten's nickname, he shouted: 'Dickie, stand there! What you did in India was like whipping your riding crop across my face!' All the other guests could hear what Churchill had said quite clearly and the party fell silent. With those words Churchill turned on his heel, left the party and never spoke to Mountbatten for another seven years.

Perhaps because of his royal connections, Mountbatten seems to have been handled with kid gloves, treated with an undeserved deference and until recently, he seemed to be 'untouchable'. During the constitutional crisis of 1936–37 involving Edward VIII and the American divorcee Wallis Simpson, the British press had observed such delicacy in their reporting that today their decorum would be laughed at. But as with Montgomery, so with Mountbatten—times change, the social mores and unwritten rules are discarded and, quite rightly, being 'royal' is no longer any protection from exposure by the media. In fact quite often it is now the reverse, for being a figure of any sort of public prominence is likely to attract rather than deter media intrusion, scrutiny and attention.

Mountbatten's public image eventually went by the board with the publication of Andrew Roberts' 1994 book *Eminent Churchillians*, where he describes Mountbatten as a lying, unintelligent and unscrupulous con man. It is speculation that Mountbatten might have responded by attempting legal action, had he still been alive, but such was his ego that, unwise or not, he probably would. Whether he would have been successful is of course entirely another question for, as the research for this book has demonstrated, Roberts' depiction was entirely accurate.

The expression *noblesse oblige* does not seem to have applied as far as he was concerned, quite the opposite in fact, for instead of noble obligations he believed more in aristocratic entitlements and rarely missed an opportunity to remind anyone present of his royal connections and patrician ancestors. In his book *The Time of My Life*, leading British politician Denis Healey recounts an occasion when he, his wife and Mountbatten were standing in line to receive a host of attachés at the Banqueting House, London. After shaking several hundred hands Healey's wife turned to Mountbatten and said her wrist was feeling sore. Mountbatten looked down at her and with condescending gravitas stated: 'My Great Aunt—the Empress of Russia—used to have a blister on the back of her hand—as big as an egg—at Easter—where the peasants had kissed it.' As Healey went on to comment, 'there was no answer to that.'[293]

On returning from India, Mountbatten immediately called in on the Admiralty to see what opportunities there might be and was given command of a cruiser squadron in the Mediterranean Fleet. Thereafter he rose to Fourth Sea Lord, then went back to the Mediterranean as commander-in-chief of the fleet, and finally in 1955 achieved what he had always felt was his rightful destiny: the post of First Sea Lord. His 4-year tenure there was one of mixed success. Denis Healey was Minister of Defence at the time and he recounts that Mountbatten's contempt for his colleagues made him impossible to work with. It had been a similar disdain for the wellbeing of others in furtherance of his own image that had been responsible for so many unnecessary deaths in destroyers, at Dieppe, Malaya and then India.

Nonetheless when the three services were combined into a single Ministry of Defence in 1959, he became Chief of the Defence Staff and remained in that role until 1965. Of that period, Andrew Roberts recounts that the Permanent Secretary at the War Office at that time had said that Mountbatten was 'probably the most distrusted of all senior officers in the three services', partly because of his practice of deliberately misreporting decisions that had been taken at various committees on which he sat. Even at the age of 65, the leopard had not changed its spots and was still distorting matters to his own advantage. Mountbatten had wanted to continue in the role of Chief of Defence Staff but when the views of forty of the top staff in the Ministry were sought, thirty-nine said no, and it was about this time that Sir Gerald Templer, a man renowned for accurate but pithy comment, said: 'You're so crooked, Dickie, if you swallowed a nail you'd shit a corkscrew.'

Mountbatten's wife, Edwina, died of heart failure in 1960 and like Montgomery he became something of a lonely man; nobody really wanted him. Like Churchill, he adored the sound of his own voice and he would appear from time to time at some relatively trivial or parochial engagement, Lions Clubs, Mother's Unions, Boys Clubs, and the like, but he managed to continue his lifelong self-promotion by starring in and directing a TV programme that celebrated his life. As would have been expected, the series presented a depiction of his career that was so distorted that it was received by those in the know with a mixture of fury and/or outright hilarity. Typical of the outlandish comments he made about himself during the series was one where he said: 'You must never let ambition interfere with the job in hand, which must be done for its own sake.' As Nazi leader Joseph Goebbels had said, 'the bigger the lie the more likely that it will be believed.'

But to give the man his due, it did apparently occur to him later that his cavalier and irresponsible handling of Indian independence may have been the cause of an enormous disaster and the problems that have erupted on the subcontinent from time to time ever since. In his book *Shameful Flight* Stanley Wolpert recounts that Mountbatten was sitting next to a BBC correspondent, John Osman, at dinner in 1965 when he confessed that he had, to use his own expression then, 'fucked up'. As Wolpert goes on to state: 'Although I could more politely and at much greater length summarize the central thesis of my book . . . I could not more pithily, nor more aptly, state my own view of Mountbatten's work in India.'[294]

These are the uncomfortable truths behind the conventional façades of three men publicly acclaimed as having been some of the main architects and performers in Britain's successes in World War II. Popular sentiment in Britain claims that 'we' won the war—Britain did not; that war was won by the United States and Russia—but Britain was fortunate to emerge on the winning side. Churchill was, no doubt, a great man, but as Alan Chalfont has written, his numerous faults were on the same huge scale as his achievements; Montgomery was little more than a vastly overrated opportunist and Mountbatten was a megalomaniac whose massive mistakes and excesses were excused because of connections with the monarchy.

The unsung heroes, Wavell and Auchinleck, and the hidden hero, Dorman-Smith, were either victims of a ruthless politician determined to retain power, or were removed by an outdated military establishment to conceal its inability to modernise.

Facts are sometimes unattractive, but truth will out.

NOTES

INTRODUCTION

1   Arnold, Michael, *The Sacrifice of Singapore: Churchill's Biggest Blunder*, Marshall Cavendish Editions, 2011.

2   Ziegler, Philip, *Mountbatten*, Alfred A. Knopf, 1985.

3   Beevor, Anthony, *D-Day: The Battle for Normandy*, Viking, 2009.

4   Charmley, John, Churchill: *The End of Glory: A Political Biography*, Hodder & Stoughton, 1993.

5   Ponting, Clive, *Churchill*, Sinclair-Stevenson Ltd, 1994.

6   Overy, Richard, *Why the Allies Won*, Jonathan Cape, 1995.

7   Corrigan, Gordon, *Blood, Sweat and Arrogance: The Myths of Churchill's War*, Phoenix, 2007.

8   Corrigan, Gordon, *The Second World War: A Military History*, Atlantic Books, 2010.

9   Harper, Stephen, *Miracle of Deliverance: The Case for the Bombing of Hiroshima and Nagasaki*, Sidgwick & Jackson, 1985.

10 Roberts, Andrew, *Eminent Churchillians*, Weidenfeld & Nicolson, 1994.

11 Barnett, Correlli, *The Desert Generals*, George Allen & Unwin Ltd, 1960.

12 Ponting (1994).

13 Moran, Lord, *Churchill: The Struggle for Survival 1940/65,* Constable, 1966.

14 Murray, Williamson and Millett, Allan R., *A War to be Won: Fighting the Second World War*, Harvard University Press, 2000.

15 Greacen, Lavinia, *Chink: A Biography*, Macmillan, 1989.

CHAPTER 1

16 Barnett (1960).

17 Quoted in Greacen (1989).

18 Corrigan (2010).

19 Orwell, George, 'The Ethics of the Detective Story from Raffles to Miss Blandish', *Horizon*, October 1944.

20 Barnett, Correlli, *The Collapse of British Power*, Eyre Methuen Ltd, 1972.

21 Chalke, Stephen, *Runs in the Memory*, Fairfield Books, 1997.

22 Stanley, Arthur P., *The Life and Correspondence of Thomas Arnold, DD*, Ward, Lock & Co., 1890.

23 Browne, Anthony Montague, *Long Sunset*, Cassell, 1995

24 Quoted in Dönhoff, Marion, *Foe into Friend: The Makers of the New Germany from Konrad Adenauer to Helmut Schmidt*, Weidenfeld & Nicolson, 1982.

25 Callahan, Raymond, *Churchill and His Generals*, University Press of Kansas, 2007.

26 Deighton, Len, *Fighter: The True Story of the Battle of Britain*, Jonathan Cape, 1977.

27 Barnett (1960).

28 Mill, John Stuart (ed. Robson, John M.), *The Collected Works of John Stuart Mill*, 33 vols, University of Toronto Press, Routledge and Kegan Paul, 1963–1991—Volume XX: *Essays on Equality, Law, and Education (Subjection of Women)*.

29 Urban, Mark, *Generals: Ten British Commanders who Shaped the World*, Faber & Faber 2005.

30 Liddell Hart, Basil (ed.), *The Rommel Papers*, William Collins & Sons Ltd, 1953.

CHAPTER 2

31 Ponting (1994).

32 Barnett (1960).

33 Ponting (1994).

34 Churchill, Winston, *Great Contemporaries*, Thornton Butterworth Ltd, 1937.

35 Churchill's speech to the Anti-Socialist and Anti-Communist Union, in Oxford, 17 February 1933.

36 Ponting (1994).

37 Ponting (1994).

38 Ponting (1994).

39 Ponting (1994).

40 *Notable Quotes* [website] <http://www.notable-quotes.com/c/churchill_sir_winston. html>, accessed 17 October 2014.

41 Ponting (1994).

42 Moran (1966).

43 Storr, Anthony, *Churchill's Black Dog, Kafka's Mice, and Other Phenomena of the Human Mind*, Grove Press, 1988.

44 Moran (1966).

45 Thompson, Reginald W., *Generalissimo Churchill*, Hodder & Stoughton, 1974.

46 Cohen, Elliot A., *Supreme Command: Soldiers, Statesmen and Leadership in Wartime*, Simon & Schuster, 2003.

47 Bryant, Arthur, *The Turn of the Tide: Based on the War Diaries of Field Marshal Viscount Alanbrooke,* The Reprint Society, 1958.

48 Slim, Field Marshal Sir William, *Defeat into Victory*, Cassell, 1956.

49 Moran (1966).

50 Kennedy, Major-General Sir John (ed. Fergusson, Bernard), *The Business of War: The War Narrative of Major-General Sir John Kennedy*, Hutchinson, 1957.

51 Moran (1966).

52 Cohen (2003).

53 Bryant (1958).

54 Corrigan (2007).

55 Bryant (1958).

56 Eisenhower, Dwight D., *Crusade in Europe*, William Heinemann Ltd, 1948.

57 Bryant (1958).

58 Granatstein, Jack L., *The Generals: The Canadian Army's Senior Commanders in the Second World War*, Stoddart Publishing, 1993.

59 Bryant (1958).
60 Ponting (1994).
61 Ponting (1994).
62 Villa, Brian Loring, *Unauthorised Action: Mountbatten and the Dieppe Raid*, Oxford University Press, 1989.
63 Connell, John, *Auchinleck: A Biography of Field-Marshal Sir Claude Auchinleck*, Cassell, 1959.
64 Corrigan (2007).
65 Moran (1966).

CHAPTER 3
66 Barnett (1960).
67 Montgomery, Bernard, L., *The Memoirs of Field Marshal the Viscount Montgomery of Alamein, K.G.*, Collins, 1958.
68 Chalfont, Alun, *Montgomery of Alamein*, Weidenfeld & Nicolson, 1976.
69 Corrigan (2007).
70 Barnett (1960).
71 Connell (1959).
72 Playfair, Major-General I. S. O. et al., *The Mediterranean and Middle East*, Vol. III: *British Fortunes Reach Their Lowest Ebb* (*History of the Second World War* series), HMSO, 1960.
73 Liddell Hart (1979).
74 Carell, Paul, *Foxes of the Desert*, Bantam Books, 1962.
75 Barnett (1960).
76 McKenzie, Compton, *Eastern Epic*, Vol. I: *September 1939–March 1943: Defence*, Chatto & Windus, 1951.
77 Corrigan (2007).
78 Barnett (1960).
79 Barr, Niall, *Pendulum of War: The Three Battles of El Alamein*, Jonathan Cape, 2004.
80 Liddell Hart (1953).
81 Ponting, Clive, *Armageddon: The Second World War*, Sinclair-Stevenson Ltd, 1995.
82 Liddell Hart (1953).
83 Royle, Trevor, *Patton: Old Blood and Guts*, Weidenfeld & Nicolson, 2005.

CHAPTER 4
84 Roberts (1994).
85 Smith, Adrian, *Mountbatten: Apprentice War Lord*, I. B. Taurus, 2010.
86 Ziegler (1985).
87 Ziegler (1985).
88 Pugsley, Rear Admiral Alan F., *Destroyer Man*, Weidenfeld & Nicolson, 1957.
89 Ziegler (1985).
90 Smith (2010).
91 Ziegler (1985).
92 Barnett, Correlli, *Engage the Enemy More Closely: The Royal Navy in the Second World*

War, Hodder & Stoughton, 1991.

93 Ziegler (1985).

94 Tunzelmann, Alex von, *Indian Summer: The Secret History of the End of an Empire*, Henry Holt and Company, 2007.

95 Smith (2010).

CHAPTER 5

96 Ponting (1994).

97 Ponting (1994).

98 Ponting (1994).

99 Ponting (1994).

100 Ponting (1994).

101 Ponting (1994).

102 Elphick, Peter, S*ingapore: the Pregnable Fortress: A Study in Deception, Discord and Desertion*, Hodder & Stoughton, 1995.

103 Elphick (1995).

104 Kennedy (1957).

105 Liddell Hart, Basil, *History of the Second World War*, Cassell & Co. Ltd, 1970.

106 Ponting (1994).

107 Ponting (1994).

108 Ponting (1994).

109 Liddell Hart, Basil, *Strategy: The Indirect Approach,* Faber & Faber, 1954.

110 Barnett, Correlli, *Engage the Enemy More Closely*, Hodder & Stoughton, 1991

111 Barber, Noel, *Sinister Twilight: The Fall and Rise Again of Singapore*, Collins, 1968.

112 Barnett (1960).

113 Gilbert, Martin, *Winston S. Churchill*, Vol. VII: *Road to Victory, 1941–1945* (Official Biography of Winston S. Churchill), Minerva, 1989.

114 Barnett, Correlli, *Singapore Straits Times*, 1997.

CHAPTER 6

115 Sheehan, William, *British Voices: From the Irish War of Independence 1918–1921*, The Collins Press, 2007.

116 Barnett (1960).

117 Thompson, Reginald W., *Churchill and the Montgomery Myth*, M. Evans and Company, 1967.

118 Beevor (2009).

119 Hamilton, Nigel, *Monty: Master of the Battlefield 1942–1944*, Hodder & Stoughton, 1985.

120 Liddell Hart (1953).

121 Chalfont (1976).

122 Chalfont (1976).

123 Cornelius Ryan in an interview with Eisenhower, Gettysburg, 1963.

124 Chalfont (1976).

125 Thompson (1967).

126 Kennedy (1957).
127 Healey, Denis, *The Time of My Life*, Michael Joseph, 1989.
128 Chalfont (1976).
129 Chalfont (1976).
130 Granatstein (1993).

CHAPTER 7
131 Corrigan (2007).
132 Keegan, John, *Six Armies in Normandy: From D-Day to the Liberation of Paris, June 6th– August 25th, 1944*, Viking Books, 1982.
133 Villa (1989).
134 Villa (1989).
135 Corrigan (2007).
136 Villa (1989).
137 Atkin, Ronald, *Dieppe 1942: The Jubilee Disaster*, Macmillan, 1980.
138 Ziegler (1985).

CHAPTER 8
139 Barnett (1991).
140 Barnett (1991).
141 Barnett (1960).
142 Barnett, Corelli, *Marlborough,* Eyre Methuen, 1974.
143 Liddell Hart (1970).
144 Douglas-Home, Charles, *Rommel*, Weidenfeld & Nicolson, 1973.
145 Barnett (1991).
146 Barnett (1960).
147 Bryant (1958).
148 Warner, Philip, *Auchinleck: The Lonely Soldier*, Cassell & Co. Ltd, 2001.
149 Connell (1959).
150 Connell (1959).
151 Connell (1959).
152 Guingand, Sir Francis de, *Operation Victory*, Hodder & Stoughton, 1947.
153 Churchill, Winston, *The Second World War*, 6 vols, Cassell & Co. Ltd, 1948–53.
154 Speech at The Lord Mayor's Luncheon, Mansion House, London, 10 November 1942.
155 Barnett (1960).
156 Liddell Hart (1953).

CHAPTER 9
157 Eisenhower (1948).
158 D'Este, Carlo, *Bitter Victory: The Battle for Sicily, 1943*, Collins, 1988.
159 Chalfont (1976).
160 Chalfont (1976).
161 Thompson (1967).

162 Corrigan (2007).

163 D'Este, Carlo, *Decision in Normandy,* Konecky & Konecky, 1983.

164 Delaforce, Patrick, *The Black Bull: From Normandy to the Baltic with the 11th Armoured Division*, Chancellor Press, 2000.

165 Patton, General George S., Jr, *War As I Knew It*, Houghton Mifflin Company, 1947.

166 Liddell Hart (1954).

167 Beevor (2009).

168 Montgomery (1958).

CHAPTER 10

169 Ponting (1994).

170 Ponting (1994).

171 Barnett (1991).

172 Harper (1985).

173 Corrigan (2010).

174 Harper (1985).

175 Slim (1956).

176 Harper (1985).

177 Harper (1985).

178 Harper (1985).

179 Harper (1985).

180 Harper (1985).

181 Harper (1985).

CHAPTER 11

182 Liddell Hart (1970).

183 Bradley, Omar N., *A Soldier's Story,* Henry Holt and Company, 1951.

184 Thompson, Reginald W., *The 85 Days: The Canadian First Army in the Savage Battle for Victory in Europe in 1944*, Ballantine Books, 1957.

185 Bennett (2008).

186 Coble, Lieutenant-Colonel Elizabeth A., *Operation Market Garden: Case Study for Analyzing Senior Leader Responsibilities,* Strategy Research Project, U.S. Army War College, 2009.

187 Bennett (2008).

188 The Urquhart here is Major-General Robert 'Roy' Urquhart, commander of 1st Airborne Division, and no relation to the intelligence officer Major Brian Urquhart.

189 Dixon, Norman F., *On the Psychology of Military Incompetence*, Jonathan Cape, 1976.

190 Ryan (1974).

191 Bradley (1951).

192 Liddell Hart (1953).

193 Ryan (1974).

194 Bourrienne, Louis-Antoine Fauvelet de (ed. Phipps, R.W.), *Memoirs of Napoleon Bonaparte*, Charles Scribner's Sons, 1891.

195 Churchill (1948–53).

196 Churchill (1948–53).
197 Coble (2009).
198 Bennett (2008).

CHAPTER 12
199 D'Este, Carlo, *A Genius for War: A Life of General George S. Patton*, Harper Collins, 1996.
200 Chalfont (1976).
201 Whiting, Charles, *Ardennes: The Secret War*, Century Publishing, 1984.
202 Chalfont (1976).
203 Bradley (1951).
204 Chalfont (1976).
205 Chalfont (1976).
206 Bradley (1951).
207 Chalfont (1976).
208 Chalfont (1976).
209 Churchill (1948–53); Vol. 6: *Triumph and Tragedy*.
210 Eisenhower (1948).
211 Montgomery (1958).
212 Guderian, Heinz, *Panzer Leader*, Michael Joseph Ltd, 1952.
213 Bradley (1951).
214 Caraccilo, Dominic J. and Pothin, John L., 'Coup d'oeil: The Commander's Intuition in Clausewitzian Terms', *Chronicles Online Journal, The Air University* [website] <http://www.airpower.maxwell.af.mil/airchronicles/cc/Caraccilo2.html>, accessed 2014.
215 Liddell Hart, Basil, *Thoughts on War*, Faber & Faber, 1944.

CHAPTER 13
216 Wolpert, Stanley, *Shameful Flight: The Last Years of the British Empire in India*, Oxford University Press, 2006.
217 Wolpert (2006).
218 Wolpert (2006).
219 Roberts (1994).
220 Tunzelmann (2007).
221 Roberts (1994).
222 Ziegler (1985).
223 Roberts (1994).
224 Connell (1959).

CHAPTER 14
225 Ponting (1994).
226 Overy (1995).
227 Moran (1966).
228 DeWaters, Diane K., 'The World War II Conferences in Washington D.C. and Que-

bec City: Franklin D. Roosevelt and Winston S. Churchill', PhD thesis, University of Texas, 2008.

229 Kennedy (1957).

230 Bryant (1958).

231 Beevor (2009).

232 Barr, Pat, *Taming the Jungle: The Men who Made British Malaya*, Secker & Warburg, 1977.

233 Barnett (1972).

234 Humes, James C., *Churchill: Speaker of the Century*, Stein & Day, 1980.

235 Overy (1995).

236 Humes (1980).

237 Moran (1966).

238 Moran (1966).

239 Corrigan (2007).

240 Thompson (1974).

241 Charmley (1993).

242 Charmley (1993).

243 Moran (1966).

244 Winston Churchill, speech at Westminster College, Fulton, Missouri, after receiving his honorary degree, 5 March 1946.

CHAPTER 15

245 Douglas-Home (1973).

246 Wavell, Archibald, *Generals and Generalship*, Macmillan, 1941.

247 Connell, John, *Wavell: Scholar and Soldier*, Collins, 1964.

248 Barclay, Cyril N., *On Their Shoulders: British Generalship in the Lean Years 1939–1942*, Faber 7 Faber, 1964.

249 Warner (2001).

250 Barnett (1960).

251 Liddell Hart (1953).

252 Maule, Henry, *Spearhead General: The Epic Story of General Sir Frank Messervy and his Men in Eritrea, North Africa and Burma*, Odhams, 1961.

253 Connell (1959).

254 Slim (1956).

255 Parkinson, Roger, *The Auk: Auchinleck Victor at Alamein*, Granada Publishing, 1977.

256 Warner (2001).

257 Parkinson (1977).

CHAPTER 16

258 Barnett (1960).

259 Guderian (1952).

260 Liddell Hart (1954).

261 Pitt, Barrie, *The Crucible of War: Western Desert 1941*, Jonathan Cape, 1980.

262 Connell (1959).

263 Parkinson (1977).
264 Churchill (1948–53); Vol. 4: *The Hinge of Fate*.
265 Connell (1959).
266 Greacen (1989).
267 Churchill (1948–53); Vol. 4: *The Hinge of Fate*.
268 Liddell Hart (1953).
269 Strawson, John, *The Battle for North Africa*, Charles Scribner's Sons, 1969.
270 Greacen (1989).
271 Greacen (1989).
272 The papers of PENNEY, Maj Gen Sir (William) Ronald Campbell (1896–1964), Liddell Hart Centre for Military Archives, King's College London.
273 Corrigan (2010).
274 Slim (1956).
275 Fraser, David, *Alanbrooke*, Atheneum, 1982.
276 Klemensits, Péter, 'A controversial figure of the Desert War: Major-General Eric Dorman-Smith and the First Battle of El Alamein', *Academic and Applied Research in Military Science*, 8:1, 2009.
277 Keegan, John (ed.), *Churchill's Generals*, Weidenfeld & Nicolson, 1991.
278 Greacen (1989).
279 Montgomery (1958).
280 Greacen (1989).
281 Barnett, Correlli, *Britain and Her Army: A Military, Political and Social History of the British Army 1509–1970*, Allan Lane, 1970.

CHAPTER 17
282 Thompson (1974).
283 Moran (1966).
284 Ponting (1994).
285 Urban (2005).
286 Baynes, John, *The Forgotten Victor: General Sir Richard O'Connor, KT, GCB, DSO, MC*, Brasseys, 1989.
287 Chalfont (1976).
288 Guderian (1952).
289 Ryan (1974).
290 Yeide, Harry, 'Patton: The German View', *Historynet.com* [website] <http://www.historynet.com/patton-the-german-view.htm>, accessed 2014.
291 Carell, Paul, *Invasion: They're Coming!*, George Harrap, 1962.
292 Corrigan (2010).
293 Healey (1989).
294 Wolpert (2006).

BIBLIOGRAPHY

Arnold, Michael, *The Sacrifice of Singapore—Churchill's Biggest Blunder,* Marshall Cavendish, 2011.

Atkin, Ronald, *Dieppe 1942: The Jubilee Disaster*, Macmillan, 1980

Barber, Noel, *Sinister Twilight: The Fall and Rise Again of Singapore*, Collins, 1968

Barclay, Cyril N., *On Their Shoulders: British Generalship in the Lean Years 1939–1942*, Faber & Faber, 1964

Barnett, Correlli, *The Desert Generals*, George Allen & Unwin Ltd, 1960

——, *Britain and Her Army: A Military, Political and Social History of the British Army 1509–1970*, Allan Lane, 1970

——, *The Collapse of British Power*, Eyre Methuen Ltd, 1972

——, *Marlborough*, Eyre Methuen, 1974

——, *The Audit of War: The Illusion and Reality of Britain as a Great Nation*, Macmillan, 1986

——, *Hitler's Generals*, Weidenfeld & Nicolson, 1989

——, *Engage the Enemy More Closely: The Royal Navy in the Second World War*, Hodder & Stoughton, 1991

Barr, Niall, *Pendulum of War: The Three Battles of El Alamein*, Jonathan Cape, 2004

Barr, Pat, *Taming the Jungle: The Men who Made British Malaya*, Secker & Warburg, 1977

Baynes, John, *The Forgotten Victor: General Sir Richard O'Connor, KT, GCB, DSO, MC*, Brassey's, 1989

Beevor, Anthony, *Inside the British Army*, Chatto & Windus, 1990

——, *D-Day: The Battle for Normandy*, Viking, 2009

Bennett, David, *A Magnificent Disaster: The Failure of Market Garden, The Arnhem Operation September 1944*, Casemate, 2008

Blumenson, Martin, *The Patton Papers*, Vol. II: *1940–1945*, Houghton Mifflin, 1974

——, *Patton: The Man Behind the Legend 1885–1945*, Jonathan Cape, 1985

Bourrienne, Louis-Antoine Fauvelet de (ed. Phipps, R.W.), *Memoirs of Napoleon Bonaparte*, Charles Scribner's Sons, 1891

Bradley, Omar N., *A Soldier's Story*, Henry Holt and Company, 1951

——, *A General's Life: An Autobiography by General of the Army Omar N. Bradley and Clay Blair*, Simon & Schuster, 1983

Breuer, William B., *Operation Torch: The Allied Gamble to Invade North Africa*, St Martin's Press, 1985

Browne, Anthony Montague, *Long Sunset: Memoirs of Winston Churchill's Last Private Secretary*, Cassell, 1995

Bryant, Arthur, *The Turn of the Tide: Based on the War Diaries of Field Marshal Viscount Alanbrooke,* The Reprint Society, 1958

Callahan, Raymond, *Churchill and His Generals*, University Press of Kansas, 2007

Calvocoressi, Peter and Wint, Guy, *Total War*, Allen Lane, 1972

Caraccilo, Dominic J. and Pothin, John L., 'Coup d'oeil: The Commander's Intuition in Clausewitzian Terms', *Chronicles Online Journal, The Air University* [website] <http://www.airpower.maxwell.af.mil/airchronicles/cc/Caraccilo2.html>, accessed 2014

Carell, Paul, *Foxes of the Desert*, Bantam Books, 1962

——, *Invasion: They're Coming!*, George Harrap, 1962

Chalfont, Alun, *Montgomery of Alamein*, Weidenfeld & Nicolson, 1976

Chalke, Stephen, *Runs in the Memory*, Fairfield Books, 1997

Charmley, John, *Churchill: The End of Glory: A Political Biography,* Hodder & Stoughton, 1993

Churchill, Winston, *Great Contemporaries*, Thornton Butterworth Ltd, 1937

——, *The Second World War*, 6 vols, Cassell & Co. Ltd, 1948–53

Cohen, Elliot A., *Supreme Command: Soldiers, Statesmen and Leadership in Wartime*, Simon & Schuster, 2003

Connell, John, *Auchinleck: A Biography of Field-Marshal Sir Claude Auchinleck*, Cassell, 1959

——, *Wavell: Scholar and Soldier*, Collins, 1964

Corrigan, Gordon, *Blood, Sweat and Arrogance: The Myths of Churchill's War*, Phoenix, 2007

——, *The Second World War: A Military History*, Atlantic Books, 2010

Deighton, Len, *Fighter: The True Story of the Battle of Britain*, Jonathan Cape, 1977

——, *Blood Tears & Folly: In the Darkest Hour of the Second World War*, Jonathan Cape, 1993

Delaforce, Patrick, *The Black Bull: From Normandy to the Baltic with the 11th Armoured Division*, Chancellor Press, 2000

D'Este, Carlo, *Decision in Normandy*, Konecky & Konecky, 1983

——, *Bitter Victory: The Battle for Sicily, 1943*, Collins, 1988

——, *A Genius for War: A Life of General George S. Patton*, Harper Collins, 1996

DeWaters, Diane K., 'The World War II Conferences in Washington D.C. and Quebec City: Franklin D. Roosevelt and Winston S. Churchill', PhD thesis, University of Texas, 2008

Dixon, Norman F., *On the Psychology of Military Incompetence*, Jonathan Cape, 1976

Dönhoff, Marion, *Foe into Friend: The Makers of the New Germany from Konrad Adenauer to Helmut Schmidt*, Weidenfeld & Nicolson, 1982

Douglas-Home, Charles, *Rommel*, Weidenfeld & Nicolson, 1973

Eisenhower, Dwight D., *Crusade in Europe*, William Heinemann Ltd, 1948

Elphick, Peter, *Singapore: the Pregnable Fortress: A Study in Deception, Discord and Desertion*, Hodder & Stoughton, 1995

Farago, Ladislas, *Patton: Ordeal and Triumph*, Mayflower Books, 1969

Fraser, David, *Alanbrooke*, Atheneum, 1982

Gilbert, Martin, *Winston S. Churchill*, Vol. VII: *Road to Victory, 1941–1945* (Official Biography of Winston S. Churchill), Minerva, 1989

——, *The Churchill War Papers*, Vol. III: *1941, The Ever Widening War*, W.W. Norton, 2001

Granatstein, Jack L., *The Generals: The Canadian Army's Senior Commanders in the Second World War*, Stoddart Publishing, 1993

Greacen, Lavinia, *Chink: A Biography*, Macmillan, 1989

Guderian, Heinz, *Panzer Leader*, Michael Joseph Ltd, 1952

Guingand, Sir Francis de, *Operation Victory*, Hodder & Stoughton, 1947

——, *Generals at War*, Hodder & Stoughton, 1964

Hamilton, Nigel, *Monty: Master of the Battlefield 1942–1944*, Hodder & Stoughton, 1985

Harper, Stephen, *Miracle of Deliverance: The Case for the Bombing of Hiroshima and Nagasaki*, Sidgwick & Jackson, 1985

Healey, Denis, *The Time of My Life*, Michael Joseph, 1989

Hook, Hilary, *Home from the Hill*, The Sportsman's Press, 1987

Hough, Richard, *Mountbatten: Hero of Our Time*, Macmillan, 1981

Hoyt, Edwin P., *The Invasion Before Normandy: The Secret Battle of Slapton Sands*, Scarborough House, 1985

Humes, James C., *Churchill: Speaker of the Century*, Stein & Day, 1980

Keegan, John, *Six Armies in Normandy: From D-Day to the Liberation of Paris, June 6th–August 25th, 1944*, Viking Books, 1982

—— (ed.), *Churchill's Generals*, Weidenfeld & Nicolson, 1991

——, *Churchill*, Weidenfeld & Nicolson, 2002

Kennedy, Major-General Sir John (ed. Fergusson, Bernard), *The Business of War: The War Narrative of Major-General Sir John Kennedy*, Hutchinson, 1957

Kerr, Mark, *Prince Louis of Battenberg: Admiral of the Fleet*, Longmans Green, 1934

Kinvig, Clifford, *Scapegoat: General Percival of Singapore*, Brassey's, 1996

Klemensits, Péter, 'A controversial figure of the Desert War: Major-General Eric Dorman-Smith and the First Battle of El Alamein', *Academic and Applied*

Research in Military Science, 8:1, 2009

Latimer, Jon, *Alamein*, John Murray, 2002

Lee, Bruce, *Marching Orders: The Untold Story of World War II*, Da Capo Press, 1995

Liddell Hart, Basil, *Thoughts on War*, Faber & Faber, 1944

—— (ed.), *The Rommel Papers*, William Collins & Sons Ltd, 1953

——, *Strategy: The Indirect Approach*, Faber & Faber, 1954

——, *History of the Second World War*, Cassell & Co. Ltd, 1970

——, *The German Generals Talk*, Quill, 1979

Macksey, Kenneth, *Military Errors of World War Two*, Castle Books, 2003

Maule, Henry, *Spearhead General: The Epic Story of General Sir Frank Messervy and his Men in Eritrea, North Africa and Burma*, Odhams, 1961

McKenzie, Compton, *Eastern Epic*, Vol. I: *September 1939–March 1943: Defence*, Chatto & Windus, 1951

Mill, John Stuart (ed. Robson, John M.), *The Collected Works of John Stuart Mill*, 33 vols, University of Toronto Press, Routledge and Kegan Paul, 1963–1991

Montgomery, Bernard, L., *Normandy to the Baltic*, Hutchinson, 1946

——, *The Memoirs of Field Marshal the Viscount Montgomery of Alamein, K.G.*, Collins, 1958

Moran, Lord, *Churchill: The Struggle for Survival 1940/65*, Constable, 1966

Mukerjee, Madhusree, *Churchill's Secret War*, Basic Books, 2011

Murray, Williamson and Millett, Allan R., *A War to be Won: Fighting the Second World War*, Harvard University Press, 2000

Orwell, George, 'The Ethics of the Detective Story from Raffles to Miss Blandish', *Horizon*, October 1944

Overy, Richard, *Why the Allies Won*, Jonathan Cape, 1995

Padfield, Peter, *Hess, Hitler & Churchill: The Real Turning Point of the Second World War*, Icon Books, 2013

Parkinson, Roger, *The Auk: Auchinleck Victor at Alamein*, Granada Publishing, 1977

Patton, General George S., Jr, *War As I Knew It*, Houghton Mifflin Company, 1947

Penney, Maj Gen Sir (William) Ronald Campbell (1896–1964)—the papers of; Liddell Hart Centre for Military Archives, King's College London

Percival, Arthur E., *The War in Malaya*, Eyre & Spottiswood, 1949

Pitt, Barrie, *The Crucible of War: Western Desert 1941*, Jonathan Cape, 1980

Playfair, Major-General I. S. O. et al., *The Mediterranean and Middle East*, Vol. III: *British Fortunes Reach Their Lowest Ebb* (*History of the Second World War* series), HMSO, 1960

Ponting, Clive, *1940: Myth & Reality*, Hamish Hamilton, 1990

——, *Churchill*, Sinclair-Stevenson Ltd, 1994

——, *Armageddon: The Second World War*, Sinclair-Stevenson Ltd, 1995

Pugsley, Rear Admiral Alan F., *Destroyer Man*, Weidenfeld & Nicolson, 1957

Roberts, Andrew, *Eminent Churchillians*, Weidenfeld & Nicolson, 1994

——, *Hitler & Churchill: Secrets of Leadership*, Weidenfeld & Nicolson, 2003

—— (ed.), *Great Commanders of the Modern World: 1866–Present Day*, Quercus, 2009

Royle, Trevor, *Patton: Old Blood and Guts*, Weidenfeld & Nicolson, 2005

Ryan, Cornelius, *The Longest Day*, Victor Gollancz, 1960

——, *A Bridge Too Far*, Simon & Schuster, 1974

Sheehan, William, *British Voices: From the Irish War of Independence 1918–1921*, The Collins Press, 2007

Slim, Field Marshal Sir William, *Defeat into Victory*, Cassell, 1956

Small, Ken, *The Forgotten Dead*, Bloomsbury, 1988

Smith, Adrian, *Mountbatten: Apprentice War Lord*, I. B. Taurus, 2010

Stanley, Arthur P., *The Life and Correspondence of Thomas Arnold, DD*, Ward, Lock & Co., 1890

Storr, Anthony, *Churchill's Black Dog, Kafka's Mice, and Other Phenomena of the Human Mind*, Grove Press, 1988

Strawson, John, *The Battle for North Africa*, Charles Scribner's Sons, 1969

Taylor, A. J. P, *The Origins of the Second World War*, Simon & Schuster, 1961

Thompson, Reginald W., *Dieppe at Dawn: The Story of the Dieppe Raid*, Hutchinson, 1956

——, *The 85 Days: The Canadian First Army in the Savage Battle for Victory in Europe in 1944*, Ballantine Books, 1957

——, *The Yankee Marlborough*, George Allen & Unwin, 1963

——, *Churchill and the Montgomery Myth*, M. Evans and Company, 1967

——, *Generalissimo Churchill*, Hodder & Stoughton, 1974

Tunzelmann, Alex von, *Indian Summer: The Secret History of the End of an Empire*, Henry Holt and Company, 2007

Urban, Mark, *Generals: Ten British Commanders who Shaped the World*, Faber & Faber 2005

Vaughan-Thomas, Wynford, *Anzio*, Longmans Green & Co, 1961

Villa, Brian Loring, *Unauthorised Action: Mountbatten and the Dieppe Raid*, Oxford University Press, 1989

Warner, Philip, *World War II: The Untold Story*, Bodley Head, 1988

——, *Auchinleck: The Lonely Soldier*, Cassell & Co. Ltd, 2001

Wavell, Archibald, *Generals and Generalship*, Macmillan, 1941

Whiting, Charles, *Ardennes: The Secret War*, Century Publishing, 1984

Wolpert, Stanley, *A New History of India*, Oxford University Press, 1993

——, *Shameful Flight: The Last Years of the British Empire in India*, Oxford University Press, 2006

Ziegler, Philip, *Mountbatten*, Alfred A. Knopf, 1985

WEBSITES

Notable Quotes [website] <http://www.notable-quotes.com/c/churchill_sir_winston.html>, accessed 17 October 2014

Yeide, Harry, 'Patton: The German View', *Historynet.com* [website] <http://www.historynet.com/patton-the-german-view.htm>, accessed 2014

INDEX